Competitor Analysis

CBI Series in Practical Strategy

Competitor Analysis

Turning Intelligence into Success

David Hussey and Per Jenster

JOHN WILEY & SONS, Ltd
Chichester • New York • Weinheim • Brisbane • Singapore • Toronto

Other Wiley Editorial Offices

John Wiley & Sons, Inc., 605 Third Avenue,
New York, NY 10158-0012, USA

WILEY-VCH GmbH, Pappelallee 3,
D-69469 Weinheim, Germany

Jacaranda Wiley Ltd, 33 Park Road, Milton,
Queensland 4064, Australia

John Wiley & Sons (Asia) Pte Ltd, 2 Clementi Loop #02-01,
Jin Xing Distripark, Singapore 129809

John Wiley & Sons (Canada) Ltd, 22 Worcester Road,
Rexdale, Ontario M9W 1L1, Canada

Library of Congress Cataloging-in-Publication Data

A catalogue record for this book is available from the Library of Congress

British Library Cataloguing in Publication Data

A catalogue record for this book is available from the British Library

ISBN 0-471-49991-9

Typeset in 11/13pt Times by Vision Typesetting, Manchester.
Printed and bound in Great Britain by Biddles Ltd, Guildford and King's Lynn.
This book is printed on acid-free paper responsibly manufactured from sustainable forestry,
in which at least two trees are planted for each one used for paper production.

Contents

Series Foreword

The aim of this series is to provide managers with books on strategy, strategic management and strategic change, which are helpful, practical, and provide guidance for the practical application of sound concepts in real situations. It is thus very welcome that a number of the books in the series should be selected for publication under the logo of the CBI, whose member organisations are very much concerned with the topics covered in the series.

In the mid 1960s when the subject of planning began to emerge, the whole literature could have been listed on one or two sheets of paper. It was easy to decide which books to read, because so few were available. This state of affairs changed rapidly, and the scope of the subject has moved from a focus on formal planning to a broader view which merges with the literature of leadership, change management, strategic analysis, and organisation. Modern writing sees the organisation and its strategies in an integrated way, and there are many, often conflicting, theories about the 'right' way to formulate strategies and practice strategic management.

Management usually does not take an academic interest in theories, but is concerned about what works best in the situation in which it operates. Hence this series. Each book is conceptually sound, and gives proper acknowledgement to the originators of concepts and ideas, but the emphasis is on using the concepts or methods, rather than academic argument. Hence, too, the choice of the six subjects initially offered under the auspices of the CBI.

There are two books which offer complementary overviews of strategic management. McNamee's *Strategic Market Planning* follows the author's belief that enduringly successful firms are those that understand most clearly, and then serve most effectively, the markets they address, and offers a blue print for this. Hussey (*Strategy & Planning*) provides essential, up to date, information for managers and practitioners of strategic management who require a practical view of the whole subject.

Segev writes on business unit strategy, and its emphasis is on analytical method for businesses that focus on one industry or product/market grouping. The remaining three books deal with specific aspects of strategy which are topical concerns for many organisations. They cover the subjects of virtual organisations (Hedberg et al), the related but different subject of multinational strategic alliances (Mockler), and competitor analysis, (Hussey & Jenster).

The emphasis of all the books is on practical application. The aim is to give the reader clear guidance on how to make the subject of the book work in his or her own situation, while at the same time taking care to ensure that the books do not over-simplify situations. Check lists and questionnaires are included when they aid the aims of the book, and examples are given. The experience of the author in actually applying the concepts, rather than just knowing about them, is intended to show through the writing.

The books are written by authors from Denmark, Israel, Sweden, the UK and the USA, which brings an international flavour, as well as helping to make complex matters understandable. We hope that it will become a catalyst that helps managers make a difference to the strategic performance of their organisations.

David Hussey, Series Editor
Visiting Professor in Strategic Management,
Nottingham Trent University
Managing Director, David Hussey & Associates

August 2000

Preface

This book was born out of frustration that, although much has been written about competitor analysis, we could not find a practical text which covered the broad spectrum of the subject, supported by examples and case histories. There are many good books which have made a major contribution, and these have been helpful in shaping many of the concepts which this book discusses, but the practical aspects of making use of the concepts in real situations has had less effective treatment. In other words the *why* and *what* of competitor analysis has been covered, but we have found few writings on the *how* and *when* which have been practical, comprehensive, and conceptually sound. So we have written our own.

Our experiences of using competitor analysis has covered both the practical and theoretical. Per Jenster has had many years' experience as a business school professor and has undertaken numerous consulting assignments in the area. David Hussey is now a visiting professor at a business school, but much of his experience has been as managing director of the European side of a US management consulting firm, where he was involved in applying the concepts in a variety of client companies, and in teaching management training programmes for specific clients. Both of us have international experience.

While anyone can study the literature to learn the main concepts, we are able to bring an additional dimension, in the shape of ways to apply the concepts to real situations, through methods we have developed which have stood the test of usage in a wide variety of organizations, and which have been further improved through such usage.

The book opens with an examination of a theoretical foundation for competitor analysis. Chapter 2 examines a number of issues of competitive strategy in both attack and defence. This, as much as anything, demonstrates the need for a vigilant study of competitors.

Chapters 3 and 4 cover industry analysis, first from an examination of the basic principles, then following with practical ways of using the concepts in business situations. Chapter 4 includes one tool for analysing the information and communicating it to others which has been found particularly useful in consulting assignments.

Critical success factors are important both for self-analysis and for an examination of competitors, and the concepts are discussed in detail in Chapter 5.

The next three chapters move from the industry, or competitive, arena to the competitors themselves, and offer ways of analysing competitors, show how to obtain information in order to undertake the analysis, and provide a case history of applying competitor analysis in a real organization. We deal comprehensively with sources of information, and offer a logical way of thinking about how and why information becomes available on competitors. The third of these chapters, the case history, shows how industry analysis and competitor analysis combine, and illustrates how information was obtained, analysed, and the strategic use which was made of it.

In Chapter 9 there is an example of how the principles of industry analysis can be applied to a country. Chapter 10 is important but much more mundane and deals with the organization and administration of competitor analysis. The remaining chapters are case studies, which provide an opportunity to think about how the principles of the book can be used in a number of different situations.

It is a book which we enjoyed writing, and which we believe will make a useful contribution to the understanding and application of the subject. As always there are acknowledgements to be made, to the authorities on whose concepts we have been able to build, to colleagues past and present who have contributed to the development of our own approaches, and to clients where we have gained valuable experience in application.

Per Jenster, Copenhagen, Denmark
David Hussey, Horsham, England

About the Authors

David Hussey is a well-known international authority on strategic management, with experience as both a practitioner in and a consultant to major companies from many industries. He was 18 years with Harbridge House (14 years as Managing Director of Harbridge Consulting Group Ltd). He is author or editor of over 25 books on strategy or management development. One of the founders of the Strategic Planning Society, and a director of the Japan Strategic Management Institute, he is currently visiting professor in strategic management at Nottingham Business School. He is former editor of the *Journal of Strategic Change*. His current interests include the development of practical strategic analysis methods, and improvements to the process of implementing strategic decisions.

Per V. Jenster is Research Professor at the Copenhagen Business School, Denmark, and Associated Director of Company Programs at the Center for Industrial Management & Industrial Development, Lausanne, Switzerland. He was previously Professor at the International Institute for Management Development (IMD), where he was Director of IMD's Managing Industrial Market Strategy program. He holds a Cand.Oecon from the University of Aarhus (Denmark) and a Ph.D. in Strategic Management and Information Systems from the University of Pittsburgh. He is author of six text books dealing with strategic management and industrial marketing, and numerous articles and case studies within the strategy and marketing area. His research interests lie in outsourcing and facility management by industrial firms and supply chain management. Dr Jenster's consulting work extends from firms in high technology industries to food processors and consumer goods manufacturers, and he serves on the board of a number of major business organisations.

1

The Foundations for Competitor Analysis

During a recent discussion with a group of managers from a large multinational company we were reminded of the old adage about the elephant and the six blind men attempting each to explain their perception of what they were encountering. One blind man, feeling the leg of the elephant, believed it to be the pillar of a grand building; another, touching the trunk of the elephant, thought a snake was moving about, and so forth. Our discussion with the managers centred around competitor analysis and how this was undertaken within their organization. A sales manager was describing the system for tracking different competitors' prices within a particular product line. A marketing manager talked about comparing brand positioning of different competitors. In production, attempts were made to benchmark the cost position of competing manufacturing sites, and the head of R&D was describing the technology path of various feuding organizations. A couple of corporate staff members described how the firm attempted to track competitors' acquisition path, in order to assess the emerging build-up of market positions and competencies. The point is that all these managers discussed some form of competitor analysis, but used the term to convey very different meanings.

In this book, we will provide the reader with an overview of the most important tools and concepts relevant to competitor analysis for strategic decision making. However, even with this limited scope, we are still covering a very broad territory of types of analyses and problem sets. We will, therefore, start this chapter with some thoughts on important dimensions to consider before engaging in any competitor analysis. We will discuss a number of factors which may aid the analyst to delineate the problem and clarify boundaries within which the analysis is to focus.

We explore the various theoretical schools of thought from academia which have contributed to a greater understanding of competitor behaviour and have provided some of the analytical tools being used to analyse competitor actions and predict future outcomes in decision making.

"IT DEPENDS HOW YOU LOOK"

Competition and the analysis of competitive behaviour is much more complex than the static phenomenon described in neo-classical economics, in which a given number of firms compete under similar assumptions, with similar products or closely related substitutes and where perfect knowledge of market conditions exists among customers and firms.

The literature and evolving management practice reveal that analysis of competitors takes on varying forms and it thus becomes critical to develop an appropriate context and a broader perspective by building on multiple streams of research.

The necessity of delineating the scope is not only felt by academics. In working with senior managers, strategic planners and marketing executives, we often observe their frustration over the quality of competitor analysis conducted within their organizations. These frustrations in management teams seem to centre around issues, such as:

1. How do we define and identify competitors, current and potential, and what criteria should be used to define the competitive landscape to be investigated?
2. The inadequate nature of traditional listings of strengths and weaknesses, which mostly reflect historical, gut-feel snapshots, rather than a dynamic future-oriented picture
3. Inability to cope with the vast amount of data from different information sources, which needs to be integrated in the analytical process,
4. The conflict which arises from the paradox that most analyses are

general in nature, whereas the decisions to be made are situation dependent
5. The sheer magnitude of the analysis, which is often presented in large volumes of reports which nobody reads, and thus results in no action
6. The analysis is only available to a few insiders in the analysis unit, rather than a broad base of line managers responsible for decision making.

The academic community has achieved great success in putting concepts and tools intended for competitor analysis into the hands of practising managers. This is particularly baffling, when one considers the academic preoccupation with questions of competitor behaviour, both at the firm level, as well as from institutional perspectives. Yet, the academic literature also mirrors the confusion experienced by practising managers, in framing the scope of the problems to be examined in a competitor analysis.

We will therefore start by discussing the point of departure of any analysis, academic or practical in nature, of competitor behaviour, namely, the definition of the focus for the analysis.

FOCUS OF THE ANALYSIS

One of the first impressions one gets from discussing competitor analysis with practising managers is their general confusion of what is meant by the term. For example, in discussions with sales managers, competitor analysis will centre around comparisons of price points, sales force coverage, seniority, professionalism, terms and conditions, service, and quality. Marketing managers will often be concerned about issues such as market share, brand positioning, advertising expenditure, distribution coverage, and product breadth and depth. In the research and development function, competitors may be examined on critical technologies among competing companies, patents, innovation performance, and so forth. In manufacturing, concerns such as competing companies' manufacturing base, economies of scale, supply chain performance, etc. And at the chief executive level, competing companies may be benchmarked on levels of operating returns and leverage, partnering relationships, etc. At the corporate level of large international organizations, competitor analyses may include such comparisons as technological platforms, degree of vertical integration, geographical coverage and locations of operating entities, and synergies between divisions.

The point is that the questions you would like to have defined and clarified depend on your departure point. Accordingly, one uses the different theoretical concepts and frameworks employed to study the phenomenon, explain competitor behaviour and predict future competitor activities and profitability of markets.

We find it useful to distinguish between a number of related dimensions which should be considered before engaging in any competitor analysis activity. The list should not be seen as exclusive, but rather as a proven group of variables which tend to influence the academic concepts and frameworks used for the inquiry, the nature of the information search, as well as impacting the shape of the conclusions to be reached from the exercise.

Decisional "Altitude"

The first dimension to observe in conducting any competitor analysis relates to the relevant organizational level of departure for the types of decisions demanding an inquiry, sometimes referred to as the unit of analysis. As already alluded to in our example, we need to understand if the competitor analysis in question relates to a sales representative who is attempting to assess a relevant bidding situation, a sales manager assessing the outcome of a new pricing strategy, a manager of a division or strategic business unit attempting to position his or her unit in the marketplace, a CEO attempting to develop an acquisition plan, or a governmental office wanting to assess antitrust matters, evaluating the impact of state subsidies or the future of foreign direct investment flows to different countries or regions of the world.

Behind a desire to define the relevant unit of analysis lies an important recognition, that it is ultimately not organizations that compete, but the coordinated market performance of different activities embedded in hierarchical structures and the associated networks with other organizations. This recognition becomes particularly important when performing a competitor analysis for the purpose of developing a platform for business strategies (see Chapters 3 and 4 which describe the concept of industry analysis).

In this book, we will also examine how competitor analysis can be performed at the level of a country, in relation to other countries competing to attract foreign direct investments, or as suggested in Michael Porter's seminal book on the competitive advantage of nations (Porter, 1990), the analysis of the underlying reasons why certain industries tend to congregate in specific countries.

In examining the different types of competitor analysis performed at various organizational levels, the literature has often attempted to distinguish between operational, tactical and strategic analysis of the competitive environment (e.g. King and Cleland, 1979).

Decisional Scope

The reference to operational, tactical and strategic analysis becomes a second dimension to consider, and centres around the immediacy of the issues, the functional base of concepts and information sources, and thus makes an implicit reference to the hierarchical nature of the decision-making unit. This can be illustrated in Figure 1.1. This view suggests, of course, that immediate competitive issues are

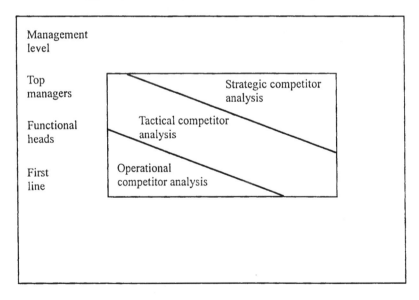

Figure 1.1 Management levels and scope of analysis.
(Source: Jenster, 1992)

> **Box 1.1** A strategic issue is one
> where the outcome or resolution has a
> significant impact on the value of the
> firm

not strategic, but operational in nature; a view with which most practising managers would disagree. Instead, the definition of a strategic issue used in this book will be one that emphasizes the impact on the value of the firm (Box 1.1).

A tactical issue does not in itself have this impact on the firm, but may in conjunction with other challenges lead to the situations which may place the organization in a strategic quandary. Following this line of thinking, an operational issue identified in a competitor analysis, usually is related to a specific customer or regional area and does not significantly impact the firm's value. In planning terms, tactical planning will typically have a horizon of 1 to 3 years, although this time span should not be taken too literally, as it is dependent on the contextual setting of the planning effort. This does not mean, however, that competitor analysis at the operational level is unimportant and should not be pursued. Lack of attention to operational competitive discrepancies can quickly accumulate and become of vital importance. We recently came across a situation with a Dutch food manufacturer who had had problems in shipments to a large retailer. The third time a shipment arrived late, the food manufacturer was de-listed from the shelves of this retailer for a six-month period. The retailer happened to buy 20% of the firm's production volume. In turn, this created the opportunity for a much smaller competitor to enter this retailer and ultimately establish itself as the "category captain" within the retailer, thus managing the category assortment for the retailer. The result over eighteen months was a devastating slide in market share for the organization. What by many would have been considered merely an operational problem escalated to a tactical issue, and then to a strategic problem.

Customer/Market Scope

The third dimension of crucial importance in competitor analysis is the delineation of a precise customer/market definition. The defini-

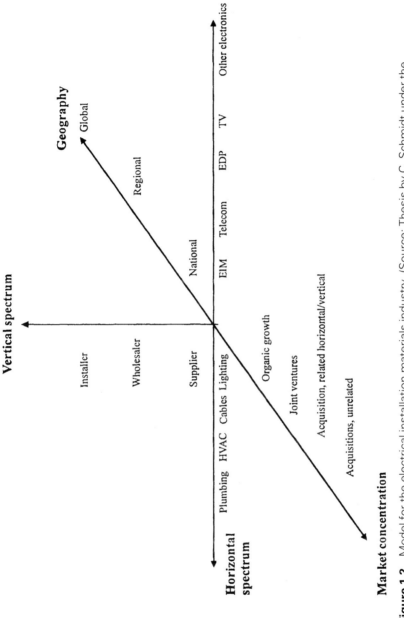

Figure 1.2 Model for the electrical installation materials industry. (Source: Thesis by C. Schmidt under the supervision of Professor P. Jenster, CBS)

tion of scope of any analysis is vital as it provides the boundaries within which the inquiry takes place. An analysis of competition in men's shoe retailing in Denmark would be distinctly different from a study of the men's shoe market in Europe, which again would differ from a discussion of the global shoe industry. This illustration also highlights the "different shades of grey" in the distinction between market and industry analysis which has often created confusion in the literature (see Hayes, Jenster and Aaby, 1996).

A company recently made an effort to understand the competitive situation in the Scandinavian Electrical Installation Material Industry (EIM). The investigation started with a delineation of the dimensions relevant to a definition of the sector to be studied in order to provide a picture of the competitive dynamics in the years to come. In Figure 1.2, we show a model which considers the vertical spectrum which defines the various critical dimensions relevant to the business, that is Customers (installers), Wholesalers, and Component Suppliers. The horizontal spectrum included Lighting, Cables, Hardware Accessories and Plumbing Suppliers, as well as those related to the Telecommunications, EDP, TV and other electronic companies, which needed to be investigated in order to understand the EIM situation. In addition, both the geographical dimension and the market strategies pursued by various organizations were clarified. This framework led to an interesting, but also challenging effort to understand the development of a number of different, but related industries, as depicted in Figure 1.3.

In a very similar way, it was necessary to understand the different client groupings among the customers to whom the industry was providing its services. In Figure 1.4, we have illustrated how the mapping of competitor formation among Electrical Installers was defined by the various companies active in related and overlapping activities, who in one way or another are competing or have the potential of competing.

Product and Technological Scope

A fourth dimension to consider before starting a competitor analysis is the definition of the product and technology boundaries framing the inquiry to be conducted. Here, a relevant aspect of "product and

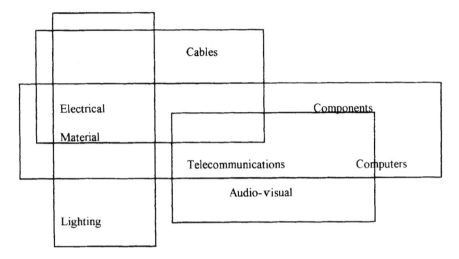

Figure 1.3 Illustration of the overlapping industries impacting the Scandinavian electrical installation materials industry. (Source: Thesis by C. Schmidt under the supervision of Professor P. Jenster, CBS)

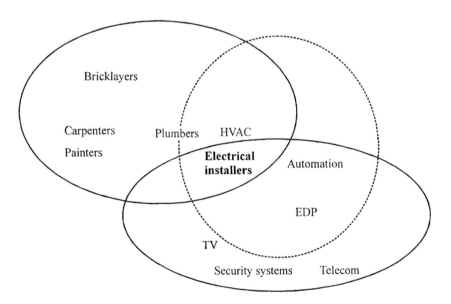

Figure 1.4 Defining the customer scope for electrical installers materials wholesaling. (Source: Thesis by C. Schmidt under the supervision of Professor P. Jenster, CBS)

gy scope" is the degree of integration to consider in the ~~ysis~~ of competitor behaviour. That is, relatively early, we must come to an agreement as to which of the critical activities involved in bringing products and services to the customers need to be considered in the discussion. This definition is particularly challenging in certain industrial settings where the technological base, and particularly the related emerging technologies, can be very difficult to assess in the context of current and future competitors.

The following example illustrates how a high-level group within Digital Equipment Corporation (DEC), called the Metaframe Group, approached the problems of finding an appropriate way of examining different competitive scenarios and communicating its findings to senior management. The firm was facing a dramatically changing marketplace and the team was appointed to "get its hands around the company's future". The task included establishing the criteria for screening joint venture partners out among its competitors.

The task force began by searching the academic community, including that of IMD and Harvard, to find useful tools which could help them in the analysis. One such useful tool to define the competitive space was identified in B. Compaine's 1985 book entitled *Understanding New Media*. The team adapted this framework and used the graph and a colour overlay from this book (Figure 1.5), to visually map out what set of competencies would be needed for the office of the future.

The Metaframe Group then developed the idea of colour-coding the competencies of different competitors or possible joint venture partners to map where various companies were positioned *vis-à-vis* "the office of the future". By using colour overlays, they were able to capture information about several companies at the same time. This also enabled the team to simulate different competitive scenarios (for example, "what if DEC makes a joint venture with ATT or buys Apple"). Although this analysis of the competitive space and the various competitors was most useful in that the two dimensions (product/service dimension and degree of content versus conduit characteristics) helped to "flush out" the possible new competitors, the team felt that more in-depth analysis was needed.

In particular, the Metaframe Group wanted to do a more detailed analysis to capture competitive information along a number of dimensions. It was, nevertheless, felt that the colouring scheme was a unique and very useful way of producing comparative data on competitors as well as possible partners. This led the DEC team to develop a unique mapping process for competitive data which was awarded US Patent 4,936,778, and is illustrated in Figures 1.6 and 1.7. Each category was further divided into sub-categories where data, such as market share, technological sophistication, skills or competency, could be shown for different competitors. This method gave the team the ability to capture massive amounts of information for analysis and, subsequently, to present it to senior management.

The above example illustrates how competitive analysis must concern itself with the definition of the competitive space, the structuring of massive amounts of information for analysis, as well as the effective communication of the analysis in a way which can be readily understood by busy executives.

Network Definition

As suggested in the illustration of the Scandinavian Electrical Installers Material Wholesalers, it is essential but often difficult to define the relevant degree of horizontal and vertical integration appropriate to consider in the analysis. This decision will be impacted by some of the previous considerations in the definition phase, as well as the nature of the transactional relationships binding the relevant activities in the value–creation chain. For example, can the textile cleaning industry be looked at as a totality or separated into garments, floor mats, general or more specific laundry to hotels, hospitals, restaurants, etc.? From one perspective, a number of the issues are similar across segments, from others, they are very different.

Temporal Dimension

The temporal dimension of how far back in the history and how far into the future the analysis should extend, that is, the time span to be covered in the competitor assessment. For example, are we to assess the evolution of European competition within electrical utilities from the start of this century? The question may rather be one of price dynamics of sales of Christmas trees in Stockholm during the month of December.

(a)

CONDUIT → **CONTENT** →

SERVICES

- GOVT. MAIL
- PARCEL SERVICES
- OTHER DELIVERY SERVICES
- MAILGRAM
- E-COM
- EMS
- TELEPHONE
- TELEGRAPH
- OCC's
- IRC's
- MULTIPOINT DSTRIB. SERVICES
- BROADCAST NETWORKS & STATIONS
- CABLE NETWORKS
- CABLE OPERATORS
- BILLING AND METER SVCS
- VIDEOTEX & DATABASE SVCS
- NEWS SVCS
- TELETEX
- TIMESHARING BUREAUS
- ON-LINE DIRECTORIES
- PRO. SVCS
- FINANCIAL SVS AND ADVERTISING SVC
- PRINTING COS
- LIBRARIES
- SATELLITE SERVICES
- FM SUBCARRIERS
- MOBILE SERVICES
- PAGING SERVICES
- MULTIPLEXING SVCS
- INDUSTRY NETWORKS
- DEFENSE TELECOM SYSTEMS
- SOFTWARE SVCS.
- SYNDICATORS AND PROGRAM PACKAGERS
- RETAILERS
- NEWSSTANDS
- SECURITY SERVICES
- COMPUTERS
- SOFTWARE PACKAGES
- DIRECTORIES
- NEWSPAPERS
- NEWSLETTERS
- MAGAZINES
- PABX's

PRODUCTS

- PRINTING & GRAPHICS EQUIPMENT
- COPIERS
- RADIOS
- TV SETS
- TELEPHONE MODEMS
- TERMINALS
- PRINTERS
- FAXCIMILE
- SHOPPERS
- AUDIO RECORDS & TAPES
- CASH REGISTERS
- INSTRUMENTS
- TYPEWRITERS
- DICTATIONS EQUIPMENT
- FILE CABINETS
- BLANK TAPE AND FILM
- PAPER
- ATM's
- POS EQUIPMENT
- BROADCAST & TRANSMISSION EQUIPMENT
- CALCULATORS, WP
- PHONO, VIDEO DISC PLAYERS
- VCR's/MICROFILM, FICHE
- FILMS & VIDEO PROGRAMS
- BOOKS

ATM: Automated Teller Machine; E-COM: Electronic Computer-Originated Mail; EMS: Electronic Message Service; IRC: International REcord Carrier; OCC: Other Common Carrier; PABX: Private Automatic Branch Exchange; POS: Point-of-Sale; VAN: Value Added Network

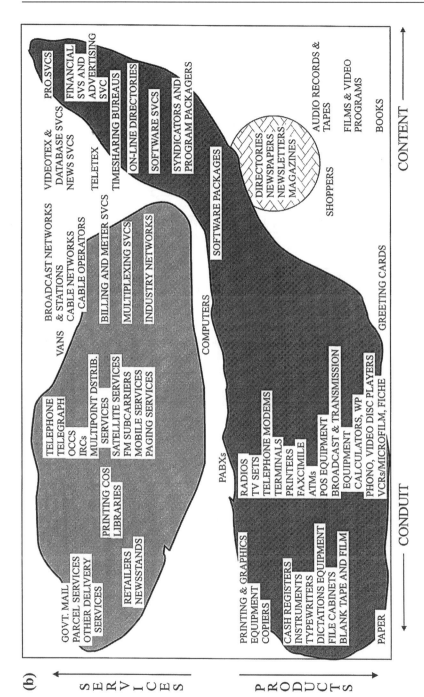

Figure 1.5 Metaframe Group: mapping of competitive positions of possible partners. (Source: Jenster, 1991)

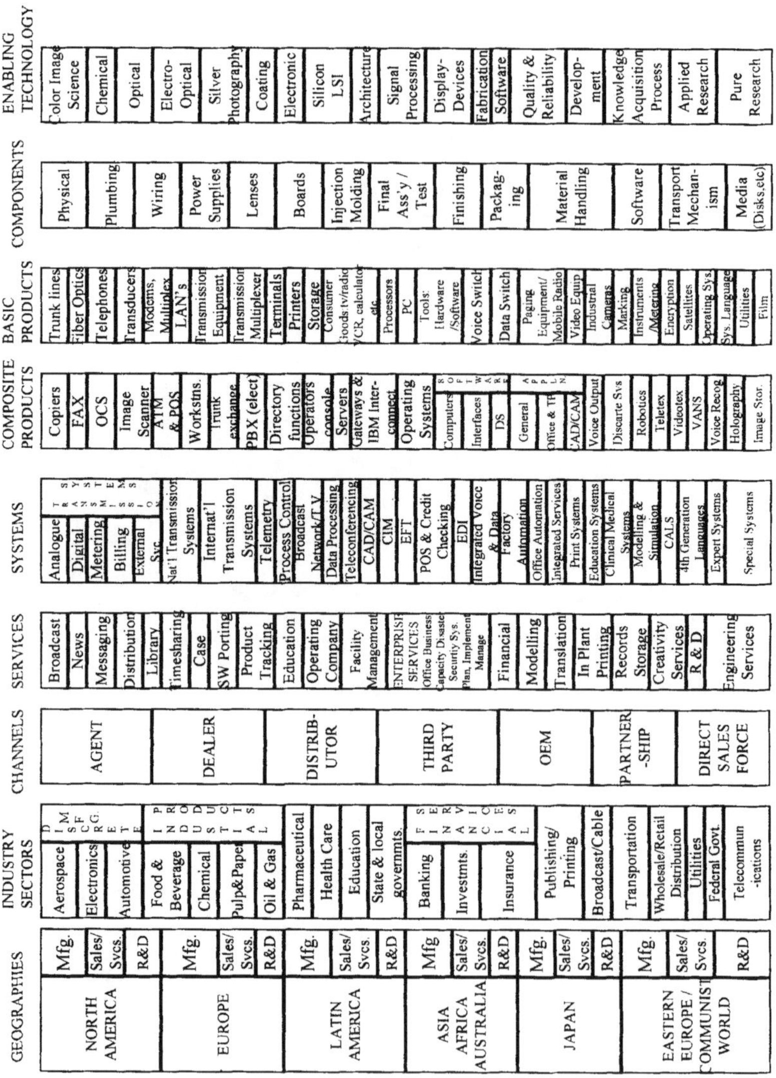

Figure 1.6 Metaframe Group: detailed segmentation for the partnering process

GEOGRAPHIES

NORTH AMERICA	Mfg. / Sales/Svcs. / R&D
EUROPE	Mfg. / Sales/Svcs. / R&D
LATIN AMERICA	Mfg. / Sales/Svcs. / R&D
ASIA AFRICA AUSTRALIA	Mfg. / Sales/Svcs. / R&D
JAPAN	Mfg. / Sales/Svcs. / R&D
EASTERN EUROPE / COMMUNIST WORLD	Mfg. / Sales/Svcs. / R&D

INDUSTRY SECTORS

Aerospace, Electronics, Automotive, Food & Beverage, Chemical, Pulp & Paper, Oil & Gas, Pharmaceutical, Health Care, Education, State & local governmts., Banking, Investmts, Insurance, Publishing/Printing, Broadcast/Cable, Transportation, Wholesale/Retail Distribution, Utilities, Federal Govt., Telecommun-icatons

CHANNELS

AGENT, DEALER, DISTRIBUTOR, THIRD PARTY, OEM, PARTNER-SHIP, DIRECT SALES FORCE

SERVICES

Broadcast, News, Messaging, Distribution, Library, Timesharing, Case, SW Porting, Product Tracking, Education, Operating Company, Facility Management, ENTERPRISE SERVICES (Office Business Capacity, Disaster Security Sys. Plan, Implement, Manage), Financial, Modelling, Translation, In Plant Printing, Records Storage, Creativity Services, R & D, Engineering Services

SYSTEMS

Analogue (TRANSMISSION), Digital, Metering, Billing, External Svc, Nat'l Transmission Systems, Internat'l Transmission Systems, Telemetry, Process Control, Broadcast Network/TV, Data Processing, Teleconferencing, CAD/CAM, CIM, EFT, POS & Credit Checking, EDI, Integrated Voice & Data, Factory Automation, Office Automation, Integrated Services, Print Systems, Education Systems, Clinical Medical Systems, Modelling & Simulation, CALS, 4th Generation Languages, Expert Systems, Special Systems

COMPOSITE PRODUCTS

Copiers, FAX, OCS, Image Scanner, ATM & POS, Workstns., Trunk exchange, PBX (elect), Directory functions, Operators console, Servers, Gateways & IBM Inter-connect, Operating Systems, Computers, Interfaces, DS, General, Office & TR, CAD/CAM, Voice Output, Discarte Svs, Robotics, Teletex, Videotex, VANS, Voice Recog, Holography, Image Stor

BASIC PRODUCTS

Trunk lines, Fiber Optics, Telephones, Transducers, Modems, Multiplex, LAN's, Transmission Equipment, Transmission Multiplexer, Terminals, Printers, Storage, Consumer goods tv/radio VCR, calculator etc, Processors, PC, Tools, Hardware/Software, Voice Switch, Data Switch, Paging Equipment/Mobile Radio, Video Equp, Industrial Metering, Camera, Marking, Instruments, Encryption, Satellites, Operating Sys, Sys. Language, Utilities, Film

COMPONENTS

Physical, Plumbing, Wiring, Power Supplies, Lenses, Boards, Injection Molding, Final Ass'y / Test, Finishing, Packaging, Material Handling, Software, Transport Mechanism, Media (Disks, etc)

ENABLING TECHNOLOGY

Color Image Science, Chemical, Optical, Electro-Optical, Silver Photography, Coating, Electronic, Silicon, LSI, Architecture, Signal Processing, Display-Devices, Fabrication, Software, Quality & Reliability, Develop-ment, Knowledge Acquisition, Process, Applied Research, Pure Research

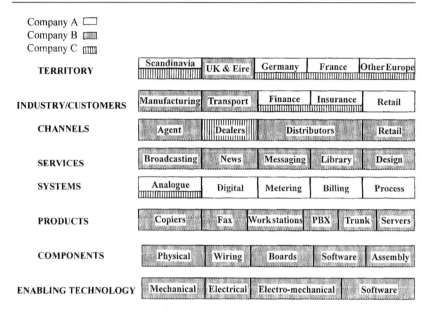

Company A ☐
Company B ▦
Company C ▥

TERRITORY	Scandinavia	UK & Eire	Germany	France	Other Europe
INDUSTRY/CUSTOMERS	Manufacturing	Transport	Finance	Insurance	Retail
CHANNELS	Agent	Dealers	Distributors		Retail
SERVICES	Broadcasting	News	Messaging	Library	Design
SYSTEMS	Analogue	Digital	Metering	Billing	Process
PRODUCTS	Copiers	Fax	Workstations	PBX	Trunk	Servers
COMPONENTS	Physical	Wiring	Boards	Software	Assembly
ENABLING TECHNOLOGY	Mechanical	Electrical	Electro-mechanical		Software

Figure 1.7 Metaframe Group: detailed segmentation for the partnering process (US Patent 4,936,778)

CURRENT TRENDS WHICH AFFECT THE COMPETITIVE BATTLEFIELD

In recent years the task of competitor analysis has been impacted by three major trends, which have dramatically changed how practising managers are addressing the topic. These major trends are (a) the fusion of industries, (b) the globalization of trade and (c) the improvements in information and communication technologies. Needless to say, other trends could be said to influence the field of competitive analysis, but it is felt that these three have had the greatest impact.

The first trend which seems to have changed the way in which firms pursue competitor analysis is the number of traditional industries and the introduction of new configurations of businesses. Most recently is the emergence of Internet publishing, which distinguishes itself from traditional publishing in so many ways, so that at one level of analysis it is no longer relevant to assess players in the traditional sectors as competitors for the new embryonic firms, such as Pointcast or Microsoft. But as we illustrated with our example of the electrical materials supply industry, we are bound to engage in much more elaborate analytical efforts than have previously been the norm. Recently, the head of strategic planning for one of the largest Danish mortgage banking firms was challenged by his analysis of the competitive activities, as the arrival of traditional full-service banks had created a situation unknown a few years earlier.

The globalization of business, and the disappearance of trade and regulatory barriers and geographical distances as constraining factors for commerce, has created competitive challenges in many markets, and the opening of borders has accelerated the flow of goods and funds. The strategic planner of the Danish mortgage banking firm would also be well advised to consider the challenges that European Monetary Union will present, when commercial developers and international firms might prefer to avoid the currency risks of mortgaging in Danish kroner (as Denmark has chosen to remain outside the EMU), and would prefer an international lender. Similarly, globalization has made it more difficult to retain price differentiation in different countries. A buyer from a large retailer recently told us that as soon as his department observed price differences of more than 3–4% on fast-moving consumer goods, he would look into so-called "grey market transfers" of products, that is, buying original products, such as Nescafé, in one country and transferring it to another, to take advantage of differences in the manufacturer's list prices.

A final development which is changing the way we view competitor behaviour and conduct analyses is the rapid development in information and communication technologies which, through speed and volume, can provide buyers, sellers, and competitors with access to information which previously was unimaginable. It is particularly the last few years with their proliferation of Internet usage, which have radically altered our view of competition. This development is likely to continue, and our ability to use this technology will be a deciding factor in the survival of business in the future.

ACADEMIC PERSPECTIVES

The academic literature has concerned itself with competitor analysis for more than two decades. It is striking, however, that the theoretical foundation and underlying assumptions vary significantly across the academic disciplines. There are, of course, several reasons why the various academic disciplines have started from different viewpoints, which relate to their underlying paradigmatic vantage points and the differing purposes of the discourse.

Most students of classical and neo-classical economic theory will have found themselves with relatively few normative tools or guidance, whereas the marketing and strategic management literature has been much more concerned with frameworks that are not only descriptive but which also emphasize normative and decision-making heuristics. In Figure 1.8 we have attempted to provide the reader with one framework to understand the various streams of literature on competitor analysis and their placement in a framework mapping the various schools of thought.

Figure 1.8 places several of the important authors, who represent specific streams of literature about competitor analysis, along two dimensions. The vertical dimension shows the scope of the perspective taken by the authors, ranging from a macro perception of societal implications to a micro level related to individual business actions. The horizontal dimension is on a spectrum from authors who assume a deterministic view (where markets are governed by a natural selection predetermined by laws of economics), to assump-

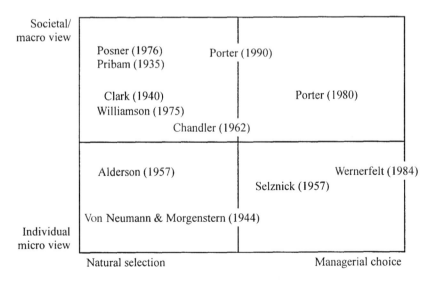

Figure 1.8 Illustrative map of the theoretical orientation of various authors on competitor analysis

tions of managerial choice (where rationality is at best limited, and certainly impacted by both psychological and sociological phenomenon).

The underlying thrust of this illustrative map of the literature on competitor analysis is to point out varying perspectives and thus potential differing outcomes in analysis and description of competitive situations, and the potential normative implications of such analysis. Thus, it is useful to reflect on one's "choice of analytical tool box" and the opportunity for selecting both complementary perspectives to underscore a certain problem set and even "opposing" perspectives in an effort to test the treatment and robustness of a certain analytical exercise.

It should be mentioned, however, that the framework introduced in Figure 1.8 represents only one viewpoint of how the literature on competitor analysis can be mapped. Other examinations of the literature, such as Day and Reibstein (1997) have looked at a number of different perspectives, such as:

1. A resource-based point of view, popularized by Prahalad and Hamel (1990), focusing on the firm's resources or assets and capabilities, and how these may provide advantages for rivals.
2. The positional view, most closely associated with the work of industrial economics, also sometimes referred to as the "Structure–Conduct–Performance" school of competitor analysis, which examines different competitors' relative positions in the industry and the forces which allow firms to sustain strategic positions (Porter, 1985). In their discussion, Day and Reibstein (1997) emphasize that the resource-based approach is concerned with *what* advantages are needed and the positional view is concerned with *how* to create advantages.
3. Game theory, which has been evolving since it was first described in ancient Chinese writings, examines moves and countermoves of competitors. Whereas this school of thought is based firmly on rational behaviour, the next stream of literature reminds us that competitors' movements may be far from "rational" (Teck and Weigelt, 1997).
4. Behavioural theory examines the cognitive and behavioural properties of decision making in competitive environments, including psychological biases and motivational forces (Meyer and Banks, 1997).

5. Public policy has, particularly in a US context, been concerned with the antitrust implications of competitive behaviour in an effort to shield the public from undesired effects of firm strategies. In many ways, the body of literature stands in contrast to the underlying motives of most of the strategic management literature which aims at equipping managers with knowledge which can help create market imperfections (Areda, 1986).

Among academics, there is a saying "there is nothing more practical than a good theory". What the above listing of various theoretical directions should point to is that the problem to be analysed may benefit from one or more theoretical perspectives, and that one cannot necessarily be said to hold a patent on the truth in the area of competitor analysis.

CONCLUSION

It would be appropriate to start a book on assessment of competitors by remembering that competitive analysis uses a broad set of analytical tools which are used to describe market phenomena and produce decision-relevant information for managers at different levels in organizations. Thus it behoves managers and other savants to think about competitive analysis with a context-specific viewpoint and not as a generally applicable methodology.

It is also important to remember that the area of competitor analysis is evolving as a result of developments in globalization of trade and commerce, restructuring of industries, and the evolution of information and communication technologies. These developments are forcing managers to go beyond the traditional definition of their businesses in terms of what they produce and market, to look at new and different configurations of how products and services are transformed in the journey to the end customer.

We can finally conclude that the academic world has been concerned with competitor analyses for many years, but that we are calling for a more integrated view to build an analytical platform from which competitor behaviour can be better described and predicted.

REFERENCES

Alderson, W. (1957). *Marketing Behavior and Executive Action*, Irwin, Homewood, IL.

Areda, P. (1986). *Antitrust Law: An Analysis of Antitrust Principles and Their Application*, Little, Brown, Boston, MA.

Chandler, A.D. Jr (1962). *Strategy and Structure*, MIT Press, Cambridge, MA.

Clark, J.M. (1940). Toward a concept of workable competition. *American Economic Review*, **30**, June, 242–56.

Day, G.S. & Reibstein, D.J. (eds), *Wharton on Dynamic Competitive Strategy*, Wiley, New York.

Hayes, M.H., Jenster, P.V. & Aaby, N.E. (1996). *Business Marketing: A Global Perspective*, Irwin, Chicago, IL.

Jenster, P.V. (1991). DEC-ITT case. *Planning Review*, September/October, 20.

Jenster, P.V. (1992). Competitive analysis: understanding the nature of the beast. *Journal of Strategic Change*, **1**, 28.1–4.

King, W.R. & Cleland, D.I. (1979). *Strategic Planning and Policy*, Van Nostrand Reinhold, New York.

Meyer, R. & Banks, D. (1997). Behavioral theory and naive strategic reasoning. In Day G.S. & Reibstein, D.J. (eds), *Wharton on Dynamic Competitive Strategy*, Wiley, New York.

Porter, M.E. (1980). *Competitive Strategy: Techniques for Analyzing Industries and Competitors*, The Free Press, New York.

Porter, M.E. (1985). *Competitive Advantage*, The Free Press, New York.

Porter, M.E. (1990). *The Competitive Advantage of Nations*, The Free Press, New York.

Posner, R.A. (1976). *Antitrust Law: An Economic Perspective*, University of Chicago Press, Chicago.

Prahalad, C.K. & Hamel, G. (1990). The core competence of the corporation. *Harvard Business Review*, May/June, 79–91.

Pribam, K. (1935). Controlled competition and the organization of American industry. *Quarterly Journal of Economics*, **49**, May, 371–93.

Selznick, P. (1957). *Leadership in Administration*, Harper & Row, New York.

Teck, H.H. & Weigelt, K. (1997). Game theory and competitive strategy. In Day, G.S. & Reibstein, D. (eds), *Wharton on Competitive Strategy*, Wiley, New York.

Von Neuman, J. & Morgenstern, O. (1944). *The Theory of Games and Economic Behavior*, Wiley, New York.

Wernerfelt, B. (1984). A resource-based view of the firm. *Strategic Management Journal*, **5**, 171–80.

Williamson, O.E. (1975). *Markets and Hierarchies: Analysis and Antitrust Implications*, The Free Press, New York.

2
Attack, Defend or Collaborate?

SEEKING COMPETITIVE ADVANTAGE

The whole purpose of competitor analysis is to build competitive advantage. Obviously this cannot be done in isolation from the market and the rest of the industry, because being better than a competitor will not guarantee success if what is offered gives little value to the customer. So any conclusions that might be drawn from competitor analysis must be considered in conjunction with these other factors.

Figure 2.1 gives one view of the strategic moves that are available to any competitor. For the purposes of this diagram, industry should be interpreted as including suppliers, competitors and buyers, and therefore includes the requirements of the market. Chapters 3 and 4 will look in much more detail at industry analysis, including the "Five Forces" approach of Porter (1980).

Every company has strategic options, although this does not mean that all options are sensible for every company. The matrix in Figure 2.1 looks at the things a company might do to build competitive advantage.

- It may choose to operate within the "rules" of the industry, without major change to what it offers. This is the top-left-hand cell of the matrix. The options here include a stronger focus on a niche strategy, seeking to identify and exploit segments where its products would have an advantage, or what might be termed improvement strategies. Those shown on the matrix are finding ways to give added value to customers, or becoming more effi-

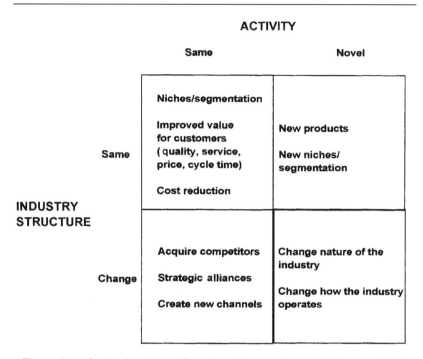

Figure 2.1   Strategic options. (Developed from a diagram in Hussey, 1994)

cient through attention to costs. Under all these strategies, most
of the changes the company would make would be internal,
looking at its processes and making only incremental adjust-
ments to what is basically the same family of products. These
options do not preclude the launch of new products, but these
would be of a similar nature to the current offering.

- The top-right-hand cell suggests a more fundamental change to
  some of the things the organization does, without any significant
  attempt to alter how the industry operates, or the balance of
  power between the industry firms and other "actors" such as
  buyers and suppliers. Strategies might again be attention to
  niches and segments, in a more innovative way than the first cell
  implies, with a willingness to add new lines. Or it might be an
  aggressive policy of new product launches. An example might be
  the automotive manufacturer which adds a new type of car to its
  list, like a sports car when previously it had offered only staid
  family cars.

- At the bottom-left-hand corner there are a group of strategic options which are designed to change how the industry is structured but without any fundamental change to what the organization does. This might include actions to reduce the number of competitors through acquisition, subject, of course, to the national monopolies legislation. Rationalization of an industry has been a traditional strategy followed by competitors anxious to improve their market position. Strategic alliances may be used for a similar reason, although, as will be seen below, there may be better reasons for making alliances. A third group of strategies is to attempt to change the channels the industry has traditionally used. So we find companies like Avon Cosmetics which do not follow the typical wholesaler/retailer route to the customers, and sell direct instead. Not on the chart but in the same category might be an attempt to work much more closely with a supplier, in a way that makes it difficult for competitors to use that supplier in future.

- The bottom-right-hand cell reflects a reinvention of the company and of the industry. It is this type of activity which Hamel and Prahalad (1994) argue should lie at the heart of competitive strategy: "... the goal is to fundamentally reinvent existing competitive space (First Direct's telephone Banking service in the United Kingdom) or invent entirely new competitive space (Netscape's Web browsers) in ways that amaze customers and dismay competitors. Sustainable profitable growth is not the product of a deal, it's the product of foresight. In turn foresight is not the product of perpiscuity, but of unconventional out of the box thinking" (page xi, 1996 paperback edition). Hamel and Prahalad argue that in order to be able to reinvent the industry, the organization must identify its core competencies, and concentrate on building the competency it will need to make the necessary leaps to a different future.

IT IS NOT ALL ABOUT AGGRESSION

One of the things that is striking whenever a competitor analysis is undertaken is that in many industries not all the competitors in an industry are in contention with each other. This does not mean that they may not become "enemies" at some time in the future, which may be a good reason for studying them, but it also provides an opportunity to gain competitive advantage through collaboration. Let us hasten to add that we are not advocating illegal actions, such as price fixing, and, as is the case throughout the book, our stance is that businesses practices' should be both legal and ethical.

There are three obvious examples of non-competing "competitors":

- The segmented market, where competitors at different ends of the spectrum offer products which are not really substitutes for each other, and have few (if any) customers in common. An extreme example can be found in the car industry with Rolls-Royce and Reliant Robin. Both companies make cars, but have little in common besides this, not even the number of wheels on the car. It is not readily apparent what either of these companies could gain from collaboration. If we had said Rolls-Royce and Morgan, both expensive cars but not competing for the same customers, it might be possible to see areas where there could be benefit from collaboration, such as benchmarking each other's processes, exchange of technological information, or sharing dealers overseas.
- The second type of non-competing competitor is the company which makes similar products to yours, but for various reasons does not offer them in the countries in which you trade. Possibly neither organization has the resources to move quickly to become global. Here a strategic alliance might be beneficial to both. This might be achieved by sharing technology, distribution facilities, or plants so that both can gain the benefits of being global, without all the costs that would otherwise be involved. Much more might be gained by both organizations than if they began to move piecemeal into each other's markets, and began to become competitors in earnest. All the commonsense rules of creating a successful alliance apply, not least being the need to understand each other's objectives for seeking an alliance, and a shared vision of what the alliance should achieve.
- A third type of competitor may be one that is in contention with you now, but perhaps in a small way, and which can be removed by collaboration. Here we are thinking particularly about the peripheral activities of someone whose original reason for establishing the competing activity was to provide services to its own organization. Activities such as corporate training colleges,

training, physical distribution, and various other services have often been set up to serve the organization and also offer their services in the market as a whole. Where there are competitors of this type, it may be possible to collaborate with the parent organization and effectively take over the competitor by persuading its owners to enter into an outsourcing deal.

When the Harbridge Consulting Group wanted to offer a Europe-wide management training service to multinational companies it could have followed a risky and expensive programme of setting up an office in every country. This could have taken a long time, but the opportunity seen existed immediately: to be able to offer a common, highly tailored training programme, which could be delivered in a variety of European languages. The alternative chosen was to create a capability through cooperation. Selecting alliance partners from competitors in each country meant that there were mutual benefits. Although some of the revenue went to the alliance partners, it created assignments and revenue for HCG that would otherwise not have been obtained. In Germany office facilities were set up within the premises of a non-competing consultancy. Although there was much more to the pan-European strategy than this, collaboration was a far more attractive method of achieving a Europe-wide presence than any of the other options.

Such methods are not open to every industry, or every organization, but they act as a counterbalance to the attack and defence strategies which may be another outcome of competitive strategy. The aim of competitive strategy is not primarily to kill the competition, but to build a position of sustainable competitive advantage. Indeed it is possible to argue that every organization needs competitors, as without them there is less incentive for creative thinking, and a tendency for the organization to become sleepy and less effective.

DETERRENCE

The concept of deterrence is as old as military conflict. Deterrence is a strategy to prevent conflict, by persuading a rational competitor that you are willing and able to punish non-compliance with your clearly expressed and understood wishes. Deterrence is a strategy for an acceptable peace rather than a war, and is a battle won in the mind of the competitor through psychological pressure rather than by physical combat (James, 1985, p. 27).

In business terms deterrence is a strategy to:

1. Persuade new entrants that the market is not worth entering, because of the way you will react, or
2. Try to stop encroachments into a segment of the market which is important to you, or
3. Attempt to keep a competitor from increasing its market share.

An example is provided by the insurance broking industry in the UK, which for decades held off the threat that the insurance companies whose products they sold would compete with them by selling direct to the market. The threat was that all brokers would cease to recommend any company that took this action, and the insurance companies held off because the speed at which they feared they would lose revenue was greater than the speed at which direct sales were likely to take off. It is only in the past decade that this threat has been overcome, and this was mainly because a new entrant to the market, Direct Line, set up to offer a direct general insurance service over the telephone, took a large market share because it was able to offer lower prices, and in many cases give a better customer service.

The best deterrence is a strong position, which makes it difficult for an attacker to gain a foothold in an economic way. This is not achieved just by having the largest market share. Indeed sheer size and past success often breeds complacency, despite the achievements of the past. It is notable that neither Xerox nor IBM, both of which can be said to have re-created their industries, were as invulnerable as they believed. IBM did not take action early enough to erect a strong position in the personal computer market, and Xerox put too much reliance on its network of patents. In both these cases the judgement appeared to be from the inside, looking out, rather than undertaking an examination of what an attacker might see as a vulnerability.

A strong position has market share as a component, and this may be most important when the learning curve effect means that high volumes give lower costs, which in turn allow prices to be set which other competitors find it difficult to meet. But it is also about technological foresight, adequate levels of research and development, and giving customers value in all respects so that they have little incentive to change.

Porter (1980) terms the tactics used by which one competitor communicates with another as market signals, and points out that they can be bluff or real. Bluffs are intended to mislead competitors into either doing or not doing something. In one study we made of the UK detergents industry we found that one competitor had sales that were considerably higher than its capacity. Investigation showed that it had announced the installation of additional capacity, but had given the impression that it was to replace old plant. In fact it was incremental, but the confusion enabled it to implement its strategy to increase market share without attracting defensive actions from competitors. Sun Tzu, wrote his treatise on the art of war some 2400 years ago. "All warfare is based on deception" he argued, and deception can have its place in the competitive battle. However, there is an added element in business battles, which is that while you may want to deceive the competitor, you rarely want to confuse the customer.

Porter gives examples of market signals, including: early announcements of new product launches, intended to persuade buyers to defer a purchase decision of a competitor's new product until both were available; announcement of capacity expansion, which is large enough for all unfulfilled marketing requirements, to deter others from planning more capacity; and speeches which try to get competitors to hold the line on prices, by giving forecasts of raw material cost rises, and expressing fears that profits are now inadequate to support the research and development needed by the industry.

When Shell Chemicals published their analytical technique, the Directional Policy Matrix, which provided an objective way of looking at prospects for different streams of products, they may well have done so for altruistic motives. Perhaps even more likely was an attempt to persuade the industry to look at data objectively, so that the then-prevailing pattern in the industry of capacity expansion on whim was changed to a less disruptive decision process. A second signal might well have been to tell competitors that they should not think on a single-country basis, as the industry had become more global.

James (1985) suggests that a deterrence strategy must have four elements:

- It must be credible, for if the competitor does not believe it, it will have no effect.

- The company applying a deterrence strategy must have the resources to carry it through, as well as the willingness to do so. If your competitor knows you can afford a price war for much longer than it can, a price war may well be avoided.
- By one means or another actions and counteractions must be communicated between the competitors, without infringing any competition laws.
- The actions should try to persuade competitors to behave in a rational manner, so that disruptive actions which are damaging to all are avoided.

Deterrence strategies do not always work, and are unlikely to be effective against a competitor who is changing the rules of the game. We once saw a pamphlet issued by a manufacturer of radio valves (and it would be no surprise today if many readers have no idea what these are) arguing that the upstart transistors had only limited use, and that valves were the long-term future of the industry. Firms who may have been leaders in duplicating machines and the older-style photocopiers could not hope to defeat the advances of the far superior Xerox machines, when these came on to the market in the 1960s. Electromechanical telephone exchanges had to give way to electronics in the 1970s. The gramophone record had almost disappeared by the end of the 1980s, in the face of competition from the CD. In the 1990s, the shape of the information industry has been changed by developments in telecommunications and computers. Lines drawn in the sand are not credible when a competitor faces such fundamental change.

ATTACK STRATEGIES

We have chosen to deal with attack strategies next, because it is logical to consider how competitive attacks may be made, before looking at defence. Sun Tzu, whose ancient writings on strategy are said to have influenced many modern Japanese companies, argued that the most important thing is to attack an enemy's strategy. Disrupting his alliances is the next best thing; next best is to attack his armies; but the worst option is to attack his cities. For competitive strategy we need to think in somewhat less murderous terms, but the underlying concept of minimum force to achieve maximum advantage is good advice.

- *Attacking the strategy of a competitor.* This can cut the ground from under the competitor's feet, and leave it in a weaker position. The most effective way is one we have already mentioned, which by applying creative, entrepreneurial thinking to a base of sound knowledge and analysis, changes the competitive arena. Another example might be to pre-empt a competitor by getting to market first with a new product, in an area which is known to be of strategic importance.
- *Attacking the competitor's alliances.* An example of this was the acquisition of Rover by BMW. There were undoubtedly many reasons for this acquisition, but one effect was to cause Honda to withdraw from the alliance it had operated for many years with Rover, and its predecessor British Leyland. Similar patterns of alliances changing allegiance have been observed in the airline industry.
- *Attacking the competitor's armies.* This is akin to choosing segments or geographical areas to attack, where the competitor may be weakest, or least able to mount a defence. Sometimes it may be the first step in a longer-term plan of attack, and may not be seen as a major threat in the first instance. When Japanese motorcycle companies entered the European market they started with the low-priced segments, but also began to expand those segments by appealing to different groups of people. This was the spearhead for a long-term attack on the market, which eventually meant that they achieved dominance in all segments.
- *Attacking the competitor's cities.* This is akin to a frontal attack where a competitor is strongest. Risks are higher, and the action ensures that the competitor so attacked will respond.

The first rule of any attack strategy is to know the industry, the market, and the competitors being attacked. If the weak points of the competitors are known, and their likely reactions predicted, the attacker is more likely to arrive at a successful strategy. It is this rational analysis which enables a decision to be made about whether the rewards of success outweigh the costs, and whether the chances of success are high enough to justify the move. The structure of the industry is, in essence, the terrain over which the battles will be fought, and will affect both what is possible and how obvious any full-scale attack might seem. In a highly fragmented market, such as management consulting, where there are no dominant leaders and a long tail of small organizations, it is possible that any attempt by any one small competitor to seize market share will pass largely unnoticed. This is because a quadrupling of sales of a company with, say, a 0.25% market share means that the impact on any one of the several hundred competitors is likely to be negligible, and even if the impact is seen, the reasons for it may not be obvious. In an industry with four or five competitors of roughly equal share, every player will be watching the others very carefully, and is more likely to notice the effect of any attack and who is doing it. Where there is a dominant player at, say, 60% market share, a follower with 25%, and three other companies sharing the rest of the market, the position may be less straightforward. It may be easier for a small company to move against the others than for either of the top two to try to improve their positions. This is because a large increase in sales of a company with a small market share may have little impact on the big company. The other companies may restrain themselves from making a violent response, because to do so would be construed as an attack on the dominant company and invite a response.

Some modern military principles can be used to guide strategy in a business situation. A comparison of the US Army field manual and principles defined by a writer on business strategy appears in Caplan (1965). They are:

1. *The objective*: every action must be directed to the achievement of a clearly defined and attainable objective.
2. *Mass*: adequate resources must be concentrated at the right time and place to achieve the objective.
3. *Economy of force*: to use only the amount of effort that the situation requires.
4. *Manoeuvre*: leave room for flexibility.
5. *Unity of command*: ensure that all action is coordinated to achieve the objective.
6. *Security*: take actions to avoid being surprised by the actions of competitors.
7. *Surprise*: attack the enemy when, where and how the attack is not expected.
8. *Simplicity*: the simple plan is usually the best.

Business is not warfare, and the objective of most competitive attacks is to secure an advantage in profit through growth, market share, or longer-term positioning. It is rarely the annihilation of a competitor, and in any case in many countries there are laws designed to prevent many of the actions that might achieve this.

The classification of attack strategies follows the thinking of Kotler (1994) and James (1985), although there are differences between these two authorities.

1. *The frontal attack.* This is the commercial equivalent of Sun Tzu's worst case: the attack on the enemy's cities. It implies a head-on confrontation where the defence is at its strongest. Some such attacks mirror the defendant's marketing strategy, and hope to achieve results through sheer perseverance. Others have only one point of difference: price. By cutting price for what is otherwise a matched offering, the attacker hopes to be able to persuade customers to switch. Only in markets where there are many niches is it possible to use the full-frontal attack selectively. It clearly does not hurt Rolls-Royce car sales if the cheapest Fiat is discounted, because the products are not comparable. In markets where the products are nearer each other, an attack on one competitor is really an attack on all of them.

   In full-frontal attacks, the victory usually goes to the strongest. However, a dominant competitor is less likely to make a full-frontal attack on a competitor, unless it is a niche operator where the effects of the warfare can be isolated. The reason is that someone with, for example, a 70% market share who has to cut prices across the board to attack a smaller competitor may find that the negative impact on profits is greater than the amount of extra market share that may be gained.

   Frontal attacks have appeal in industries where very large cost reductions can be gained from increases in volume, and where price reductions may stimulate growth in the market as well as stealing share from competitors. This is a feature of markets such as pocket calculators, and various consumer electronic products, where gains in volume can bring considerable competitive benefit.

2. *The flanking attack.* Instead of attacking where a competitor is strongest, the flanking attack goes for areas of weakness. This may be to find geographical areas where the competitor is not performing as well as elsewhere, or to identify segments of the

market which have either not been spotted by the competitor, or are not catered for as well as they might be. In both of these situations the attack may be partly concealed, because if that portion has not been served well, attention to it may expand the market as well as taking sales away from the competitor. If the product has been specifically designed for the segment, it may be some time before the defender can respond. One example of the flanking attack is provided by Simon Aerials in the USA. This was a company that made truck-mounted aerial platforms, of the type that would hoist a worker to the top of a tree or building, and provide a secure platform from which tasks could be undertaken. These heavy vehicles were also used on construction sites, but were not ideal for all jobs because of their size and weight. The company designed a vehicle specifically for the construction industry. It was a fraction of the size and height of the trucks, but would give the same weight, with greater capability to reach awkward places because of the way the lift mechanism worked. Its smaller size meant that it could work inside a building, and had greater manoeuvrability and flexibility. It could also be manufactured at a much lower cost, and could be offered at a cheaper price than the less suitable vehicles traditionally used on construction sites. Because vehicles were smaller, a greater volume could be made in the existing plant, thus capacity was increased without major investment. This flanking attack was successful, as there was little that the competitors could do in the short term, since cutting prices to meet the new machine would have been uneconomic, and would have resulted in unwanted losses in the other markets to which the machines were sold. In any case, the new machine was still better for the construction industry. A comparable product could not be offered until it had been developed.

One example of geographical flanking attacks is the supermarket which erects its new store in an area where its rivals are weakest. Another is First Direct which established a telephone retail banking operation, which not only avoided the need for branch offices but also enabled the company to accept only the business it wanted, thus cherry picking the more profitable segments. EasyJet, a small company, established a cut-price service from the UK to various destinations on the continent of Europe, taking from British Airways both low-margin holiday traffic and some of the premium business travel. Flanking attacks have also been carried out successfully on companies that supply products like tyres and batteries to an original equipment manufacturer. Traditionally the OEM sales have been made at low margins, in order to gain the more lucrative aftermarket for replacements. The flanking attack has been for competitors to enter the replacement market, possibly offering a price advantage, thus picking off a slice of the more profitable business, and leaving the OEM business untouched.

3. *Encirclement.* Under an encirclement strategy the attack is made on several fronts at once. Successful encirclement strategies usually attempt to identify and exploit new niches, and to beat the offer made to the customer by competitors. The attempt by US retailers Sears Roebuck to change the financial services industry in the USA was an encirclement attack on competitors from several different industries at the same time. The in-store credit card was converted to Discovery, a full credit card, a chain of estate agents was acquired, as was a major securities organization. Allstate Insurance had been part of the Sears Roebuck group for many years. The new niche the company hoped to conquer was the private consumer who wanted one-stop shopping: to buy a house, furnish it, obtain all necessary loan facilities, and insure everything in any Sears store. The strategy failed, because the niche was not large enough. The acquisitions therefore did not upset the competitive situation in their industries, and the Discovery credit card became a frontal attack on existing credit card competitors. At one time Sears were reported to have secured the record for signing up the largest number of defaulting clients in the shortest time.

4. *Unconventional or guerrilla warfare.* This is a continuous series of attacks on the competitor's weak areas, particularly where it is possible to avoid a crushing response. The aim is to build market share and thereby gain a stronger overall position. In marketing terms it may mean attacking in countries or regions which may not be of large importance to the competitor, or following a policy of selected price discounting. Guerrilla actions may also include deliberate attempts to entice executives away from a competitor, a not-infrequent occurrence in the financial services industry, and exploiting any opportunities in the legal process (for example, anti-monopolies legislation,

and planning applications) to increase the competitor's costs, or frustrate its intentions.

The military analogies are useful, but they show how actions might be applied, rather than what actions to take. The list below owes much to Kotler (1994), but extends the list of headings that he suggested.

- *Price discounting.* The aim is to offer a comparable product at a lower price. However, the buyers have to be convinced that it is a comparable product, and will take other factors into account, such as after-sales service. The strategy will bring more economies to the challenger if it is linked to actions to reduce the overall costs of the challenger, through actions such as business process re-engineering or the experience curve effect.
- *Lower price, lower quality.* In essence, this strategy tries to appeal to that segment of the market which is only interested in price, or the segment which believes that the current offerings are overspecified. The Ratner jewellery chain in the UK expanded the retail jewellery market, and achieved large growth between 1984 and 1991, by virtually creating a new segment of the market for very cheap jewellery. This brought the resources which enabled the group to buy chains that operated in higher-price/quality segments. Amstrad, a British company, obtained considerable success in the personal computer market by producing a low-priced product which exploited obsolete technology. Because of the rapid changes in technology, component suppliers had large stocks of 8-bit computer components, which ran on the CP/M operating system, instead of the modern DOS. There were also stocks of obsolete 3-inch drives and disks. Amstrad designed a computer around the old technology, taking advantage of the very low costs of these components. It had the user in mind, and drives, computer, monitor and printer were easily connected, and were plugged into the mains by one ready-fitted plug. It was promoted as a word processor that would do other things, and was the first serious computer to penetrate the home market in volume, as well as appealing to small businesses and schools. Here was a low-price product which could not match the specifications of the DOS machines, but which nevertheless gave its users the quality and reliability which they found acceptable.

- *Same price, higher quality.* The offering of a better product at the same price as that of the competitor. How many times do you see "new improved" on a product label as you walk round a supermarket, and how many times do you believe it? Success requires that the customer accepts that the quality is higher.
- *Higher quality/higher price.* Kotler terms this a prestige goods strategy. Essentially it is an attempt to serve a niche which the competitor has neglected.
- *Product proliferation.* Under this strategy the product category is expanded by the launch of additional varieties of the product, giving more choice to the buyer. So instead of a copy of the competitor's product, several varieties are offered.
- *Product innovation.* An innovative version of an old product, or in some cases a new way of packaging it, may be the main feature of an attack. Miller took its US market share to second place by the introduction of a light beer, in an innovative packing. Such a strategy, if successful, usually works by its ability to satisfy a niche that had previously been unidentified. In the UK the introduction by Mars of an ice cream bar version of the chocolate-covered Mars bar not only gave them a good position in the ice cream market but also changed the market as competitors strove to launch products to compete with it.
- *The innovative product to bypass the competitors.* The hardest strategy to devise, and the hardest for competitors to react to, is one that we have mentioned earlier. It is the innovative attempt to change the industry so that new norms are established and the existing competitors are all left isolated, with obsolete products based on old technology. The fax, for example, has driven out the telex because it is simpler to operate and the machines have steadily come down in price over time, and it has dramatically expanded the market for the transmission of hard copy over the telephone system. Other examples have already been given.
- *Innovation of distribution.* New ways may be used to get the product to the ultimate buyer, either through the creation of new channels or the modification of old ones. The example of First Direct has already been mentioned.
- *Advertising and promotion.* A significant increase in advertising and promotion may be used. However, it should be remembered that a brand share may have been built up over many years of promotion matched by the performance of the product, and

merely outspending the competitor for a short period is unlikely to be effective unless there are weaknesses in its position.

A few of these strategies are mutually exclusive, but most can be used in combination with other actions. So it is a question of choosing the most appropriate mix to achieve the objective which lies behind the attack.

DEFENSIVE STRATEGIES

Competitive positions are being attacked all the time. Strategies of deterrence may not hold off the enemy for ever, and in any case are not available to every competitor. Smaller competitors in a market where there is a dominant leader may be able to offer few credible deterrents.

The first issue is to know when there is an attack. Sun Tzu stressed the importance of information. In all markets there is competitive activity, but this does not always imply a serious threat and may be countered by what might be termed the normal actions of marketing. The danger signs are:

- New entrants to the market
- Existing competitors who are trying to move into different segments
- Attempts to change how the market works, which may be through technological change, alterations in the channels of distribution, or changes in relationships with buyers and suppliers
- Abnormal marketing activity, that is outside the expected pattern, such as the enlargement of the sales force, price cutting, expansion of capacity beyond that justified by current market shares, large increases in advertising, or increases in R&D capability.

The first decision when a market position is under obvious and serious attack is whether it should be defended at all. This should be a consideration of the fit of the activity with the strategic vision of the company and an assessment of the resources needed to mount a successful defence. There is a warning, in that retreat from one segment can strengthen the attacker, and put it in a good position to attack the next segment. It may not be long before the core of the business is vulnerable. The companies in the British motorcycle industry followed a path of segmental retreat in the face of competition from Honda, and eventually surrendered the whole market. The belief that Honda and other Japanese companies would stop at the bottom rung of the ladder because they did not have the engineering skills to make quality medium-sized and large motorcycles was a total misreading of the competitive situation.

However, there are times when it is better to give up than to fight for something which is not seen as important for corporate success. Retreat may be a question of letting the market decide, and taking no particular actions to counteract the actions of the attacker. It may be a question of selling the activity, probably to a competitor which may even be the aggressor, thus recovering capital. Alliance may also be a way of reducing the level of commitment needed to resist a determined attack, in that a joint venture between two competitors may mean that a position can be defended at a shared cost. However, if the motivation of one of the parties is to reduce commitment to the market, there may be a recipe for failure.

- *Position defence.* In military terms this is the defence of a previously prepared strong position, the "cities" of Sun Tzu, or the French Maginot Line of the Second World War. The aim is to build an impregnable position, through product differentiation: achieved through image, levels of service, design, quality, reliability, and every other possible way, and by being a low-cost producer. This all-round bastion is better as a deterrent than as a defensive strategy, since a protracted siege may be costly to the attacker: however, if it starts it may also be costly to the defender. Kotler (1994) argues that position defence is often a form of marketing myopia, and it is all too easy for a strong position to turn out as something the attacker can walk around. Position defence implies matching what the attacker does, which leaves the initiative with the aggressor. Sun Tzu advises against a protracted war, as it leaves even the winner in a weak state and vulnerable to further attacks from elsewhere.
- *Counterattack.* The counterattack is an attempt to ward off the intrusions of the attacker. The most effective counterattacks are those which identify an area of weakness in the attacker, and result in carefully chosen, cost-effective responses. It is sensible

to examine the competitor as a whole, and not just the brand or product, as it may be better to attack something important to the competitor than to mount an expensive defence of the product being attacked. This may be a product or a geographical counterattack.

For example, if you and your competitor both make canned cat and dog food, and one of your product lines is attacked on price, it would be worth considering whether to defend this product or to choose the product that contributes the most to the competitor's profits, and make a massive attack on this instead. Or if the competitor is attacking your organization in a country where its present market position is weak, consider attacking it in one of the countries which is more important to its profit and loss account. In this sort of game, there are advantages to the competitor which not only operates in many countries but also has a global approach to marketing, because this gives it the information and the capability to switch the attack to a different country. Companies which operate as a series of local businesses, with local managing directors held responsible for their own profitability, find it much harder to respond in this way, and are easier to attack because of this.

The strategic options available for a counterattack are largely those listed under the attack strategy. The difference is that they are the tools of response rather than aggression, and should be chosen in relation to the attacker's strategy. Would the best counterattack to a massive advertising campaign by a competitor be to respond in kind, to bring forward the launch of the "new improved product" or the innovative packaging change, or to do a money-off promotion? The right answer, and this is not a full list of options, depends on the nature of the attack, and the weaknesses identified in the competitor.

In the Simon Aerials example mentioned earlier, there was little short-term action the competitors could take. The product's price differential was too great to allow for an effective reduction of prices, and it was much more suited to the purpose for which it was aimed than the competitor's products. The medium-term response was to accelerate development of competitive products. As contractors would not all replace their old equipment at once, this meant that competitive products launched within a reasonable time would have a chance of capturing sales. So the main defensive strategy they might have used would be to persuade previously loyal customers that a better version of the product was on its way, and that they should delay any decision to change.

- *Pre-emptive strike.* Anticipating a competitor's moves and frustrating them by attacking first carries the advantage of surprise. In Chapter 7 we will give the example of an advertisement which gave information about the recruitment of a large number of additional sales posts as part of an expansion plan in a particular market segment. A pre-emptive strike might do much to reduce the impact of these moves. There is an old story, probably apocryphal, that when Heinz first suspected that Campbell might be planning to enter the UK market with a range of condensed soups, they frustrated the move for many years by launching a range of condensed soup which was clearly inferior to the traditional canned soups. This established that canned soups were an inferior product to the real thing. The story may well be untrue, but it helps to illustrate the ingenuity which may be used in formulating a pre-emptive strike.

- *Flanking defence.* The flanking defence is an attempt to create positions away from the core of the business, which may either make it more difficult for a competitor to attack or may serve as a basis for counterattack. In this example, we have had to hide the product and the industry, but the actions are substantially correct. The global market leader in the manufacture of a particular type of plant had suffered a series of attacks in Europe from a much smaller competitor which, for the sake of this example, we will say was based in Holland. This was a country that the multinational had avoided because of the extremely strong position of the competitor, and a belief that it would be impossible to make profits there. In turn this meant that the competitor had an extremely profitable home market, which enabled it to fund its gradual erosion of the larger organization's global market share. The flanking strategy was to establish an operation in the competitor's home base, accepting that it would make losses for a long period. This would also provide a base to counterattack the competitor where it might hurt most, should this become necessary in the future.

Both attacking and defensive strategies are most effective when based on a sound knowledge of the competitive arena, and of the key competitors. This is the journey we begin in the next chapter.

REFERENCES

Caplan, R.H. (1965). Relationships between principles of military strategy and principles of business planning. Appendix B of Anthony, R.N. (ed.), *Planning and Control Systems: A Framework for Analysis*, Harvard University Press, Boston, MA.

Hamel, G. & Prahalad, C.K. (1994). *Competing For The Future*, Harvard Business School Press, Boston, MA.

Hussey, D.E. (1994). *Strategy Management: Theory and Practice*, Pergamon, Oxford.

Kotler, P. (1994) *Marketing Management: Analysis, Planning, Implementation and Control*, 8th edition, Prentice Hall, Englewood Cliffs, NJ.

James, B. (1985). *Business Wargames*, Penguin, London (first published by Abacus, 1985).

Porter, M.E. (1980). *Competitive Strategy*, The Free Press, New York.

Sun Tzu (*c* 400 BC) *The Art of War*, The translation used: 1993, Wordsworth Editions, Ware, Herts: translation by Yuan Shibing.

3
Industry Analysis: Key to Understanding the Competitive Arena

THE IMPORTANCE OF INDUSTRY ANALYSIS

Businesses do not operate in a vacuum, and in order to understand the likely behaviour of a competitor we first need to understand the context in which it operates. One element of this is the external business environment in the countries in which the industry operates, a topic which we will return to later in this chapter. The second element, which is what this and the next chapter are mainly about, is the balance of forces which determine competitor behaviour within an industry. This is not just about the relative size of the competitors, but goes backwards to the relative influence of suppliers of the industry and forwards to that of the buyers.

An understanding of the principles is important because it helps us to interpret what a competitor is most likely to do in particular situations. This is never a certainty, but even when a competitor behaves in a way that we did not expect, a knowledge of the principles helps us to understand the most likely results of this behaviour. By using industry analysis in a dynamic way, it is possible to identify what actions might be taken to change the balance of power, and which actors across the whole spectrum could take this action.

So industry analysis is an essential first stage in competitor analysis, and one which if done well helps us to ask the right questions and to make better use of the information we collect on individual competitors. It helps to bring a measure of order to the data we have on the industry, and on the individual competitors within it.

THE CONCEPTS OF INDUSTRY ANALYSIS

The credit for much of the thinking on industry analysis goes to the industrial economists, and notably Michael Porter, who pulled together and further developed much of the thinking about what influences the profitability of an organization in a competitive situation (see Porter, 1975, 1980). Part of his thinking resulted in what has become known as the Five Forces model, i.e.:

- Rivalry among competitors in the industry
- Bargaining power of buyers
- Bargaining power of suppliers
- The relative attraction of substitutes
- Entry/exit barriers.

Within each of the categories are factors which affect the balance of power between the competitor force and each of the others, and between competitors within the industry. Later we will discuss these factors. One main value of the Porter concept is that it broadened thinking, both about the number of forces that should be considered and the factors within each. Traditionally some thought has always been given to competitors and to customers, but Porter demonstrated that this was inadequate to fully understand the industry.

Figure 3.1 builds from the Five Forces. It owes a debt to Porter's work, but makes two different points of emphasis, and adds another important force which is not in the Porter model. The figure makes it clear that substitutes are really two different forces: between suppliers and the industry, and between the industry and its buyers. Entry and exit barriers have been separated, because they are totally different forces, which work in different ways. The totally new force is influencers. A critical element between the industry and a buyer is often an organization or person who determines a key aspect of the buying decision. One example is given in Chapter 7 in the role of the consulting engineer in the ASH case. Another, which everyone will be familiar with, is found in ethical pharmaceuticals. Take a situation where a child is ill. A doctor determines what drug is necessary

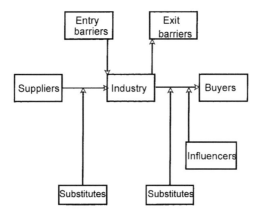

Figure 3.1 Components of industry analysis

and writes a prescription: the doctor does not buy the drug, but without the prescription the chemist cannot dispense it. The parent collects the prescription from the chemist. In some countries he or she does not "buy" it, as it may be paid for by a national health service: in others cash may pass, or there may be a minimum prescription charge which has no relation to the price of the drug. If we wanted to study the ethical pharmaceuticals industry we need to take the doctor into consideration, for if he or she does not prescribe our product the chemist will not stock it. But in this industry there may also be a national health service, which in one sense is the ultimate buyer, but not the user, of the product, and may influence the market by urging doctors to prescribe a generic version of our product, because it is cheaper. The complexities in this brief and incomplete example take us beyond the scope of Figure 3.1, and are something we will return to later. For the time being our figure is all we need to consider the factors which will affect the profitability and competitive strength of any firm in the industry. Real-life situations will bring us more issues to consider, but will not change the underlying principles.

FACTORS WHICH INFLUENCE THE COMPETITIVE POSITION

One of the difficulties of writing about the factors that influence competitive success is that the points have to be set out sequentially.

In a real situation only some of the factors will affect a particular competitor in the industry, and they are not necessarily the same factors for every competitor. It is how the individual organization manages its situation to achieve the most favourable balance of factors across all the forces that is the ultimate determinant.

In discussing the factors, and to avoid repetition, we have given one list of factors which covers both the buyer and supplier components of the model. Of course, there needs to be some mental manipulation, for whereas the industry is in the position of a supplier to its buyers, it is a buyer to its suppliers. So when we look at what strengthens or weakens the power of a buyer this can be interpreted as what strengthens our buyer's power weakens us: but when we are the buyer, it strengthens us in relation to our suppliers. The opposite applies to the factors which weaken a buyer's power.

When undertaking industry analysis it is important to remember that the profitability of the whole chain in the industry may not necessarily be driven by the competitors in the industry. Intel at the supply end and Microsoft as both a supplier and a creator of overall demand through software sales have shifted much of the power in the personal computer industry to themselves from the manufacturers of personal computers.

The structure of industries changes, so it is important not to rely on static analysis. A dynamic view is essential (see later). Failure to understand the changes that are taking place can give rise to serious strategic errors, as, for example, when Xerox failed to see the threat posed to it when Canon entered the market, and when IBM underestimated the changes that the personal computer would bring.

When looking at the factors which should be considered when analysing an industry it is important to take a balanced view. A negative impact of one factor may be cancelled out by a positive impact elsewhere. But to understand the factors we do need to look at them separately. They will be considered in relation to the headings of Figure 3.1.

Competitors in the Industry

1. *Number of firms and relative market shares.* A fragmented industry where no one firm has a significant market share tends to be more fiercely competitive than one which has a clear market

leader who is in a dominant position. A lack of clear market leaders may be because the industry is emerging and is in a condition of considerable turbulence and uncertainty, or it may be a more mature industry where there are low entry barriers and few advantages to size. The ferocity of competition is also affected by the degree of "protection" given by locality. There may be thousands of hairdressers in a country, but because they supply a relatively local service the strength of competition is related to the size of the local market in relation to the number of firms in that market. In this situation market share may be less important than whether there is enough business to allow profitable trading for all the competitors.

When a market has a dominant leader, whose market share is considerably higher than any of its competitors, competition may be less violent. As long as those firms holding the smaller shares do not threaten the leader, behaviour in the industry can be summed up with the word "gentlemanly". This was the position in the computer industry until the advent of the personal computer, where for years IBM was the dominant player.

2. *Growth rates in the industry.* Competitive behaviour tends to be less aggressive when growth rates are maintained, because each firm can achieve its growth objectives without having to steal market share from others. This may not hold true for an industry at the early phase of the product life cycle, when existing competitors are striving to attain a sustainable position and high growth is attracting new entrants. What is often a trigger to more aggressive competitor behaviour is a change in growth rates. Competitors in all industries tend to take actions to maintain volumes in times of recession and may break the behaviour pattern of the past. When an industry matures and growth slows, there is often a period of intense competition as some players are shaken out of the industry. This means that an industry whose growth rate has plunged from 10% to 1% is likely to be more competitive than one whose growth rate has been 1% over a long period.

3. *Nature of the product.* A perishable product which may be a physical product, which cannot be stored for any length of time, or a service such as a seat on an aeroplane or the time of a management consultant tends to be more susceptible to random moves by competitors as they strive to avoid loss. This may be

offset to some degree by the success the competitor has in obtaining prices that are high enough to cover part of the loss. Management consultancies and solicitors may be able to sustain a certain amount of downtime without slashing prices: a low-margin product, such as fresh fruit, may leave the competitors few options other than to cut prices to try to dispose of surplus stocks.

4. *Degree of differentiation.* The closer a product is to a commodity, the more intense the competition in the industry will be. Where product differentiation is high, and there is less of a substitute effect between the products of the various competitors, the tendency is for some protection to be obtained against the actions of competitors. Protecting this degree of differentiation should be a key element of the organization's strategy.

5. *General level of profits in the industry.* A very profitable industry often tends to be somewhat complacent. If all competitors are profitable there is no incentive to rock the boat by aggressive actions. A decline of profitability, like a fall in growth rates, may be a trigger for less tolerance of competitors.

6. *Level of fixed costs.* When investment is large and highly specialized, and fixed costs are a relatively high proportion of total costs, competitors tend to "hang on", selling at less than full costs, when the market slumps or there is overcapacity for some other reason. Shipping, oil refinery, and petrochemicals are examples of such industries, where competitive behaviour has led to continued trading at low profits or losses over a long period, because the alternative is plant closure at a time when assets cannot be realized.

7. *Economies of scale/experience curve.* In some industries there are clear advantages to being big, as the experience curve effect means that increases in volume bring predictable decreases in costs. When demand is elastic, such as with consumer electronic products, a lower-cost producer can expand the market, and each increase of market share fuels further decreases in cost, making it much harder for competitors to stay in the market. While these conditions are maintained, competitive rivalry will tend to be fierce.

8. *New owner or chief executive.* Another factor that may increase or decrease the fierceness of competition is a change either of ownership of a competitor, or of its chief executive.

Often an industry will settle down to an established pattern of competitive behaviour, where certain unwritten rules become established, and each member of the industry recognizes certain no-go areas. So no one ever goes in for aggressive price cutting, or launching products that are intended to damage part of the business of a competitor. Then a competitor is acquired by an organization that is not in the industry, and the new owner either does not know the unwritten rules or has no interest in maintaining them. The same effect can occur when a new chief executive is brought in from another industry.

In competitor analysis any change of this type is a danger signal. Although an increase in aggressiveness is not inevitable, it is a time to consider the possibility. It is also worth challenging the assumptions under which the company's managers act.

Buyers (the converse of these factors applies to suppliers)

1. *Dependencies.* If one party is highly dependent on the other, its power increases. The industry firm that depends on one buyer for most of its profits may find that it has to dance to the buyer's tune. Similarly, the sole supplier of a critical component may be able to determine its own level of prices. The ratio of industry firms to buying firms is an important indicator of whether the balance of power lies with the industry or with the buyer. The position is complicated by switching costs. If a buyer can only change a supplier at some expense, which may be additional capital and revenue costs, or lost profits because of production shutdowns while the switch is being made, the industry firm's power will increase. This was once the position with computers: if you started with IBM, expansion and upgrading tended also to be IBM, although it is not the same with personal computers, where it costs little to switch (unless to and from Apple). Looking at ways to increase switching costs for its buyers is one strategy that can be applied to help an industry firm retain the initiative, or to neutralize an advantage a buyer has over it.

2. *Relative size.* If the industry includes firms that are considerably larger than their customers, sheer weight of resources may put them in a dominant position. The converse may apply when the buying organizations are the largest. This is not a universal

rule as other factors may outweigh it. For example, access to the UK grocery markets is largely controlled by a few supermarket chains, who not only control most of the sales volume going to consumers but also have arrangements with contract packers to make own-label products for them. These can be adjusted in volume, space, and shelf space if branded manufacturers do not toe the line. In this way they may determine the profitability of manufacturers, although these may be parts of giant global corporations.

3. *Profitability of the buying industry.* The industry firms are likely to be in a healthier position when they are selling to a profitable industry. When buyers are unprofitable, or have low profits, there is likely to be strong pressure on the industry to reduce prices, or at best to hold them stable. Resistance against price increases, and an increased tendency to change suppliers, may be greater when the buyer faces an elastic demand curve and cannot pass on price increases. The modern tendency is for buyers and suppliers to try to work together so that both are profitable, but this does not apply in all situations.

4. *Experience of buyers.* Although experienced buyers may instigate actions to work more closely with the industry, they are also more likely to be aware of all the competitors, the levels of quality and the prices at which they are available, and to have coordinated their needs across the whole organization in order to ensure one standard price is paid to their suppliers. Less experienced buyers, or buyers in an emerging industry, may not be in such a strong position, either because of lack of information or because the requirements are changing so fast that there is no time to understand the suppliers.

5. *Threat of integration.* The possibility of integration forwards by an industry into its buyer's business or backwards by the buyer to the industry may be a considerable source of power. Whichever party can offer the implied threat gains a potential advantage over the other. The threat has to be credible. It may, for example, be entirely possible that a giant multinational oil company could decide to move into the management training business, or as a minimum undertake in-house the services it was buying: it is not credible that the modest-sized consultancy it was using to provide its training could offer a credible threat to challenge the oil industry. A threat does not have to be

implemented, or even made explicit, for it to influence the balance of power. It is interesting to speculate whether the 1997 Microsoft deal for Viglen, a British manufacturer of personal computers, to produce a Microsoft-badged range of PCs is a way of making an implied threat to move seriously into the hardware business, thus erecting another bastion around Microsoft's already strong position.

Entry barriers

One way to think about entry barriers is to compare them to a boundary around an orchard. If the fruit trees were diseased, and the fruit sparse and of poor quality, the weakest of fences would be enough to deter thieves. A good-quality orchard might find that a security fence was essential, and that even with this some determined predators could find ways of breaking into the orchard. If the fruit had unique properties, perhaps the apples were from the original stock from the Garden of Eden, security alarms and guards might be necessary to try to keep thieves out. In other words, entry barriers which might deter a new entrant from going into a poor industry may be inadequate to keep out someone from attacking an industry with strong growth and profit prospects. So any discussion about entry barriers should be interpreted according to the situation.

New entrants to a market should be of considerable concern in competitor analysis, as they are difficult to predict. There are four types of possible new entrants:

- Organizations that are in the industry already but in a different part of the world. The forces of globalization have led to much more cross-border movement of companies and products, and the process has not yet ended.
- Organizations that are in closely related businesses.
- New businesses set up by individuals who have been employed in other firms in the industry and therefore already know the business. This is very prevalent in service businesses where entry barriers are low, but is not restricted to this as well-connected individuals are often able to obtain financial backing which enables them to overcome many of the barriers.
- Rank outsiders, of whom little may be known. Given the move-

ment by Sears Roebuck into financial services in the 1980s (although they had owned an insurance company for many years longer than this), it was not surprising to see Marks & Spencer add banking services to their activities in the UK, and not totally unpredictable that major supermarkets would follow suit. However, who would have expected Virgin, with (at that time) its interests in the music industry and retailing, to open an airline?

A determined entrant may try to avoid many of the barriers by alliance with, or acquisition of, one of the existing players. When such moves occur, it becomes even more important to assess the strategic reasons behind them. A change of ownership may not necessarily imply more than that, but when an organization in a related business, or the same business in another country, makes such a move there may be much more reason for concern. For example, when Otis Elevators bought into lift companies in central and eastern Europe it would have been a mistake for any competitors in those countries to assume that this would bring no change to the local competitive scene.

It is in the interests of competitors in an industry to raise entry barriers when this is possible (and legal), and this is an action that can be seen in practice. The attempts by the British security services industry to obtain legal regulation of their industry have less to do with its declared intention of working for the common good than to stem the flow of new security firms which any individual can easily establish. Although some of the high-tech parts of the industry have higher barriers, the guard and patrol business has become a commodity because of the volume of competition.

What creates entry barriers?

- A high level of differentiation will raise entry barriers, since any newcomer will have to make a significant marketing investment to gain any significant market share.
- Patents may prevent others from competing because the technology is not open to them, but this can also create an unfounded complacency. Xerox ignored the threat from Canon until it was too late, because in order to enter the market Canon had to develop products that did not infringe Xerox's 600-plus patents. Had the copier industry not had high growth and profitability characteristics, it is unlikely that Canon would have expended the enormous effort to do this.

- The cost structure of the firms in the industry. If a critical element in profitability is determined by economies of scale or the experience curve, it follows that any newcomer will have to make a large investment in capacity, and may face losses and considerable risks when trying to build up to the volume needed. However, it must be remembered that many such products are no longer made on the basis of a factory in every country, and the barrier may be non-existent for a company that is not in your market but which can ship products in from operations in other countries.

- In addition to patents, there may be other factors which make it difficult for others to gain a foothold in a particular market. These may be government restrictions: for example, a new airline can only operate if it has landing slots, and as there are a finite number of these it is rare for there to be spare slots available. Long-term contracts with buyers can make it harder for others to break in. The modern tendency to have "preferred suppliers" makes it harder for another to gain a foothold. Control of distribution outlets may also create barriers, but this should not be overestimated. When Honda attacked the British motorcycle industry there were no dealers available to distribute their products, so they set about creating new dealers by persuading bicycle retailers to convert, a task made easier because the first Honda motorcycles were not much bigger than a bicycle.

Exit barriers

Exit barriers work in quite a different way. They imprison an organization so that it cannot escape from the industry without loss, and will therefore continue to operate as long as there is cash to support it. The oil-refining industry in Europe continued to add capacity after the OPEC oil crisis of the early 1970s, despite the fact that demand for petrol fell dramatically throughout the decade. No companies were willing to abandon partly built refineries. The industry continued to have severe overcapacity through the 1980s, with the consequent effect on competitor behaviour, until BP began to lead a move to close down some of its refineries. Highly specialized assets may be impossible to sell when there are conditions of overcapacity, and the inability to take the capital loss (and sometimes the obligation to clean up an abandoned site) means that it is extremely difficult to exit. The stronger these exit barriers are, the more likely it is that there will be periods of extreme competitive aggression whenever trading conditions are bad.

Substitutes

For reasons described earlier, substitutes appear in two positions on Figure 3.1. However, the effect they have on the competitive arena is similar, and if we describe the impact on the industry firm/buyer relationship there should be no difficulty in reinterpreting this for the supplier/industry firm relationship. It would be possible to argue that there should be no separate consideration of substitutes, because if they exist they should be brought into the industry definition. Most people would agree that it would be pointless for a company that made canned dog food to insist that dried dog food was a substitute and not really part of the overall pet food market. The glass bottle industry would be foolish not to consider the manufacturers of PEP bottles and drink cartons as competitors. Similarly we can see without difficulty that a company which made steel cans would be very shortsighted if it excluded aluminium cans from its definition of the industry. In such examples it makes much more sense to treat the substitutes as part of the industry, and the firms in it as competitors. As we will see in the next chapter, there is room to examine various segments when analysing competitors.

The position when a more general view of substitutes is taken is somewhat different. Although both are forms of transport, a bicycle is hardly a substitute for a plane ticket. Yet even here things change, and fast trains through the Channel Tunnel are certainly now in direct competition with flights to some destinations. Often the impact of a broad substitute is on the market: a government may tax and regulate private cars so that buses and trains are used instead. This may affect the demand for cars, but it is not really realistic to consider a local bus company as a competitor to Ford or BMW.

When a substitute offers a real or likely threat to the current industry products, it should be studied in the same way as the industry. When it does not, it may be a relevant factor to consider when looking at the future of the market, but it is only a matter for industry and competitor analysis if the buyer is able to use it as a threat to gain advantage over the seller. The availability of real substitutes strengthens the position of the buyer.

Influencers

The difficulty with influencers is that they are not always obvious, but this does not make them any less important. What is important in any study of an industry is to assess whether influencers play a role in the buying decision process, and to set strategies to either influence the influencers or to eliminate their role. This means obtaining good information about the businesses which influence the buyers, and using that information to formulate a plan of action.

THE INDUSTRY AND THE EXTERNAL BUSINESS ENVIRONMENT

Figure 3.2 adds a further step in the analysis of an industry. This is the elements in the external environment which affect the demand for the product and the businesses of the "actors" on the competitive stage. The figure is intended to mirror the reality, that every industry operates within an environment, and that that environment is continually changing. So our industry analysis diagram is set within a diagram of its external world.

The outer octagon offers some broad headings that might be used as a check list to aid thinking about what is going on in this outside world. They are, of course, very broad headings, and there are many subheadings which should be considered under each. For example, under the economic heading there are factors like the level of unemployment, inflation, growth or decline of GDP, and foreign exchange rates.

The faint lines which connect every point to every other are intended to imply that everything has a potential influence on everything else. Thus changes in economic circumstances may trigger different social trends and opinions, which may then cause political pressure to be brought to bear, and eventually the political view may result in changes in legislation. (See Hussey, 1998, if more information is needed about this view of the environment, and methods of assessing it.)

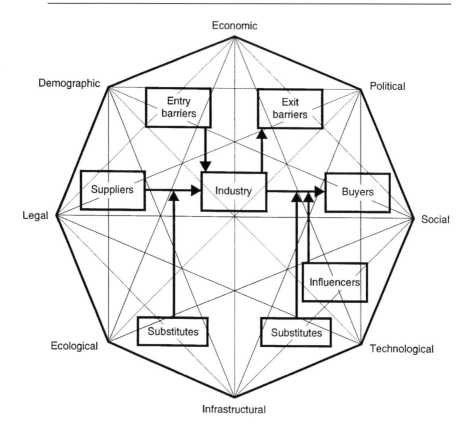

Figure 3.2   The industry and the business environment

It is tempting to argue that external factors affect everyone in the industry in the same way, and that they are important for looking at market trends but can be ignored in competitor analysis. This would be a naive conclusion. First, the products of every firm in the industry are rarely identical, nor are they all manufactured in the same country. So changes in economic factors, such as inflation, will not hit every competitor in exactly the same way, because labour costs rises are not identical in all countries, and a different mix of components and raw materials may mean that rises in these costs are not evenly spread, even when the competitors manufacture in the same country.

The different segments where competitors have their strengths may not all have identical vulnerability to, for example, changes in unemployment levels. In fact, in some markets, if a premium segment of the market becomes smaller, it is possible that a low-priced segment may increase. A competitor in the higher-priced segment may be tempted to move into another segment in order to offset a decline in sales.

A consideration of change in the business environment in relation to the industry is one of the important steps which helps to change industry and competitor analysis from an examination of the past to a dynamic appreciation of what may be different in the future. Further ways of ensuring a dynamic view will be discussed in the next chapter.

THE LIFE CYCLE AND THE INDUSTRY

Figure 3.3 draws attention to another factor which affects behaviour across the whole industry. This is the position in the life cycle of the industry. Before discussing this figure, we should stress that it is a generalization, and what actually happens in any one industry will depend on all the factors we have already discussed. If entry barriers are high, some of the issues suggested, for example in the emerging industry, may not happen as the diagram suggests. A lot also depends how long a phase of the industry life cycle lasts, and how dramatic is the change from one phase to another. In the modern world, many industries may move rapidly from one phase to another, and sometimes be overtaken by the merging of industries, or under the onslaught of new technology. The figure should be used as a very approximate guide to some of the things that might be expected, rather than as a firm statement of what will happen.

The emerging industry, particularly if the technology is new, is characterized by uncertainty. A typical situation is of a period of negative cash flow, as capital requirements chase the expansion of demand, and as markets are developed. If growth is high, newcomers may enter the industry. The learning curve effect may be very noticeable in certain types of industries, such as manufactured products where there is an elastic demand, and the pioneers try to build volume fast in order to gain the cost advantages of high cumulative volume.

We have not illustrated what may be a fairly consistent period of growth as the industry takes off, although a little thought will show that this would be a very different situation for the competitors in an

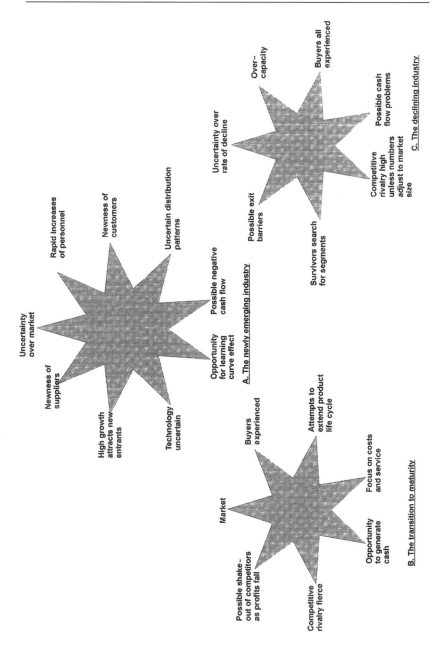

Figure 3.3   The effect of the product life cycle on industries

industry. We join the life cycle again at a point where the industry is moving towards maturity. Growth rates are slowing dramatically, and competition might be expected to become fiercer as each competitor strives to obtain its historic pattern of growth. This may cause a fall in profits, and lead to a shake-out in the industry. It depends on the number of competitors, and their relative market shares, and in some situations emphasis on costs, and attempts to extend the life cycle through product enhancements and add-ons may enable profits to hold up. In many industries, the slowing growth of the industry may bring an opportunity to generate cash, as there is no longer a need to expand capacity. However, this depends on the lead time of investments. It was noticeable that the European oil refinery industry continued to expand capacity for several years after the OPEC oil crisis of the 1970s. Although demand slumped and continued to decline over several years as buyers were motivated to save energy, much of the new capacity was already partly built, and the oil companies felt they had no option but to complete its construction. It was not until the 1980s that the industry began to close capacity.

We have skipped the period of maturity, which can, for the reasons given earlier, be a time when the industry's cash inflow considerably exceeds its outflow. Such a period may last for many years: an example is the tobacco industry in the USA and most of Europe.

Our final illustration is the industry which is in decline. Once again uncertainty is the order of the day. There may be a frantic scramble to find new segments. Unless there is a shake-out, it may be a period of low profit or even losses. Competitors are especially vulnerable to recession. In the rare situations where the shake-out leaves only one or two players, with the obvious reduction of rivalry, it may be possible to do very well in a declining industry, but this is the exception.

WHAT IS THE "INDUSTRY"?

So far we have left open the critical issue of determining the parameters of the industry we are studying. When we discussed substitutes we suggested that real substitutes might be considered within our industry definition, effectively taking more of a market view of the industry than the more traditional technology view. The definition of the industry should be related to markets, but not too narrowly. In other words, it would be a mistake to analyse only the product/segment of an industry that we had chosen to operate in, and to ignore other product/segments which form part of the overall market. For example, if we only manufacture wheat beer, it would be very silly to analyse only the wheat beer market. This would deprive us of a full understanding of the whole industry, and would stop us examining competitors who did not currently make our product, but could easily do so if they wished.

Almost every marketing manager likes to be able to claim brand leadership, and this is nearly always possible if the segments are narrowed down enough. However important this narrowing may be for marketing claims, it would be disastrous for industry analysis. We have several times had experience with organizations which once provided particular types of plant and machinery to the world but which have not kept their technology up to date, and have ended up losing markets in the developed world, and supplying only the less sophisticated markets of the Third World. However, as these markets either move to world standards for the industry, or disappear, it follows that analysing only the low-technology end of the industry can deliver misleading information.

There is another important aspect to consider. This is the geographical area in the investigation. We may operate only in one country, and at this time this is our only important market. But can we sensibly think of our industry only in parochial terms? Instead of thinking, for example, of just the French industry, should we not extend our thinking to the European Union? Is there any reason why this restriction is appropriate? Should we be thinking even more globally?

Clearly in this case we should want to look at the French industry in detail. If we have a number of competitors which are multinational companies, we cannot begin to understand them unless, as a minimum, we extend our analysis of the competitors to their total operation, and if the market is truly global we may be forced to paint our picture of the industry on a wider canvas.

Our experience has been that often too narrow a view is taken, with the company limiting its focus to the things it does itself. Thus we have found a machine tool manufacturer who believed that it needed to consider only the British industry, because it itself was restricted by a technology agreement from offering its main product in other countries: yet all its competitors in its narrow product segment were from Japan or Germany. There was the fast-moving grocery products company that undertook a European analysis (restricted to the countries in which it operated). One major multinational competitor operated in only one or two of the countries in Europe, and the conclusion was that it could almost be ignored, as its interest in the product category was so small, and appeared to be more of a matter of historical activities rather than a deliberate strategy. When this competitor was considered as a total business, it was found that it was making massive investments in this industry, acquiring marketing and manufacturing businesses in a number of countries around the world, and building up strong R&D capability in North America and elsewhere. It simply had not got round to extending the global strategy across Europe, but it was clearly an error to assume that it had no real interest in this product area.

The only guidance that can be given is to think very carefully about what is an appropriate scope for the industry. There are still some industries where a country analysis is completely adequate. There are many others where the old definitions are suspect, and there is a need to extend the thinking. By all means begin by looking at a particular country, but always be willing to extend the analysis as it progresses, and deliberately seek out any indications that this should be done. The worst assumption to make is that the industry is only what you happen to do, rather than what it really is.

In the next chapter we will explore some ways of applying and interpreting industry analysis.

REFERENCES

Hussey, D.E. (1998). *Strategic Management: Theory and Implementation*, 4th edition, Butterworth-Heinemann, Oxford.

Porter, M.E. (1975). *Note on the structural analysis of industries*, Harvard Business School, Cambridge, MA (a teaching note in the case study collection).

Porter, M.E. (1980). *Competitive Strategy*, The Free Press, New York.

4

Industry Analysis in Practice

GETTING STARTED

There is always a difference between understanding a concept and actually applying it in a real situation, and there are at least three questions that the analyst has to answer before a start can be made. What information do we need to undertake industry analysis? What do we have at present? How should we use that information? In considering the last point, it is worth also thinking about how the information will be communicated to others once it has been analysed.

Industries vary in the amount of good statistical data that is available, and organizations vary in the attention they have paid in collecting relevant information. As a generalization it is true to say that consumer products companies tend to have much more information about markets, channels, consumers and competitors than do industrial products companies. Professional services organizations tend to have much less hard information about their industries than even industrial products organizations. Lack of information at the start of the analysis does not mean that nothing can be achieved, as the case history in Chapter 8 demonstrates, but it does make it harder to get started.

The first step for the analyst is to collect together the hard data that is available, and to tap into managers to obtain the soft data that they all possess. The term "analyst" is used here not as a job title but meaning no more than the person doing the analysis, who may be the managing director, a staff specialist or a manager in any position or at any level.

One of the things that in most organizations will become obvious the minute anyone takes the first serious step to undertaking industry analysis is that the headings in the Porter Five Forces model, and even in the expanded version we have used, are too broad. There is a need to categorize buyers, and also to think of whether they sit at the end of the chain or are part of the channel which enables the products to reach the final consumer. Two examples will help to clarify this.

A company like Heinz will make its sales to retailers such as the supermarket chains. It may also sell to wholesalers, to cash-and-carry warehouses, and to specialist retailers who may vary with the product (chemists may be important for baby food but not for baked beans). All these buyers sell on the products to consumers, and Heinz will be as interested in the end users as it is in its buyers. The consumers are indirect buyers but behave very differently from the trade customers. However, they do not all have the same requirements, and need to be thought of in terms of market segments, because the Heinz competitive position may vary between segments, either from choice or because of competitive rivalry. And different types of trade buyers exercise different levels of influence over Heinz, and Heinz again may have greater strengths in some channels than in others. Just as we think we have got all this sussed out, we suddenly remember that Heinz products may also be sold to the catering industry, which has a different pattern of buyers and ultimate consumers. So we have to think this through too. This would then bring us to a point when we should define the industry further. In a broad sense we can say that Heinz is in the food industry, but it is unlikely that the competitors for soups, baked beans and baby foods are the same for each classification. So although we might come to the same conclusion about the relative power of Heinz and Tesco we would probably want to make a different analysis for each of the products, as the competitors and consumers are different.

Now let us take a company which makes batteries for vehicles such as forklift trucks. There are two markets here, the original equipment manufacturers (OEMs) for inclusion in their products and the replacement market. It is likely that not all competitors will serve both. OEMs almost certainly will buy direct from the battery companies. Replacement sales will be made to wholesalers, service centres, OEMs, and sometimes direct to those organizations which operate large fleets of forklift trucks. So again we have a far more complex situation to analyse and consider.

The supply side of our analysis may be equally complicated. It does not make sense to throw all suppliers into one box. Every organization uses office stationery, yet the power that the suppliers of this exercise over organizations is almost non-existent. But what about the suppliers of chips for computers, where there may be only a few suppliers for the whole world? Clearly we need to separate the suppliers into categories, and not waste time on detailed examination of the unimportant. But our suppliers may not be at the start of the chain, and we may need to look behind them in some cases to look at their suppliers.

There is something else we have to decide before we really get started, and this is how far along the chain from the first raw material to the ultimate consumer we need to analyse. Take the travel agency business as an example. This divides into two businesses. One is a leisure business offering services, mainly package holidays, to the individual. The other activity is business travel, dealing with the requirements of companies for the travel arrangements of their staff. Here package holidays are only sold to individuals in the client businesses. Business travel bookings made have to match the needs of the customer. This is straightforward so far. When we look at suppliers we have to stretch the definition a little, as the role is agency or consultant, but this does not impede the analysis. The leisure side deals with package holiday companies as well as with individual rail, air, ship, ferry, coach, car hire, and hotel bookings, and insurance. The package holiday companies also deal with these other suppliers, often to a greater extent than do any of the firms of travel agents.

The situation is made more complex by the fact that some package holiday firms own travel agents and airlines and hotels. Some airlines own hotels and travel agents, although this tendency is less marked now than it was twenty years ago. Airlines are major buyers of equipment and services, the most obvious of which are the aeroplanes. But sometimes they lease these planes, even from competitors.

If we were leisure travel agents we would want to make a study of the package holiday companies, because some of them are also competitors in our business, and because they are our major suppliers. We might want to understand the airline industry, but we certainly would not want to consider their suppliers, such as the airframe and aero-engine companies. However, if we were an airline, we should certainly be considering these suppliers in depth, as well as looking forward at both the package holiday and travel agents industries, right to the ultimate user of our services (we would also want to review charter and scheduled airline competitors, and add the airfreight business to what we had to study).

The point is that although we could argue that all the suppliers and the travel agents are part of the travel industry, we would choose a different arena to analyse depending on where we sat in that industry. A decision has to be made of what makes sense, and will give useful results.

MAKING SENSE OF A MASS OF INFORMATION

These brief examples have begun to show the complexity of the analysis, and we already know from the previous chapter that we need to answer a number of questions, which requires the manipulation of a great deal of information. One method developed by Hussey is to chart the industry, creating a block diagram to represent the various groups of "actors" we want to consider, so that we have a visual picture of the industry. Key information is then recorded on this diagram in note form so that interpretation becomes easier, and communication with others is facilitated. The implications of the analysis are recorded on a separate sheet, and, of course, extra information may be added either on this sheet or in an appendix.

This approach has been used in a variety of consulting assignments, and the normal presentation has been to use A3 paper, and to bind the sheets so that the chart and the implications are on facing pages. Sometimes one such pair of pages is adequate, but more likely an organization will have several pairs to cover different products and/or geographical areas. The advantage is that complex situations can be expressed in very few pages. Typically, the analysis would be supplemented by one-page charts of key competitors, and possibly key buyers and suppliers. These contribute to the understanding of the situation, and have another use which we will come to later, in using industry analysis in a dynamic way.

The examples given here are compressed to fit the book, and the data recorded has been simplified for the same reason. Colours can be used in a real situation, and this can expand the information that can be displayed, as it reduces the amount of explanation. For example, the normal path of distribution for the industry might be shown through black lines connecting the boxes that represent the groups of actors, while your company's path might be shown in a colour. This immediately shows the difference without the need for long explanations. The percentage of product that goes through each channel may be indicated by numbers written on the lines. But we are getting a little ahead, and need to give some examples of how to undertake this type of analysis.

The Outline Diagrams

The first step is to prepare a block diagram for the industry as you have defined it for the analysis. The starting point may be what your company does, but it would be a mistake not to check this against the broader canvas of the rest of the industry. First, we are interested in identifying all the means by which the product reaches the customer, not just the method your organization has chosen. Thus in our example in Figure 4.1 of a toiletry such as a haircare product most competitors do not supply direct to the consumer, but to ignore this would mean that we omitted organizations such as Avon. Second, we need to ensure that the chart is not just restricted to the product activity which we undertake. Not all toiletries manufacturers are in the own-label business, and many companies make this their only business. To ignore this activity would be to run the risk of not fully understanding the dynamics of the industry.

The outline block diagrams can usually be drawn from discussions with managers inside the organization, supplemented by market research reports. However, our experience is that managers sometimes ignore those aspects of the industry in which they do not participate, so great care should be exercised when they are the primary source of information, and a lot of prompting may be needed to ensure that every aspect is captured.

Figure 4.1 gives a reasonable first picture of the way the industry works, and might be what results from the first round of thinking. The three key groupings of suppliers represent raw materials, packaging, etc., and there may, of course, be more than three, in

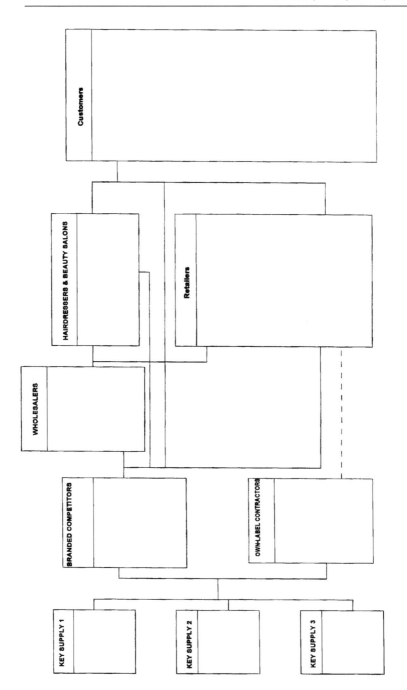

Figure 4.1   Outline chart for a toiletry product such as hair care

which case we add more boxes. Competitors are divided into the two parts of the industry, both of which use similar raw materials, although if we wanted to include advertising services this would not be of interest to contract packers. The branded products reach the industry through wholesalers, retailers, and the hairdressers and beauty salons. Contract packers deal only through retailers.

When we move into the checking phase, other things become apparent. First, we have forgotten hotels and airlines, both of which may be customers of the branded and contract packing parts of the industry. Second, we need to separate the different types of retailer: the supermarkets have a stronger influence on the profitability of the indusry than chemists, chains such as Woolworth's, and departmental stores. Similarly, we should at least consider whether we should separate out the different types of wholesaler. Third, we need to give thought to the consumers, and perhaps look at them in segments.

Next, we need to consider substitutes, make sure that we have not neglected to think about any influencers, and add a space to note information about entry and exit barriers, although if the sheet is getting cramped this could appear on the facing page. There is considerable variation in outline charts for different industries, but the principles for constructing them are the same. Further examples can be found in Hussey (1998).

Completing the Chart

What we want to try to put on the chart are as many of the facts that answer the questions raised in the previous chapter as we can. In order to illustrate the sort of things that might be entered, we have begun to complete a chart for the UK travel agents industry (Figure 4.2). The chart is incomplete, partly to make it easier to follow, given the space limitations of this book, and partly because we have restricted the information to what is in the public domain. Some of the issues that affect this chart were mentioned earlier. Our stance is that we are looking at the broader travel and tourism industry from the viewpoint of travel agents.

As suggested earlier, we have divided the travel agents' business into leisure and business. The critical success factors for the two types of activity have many differences. As the diagram shows,

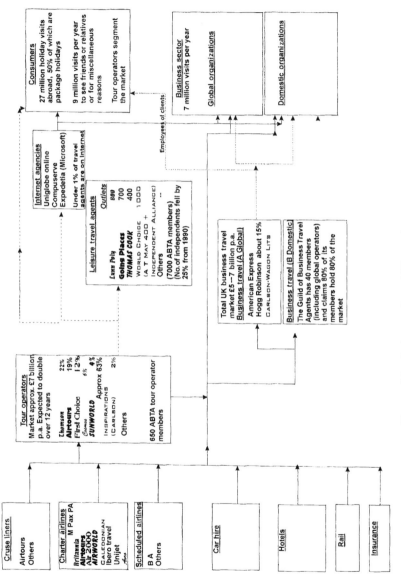

Figure 4.2 Industry chart: UK travel agents

business travel agents frequently establish dedicated offices in the premises of their large customers to improve service levels and to make it slightly less easy for clients switch top competitors. Shops are not needed, as much business is conducted by telephone, with tickets couriered to the clients' premises. In fact, business travel agents may sell leisure travel but only to individuals employed by their clients, and usually through requests by telephone.

Increasingly the business travel business has to be global. Although the chart refers to the UK, only those competitors with global networks can obtain the business of those clients who want a global service. The top three competitors (Hogg Robinson, American Express and Carlson-Wagon Lits) have built up comprehensive networks through alliances and acquisitions, which gives them a competitive edge over those competitors which are more local in orientation.

Large airlines exercise power over the industry. For example, in January 1998 British Airways reduced the rate of commission paid to travel agents from 9% to 7%. Although some competitors had already changed their business from a commission-based agency obtaining revenue from suppliers to a fee-based consultancy obtaining the best prices for clients and charging a fee to the clients for services provided (with annual bonuses based on savings achieved), most had not made the switch.

The buyers' section of the chart shows two segments, the global companies and others. There are, of course, more segments than this, which would be identified by anyone extending this example to a full analysis. Few buyers want to deal only with one airline, which means that the business travel agencies draw strengths from their role in the overall value chain.

The leisure travel agency business is now dominated by firms owned by the package holiday companies. Because sales of package holidays are to domestic consumers, however international the product itself, there are no particular advantages in these competitors having global networks. However, the package holiday companies themselves have begun to expand into similar businesses in other countries: as well as opportunities for profitable operation, it enables them to increase their bargaining power over their suppliers.

Although the major proportion of business is in the package holiday, there are other types of leisure travel agents, such as those who operate "bucket shops" selling cheap tickets, and those which specialize in round-the-world tickets for globe-trotting students. Some package holiday companies sell direct to the consumer, particularly those related to affinity groups such as ramblers' holidays and HF Holidays. Again only a rudimentary segmentation has been shown for buyers, but this is enough to show that there is opportunity for specialization.

All this information can be read from the chart, and in a real exercise much more would be added. Of course, it is possible to interpret the industry without drawing the chart, but the two main advantages of this method are that the exercise helps to ensure that the right questions are asked, and the resultant chart communicates a great deal of information in a compressed way to other people. Strategies to respond to what is discovered rarely emanate from only the analyst, and information has to be shared with, and the issues fully understood by, other key managers. The charting approach helps do this, and also provides a framework for keeping information up to date.

Another benefit we have found from this approach is that it reveals where information is lacking, and often shows up other problems. It is not uncommon for different parts of an organization to be using different figures for the market or market shares, and this approach makes these differences very clear. Our experience is that the method often shows that a piece of information that the organization has relied on in the past is inaccurate, occasionally dangerously so. Market size, for example, may be calculated from a variety of sources, not all of which are as complete or as accurate as they might be. It is rarely easy to take market information from several overlapping sources without exposing some areas of doubt. Any mechanism that shows that if "fact" A is correct, "fact" B has to be untrue is potentially very helpful, and may reveal that assumptions that have been used in the past are unreliable.

Because the chart in Figure 4.2 is developed only far enough to demonstrate the concept, no attempt has been made to assess entry and exit barriers. There has been movement in the recent past. For example, Hogg Robinson sold its leisure travel business with its high street shops to Going Places (part of Airtours) in order to focus on the business travel side. It is also clear that the entry barriers to business travel are higher now than they were in the past, as the requirement to offer a global service has increased. However, our purpose has not been to develop strategies for the industry but to illustrate a method that can be used in any industry.

MAPPING STRATEGIC GROUPS

It will have become apparent that what has been suggested so far is only part of the analysis of competitors, and that even the analysis of the industry requires much detailed knowledge about the competitors. The nature of this knowledge, and how to obtain it will be the subject of subsequent chapters. However, even on what we have looked at so far, we can see that understanding may be improved if we can cluster competitors into groups that have similar strategic characteristics. This may be essential in an industry where there are hundreds of competitors and it is impractical to study every one of them in detail. It may be desirable when the numbers are manageable, but it is helpful to get a fix on who is competing and where. Porter (1980) developed the idea of "strategic groups", which could be mapped on a diagram to show the variations in competitive activity. One value of this is that it may show up which are the real competitors and which are in the same industry but are not really a threat.

Porter suggested a matrix with specialization (narrow to full line) on one axis and vertical integration (high to assembler) on the other. However, this is illustrative, and what he advocates is a matrix which shows the way in which the firms are similar to other firms in the competitive strategy they are following. The two sides of the matrix might in another industry be quality brand image and mix of channels. The groups are illustrated by circles which diagrammatically represent the collective market share of the firms in the group, and the names of the firms are written in each circle. Figure 4.3 provides an example, using two strategic parameters for the business travel industry. The circles' sizes in this example should not be taken as accurate representations of market share.

The purpose of the exercise is to help explain differences in profitability of the various competitors, identify barriers to mobility between the strategic groups, provide a basis for charting movements of competitors, to analyse trends and assess likely reactions. Although the technique is helpful, its value depends on the ability of the analyst to determine the most appropriate parameters for the

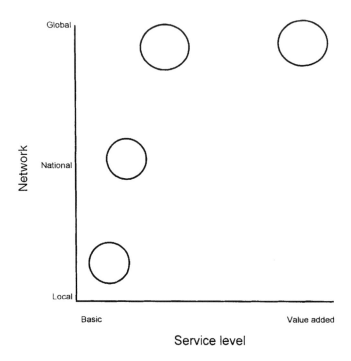

Position the business travel agents you know on this diagram

Figure 4.3   Strategic groups: business travel agents

matrix. Selecting two from the many is not always an easy task, and
the wrong choice will result in an inadequate assessment.

It follows that the only sensible route to the choice of parameters
would be to begin with a larger matrix which listed all the main
competitors (and some representative competitors from the lesser
ones) on one axis and all the key strategic variables on the other. By
marking which of the parameters is used by each competitor, it may
be possible to arrive at the sort of two-dimensional map suggested
by Porter.

Although it does not appear in much of the literature on industry
and competitor analysis, there is some value in considering the
approach suggested by Abell (1980). At the very least, the Abell
approach might be borne in mind for use in the individual competitor analysis methods covered in Chapter 6. He suggests a three-
dimensional matrix to examine the strategic variables, although he

sees this as an exercise in analysing the business and making similar analyses of the businesses of competitors.

Abell's three variables are customer functions, customer groups, and alternative technologies. He suggests variations in what is examined under each heading, based on the circumstances of the industry. Customer groups may, for example, be standard business definition such as airline, banks, hospitals, etc., or they may be something about the buying requirement (as in our business travel example, where global customers want an organization that can offer a global service, something not needed by a purely local customer). Customer functions are how the customer is satisfied by the product. If we use the business travel example again, we can see that some customers want, and are offered, the basic requirement of travel arrangements. Additional functions, which are not offered by all suppliers, might include reducing or monitoring travel costs and other consultancy services. In another industry, the functions would be different.

Alternative technology is best illustrated through another industry: elevators. The main technologies are around the electric lift, and most modern lifts include a quota of electronics. One alternative technology is the hydraulic lift, which has a particular advantage for low-rise buildings where overall roof height is limited for environmental reasons (the electric lift requires a building on the roof to house the lift machinery: the hydraulic lift has its driving force housed in a pit at the bottom of the lift shaft). A third technology is the stair lift, designed for infirm people, where the lift seat moves on rails around one side of the stairs. This is not the end of the story, but is enough for our example. There are competitors which are limited to only one of the technologies, while others could cover all three.

For illustration purposes, Figure 4.4 develops the lift example, to show the application of Abell's concept. The three-dimensional diagram could be seen as being made of a series of bricks, every competitor choosing the bricks it will use to build its own strategy. Do not take the analogy too literally, as you have to imagine that some bricks may defy gravity and be held in mid-air!

There is no reason why a three-dimensional approach cannot be used in strategic group mapping, although it may be easier to indicate the third dimension through colour or shading than to try to draw three dimensions on a flat piece of paper. An option is to map the strategic groups against a number of different strategic

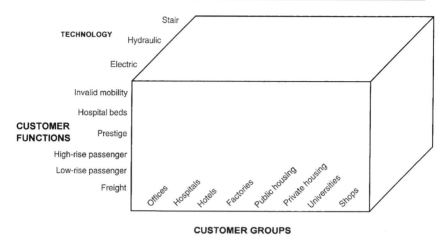

Figure 4.4   Abell's approach to business definition: elevator industry

parameters, so that each delivers some insight and helps the assessment of whether there is likely to be migration of the firms in each group into a different position on the chart.

TAKING A DYNAMIC VIEW

Although we have hinted at change, much of the description so far has been about taking a snapshot of the current position. Yet we can all see how many industries have changed not just in their structure but also in the relative power of industry firms, suppliers and buyers. In Chapter 2 we discussed the idea of deliberately setting out to change an industry, and if this is something which we might consider we have to accept that the other actors in our drama might also have similar thoughts.

One method we have found to be useful in using industry analysis in a more dynamic manner is to chart the industry in the way described at the start of this chapter and to complete the mapping of the strategic groups. Ideally we should have also collected enough information to gain an understanding of each competitor. This is something we will explore in more detail in subsequent chapters. The best analysis will also include collecting detailed information about key customers and suppliers. Our industry analysis so far helps us to see how the industry works, but as we move into a more dynamic analysis there is a need to understand the motivation and capabilities of the rest of the industry as change may be initiated at any point in the chain from raw materials through to the final consumer.

The next stage is to try to think of all the ways in which either the structure of the industry might change or the balance of power be shifted from one part of the chart to another. This requires us to add thinking from trends in the external environment, to which we referred in the previous chapter. Often the structure of an industry may undergo change because of the availability of a different technology, either affecting the product itself or how it reaches the customer. For example, automatic teller machines, now an accepted part of the retail banking system, were one of the technological advances that made it possible for First Direct to launch an effective telephone banking service, thus changing the competitive structure of its industry.

The next step in the analysis is to examine the list of what could happen, to see which of the "forces" (suppliers, competitors, buyers, influencers, and new entrants) might initiate such a change. We can then be more specific, and examine which particular organizations shown on our industry chart could initiate such a change with success.

From this thinking it is possible to develop some scenarios of the way the industry could change, and to consider our own strategy in relation to this. We may want to be the organization that causes the change, or we might want to take pre-emptive action to make it more difficult for such a change to be initiated. What should be borne in mind is the fact that the structures of industries do change, and very few are totally static. Dynamic industry analysis can help to prevent a competitive position from being eroded because someone else has rewritten the "rules" of the industry.

REFERENCES

Abell, D.F. (1980). *Defining the Business: The Starting Point of Strategic Planning*, Prentice Hall, Englewood Cliffs, NJ.

Hussey, D.E. (1998). *Strategic Management: Theory and Implementation*, 4th edition, Butterworth-Heinemann, Oxford.

Porter, M.E. (1980). *Competitive Strategy*, The Free Press, New York.

5
Using Critical Success Factors in Planning

This chapter introduces a strategy planning and strategic control process which is designed to aid directors and senior managers in executing and monitoring their strategies. On the basis of this research, the author provides a detailed description of this method for developing, monitoring and integrating critical information into effective strategic management decision support. This design method incorporates nine steps:

1 Provide structure for design process
2 Determine general forces influencing strategy
3 Develop a strategic plan or review/modify the current plan
4 Identify a selected number of critical success factors (CSFs)
5 Determine who is responsible for which critical areas
6 Select the strategic performance indicators (SPIs)
7 Develop and integrate appropriate reporting procedures
8 Implement and initiate system use by the senior personnel
9 Establish evaluating process and procedures.

Through appropriate introduction, this approach can create an integrated strategic context within which top management and key personnel can execute the strategy and maintain a competitive advantage for their firm.

Successful strategy development and implementation relies on the quality of the available information. Further, this information is often seen as a vital resource which can make or break a firm's chance of success. The availability of information to senior man-

Reprinted from *Long Range Planning*, **20**, No. 4, 102–109, 1987.

agers, however, is usually not the problem. On the contrary, they are generally inundated with data (see Calingo et al, 1983).

Thus, in this increasingly complex and information-oriented world the main challenge confronting managers is the identification, selection and monitoring of information which is related to the strategic performance of the company. (Depending on the nature of the business, this methodology is appropriate for smaller to medium-sized firms.) Also, the right information requested and communicated by the managers will help shape the way in which other members of the organization define their tasks, interpret the firm's strategy, and determine what is important and what is not.

A leasing firm recently brought in a new president. The previous manager had received summary reports from several accounting systems which were considered state-of-the-art. The new president identified the firm's "spread" (i.e. the difference between the firm's cost of funds and the firm's yield on an annualized basis) as one of his primary concerns. However, not only was this figure not available in current reporting, the data required to provide the "spread" figure resided in external as well as internal databases. Once the reporting was realigned, a key measure replaced and/or supplemented multiple reports.

More important, consider the strategy implication of the new margin figure, as compared to the previous segmented reporting. The single measure provided the president with the "pulse" of the firm on a weekly basis. Thus, he was able to have a generalized feel for the firm's exposure, its position *vis-à-vis* other firms, and trends indicating the need for asset or liability repositioning. Additionally, he was no longer required to analyse multiple reporting sources, except when conditions warranted accessing the detailed information.

This chapter introduces an information-based approach to strategy development and control which can aid managers in turning their strategies into action. The author provides a method for designing a planning and control process whereby crucial information can be identified, organized, evaluated and communicated in a manner which supports execution of the strategic plan.

INFORMATION FOCUSED ON FACTORS INFLUENCING STRATEGIC SUCCESS

An increasingly popular approach for identifying "strategically relevant" information is through the critical success factor method (Hise and McDaniel, 1984; see also Daniel, 1961, 1966). Critical success factors (CSFs) are events, conditions, circumstances or activities. Specifically, they are "the limited number of areas in which results, if they are satisfactory, will ensure successful competitive performance for the organization" (Rockart, 1979). These factors may also result from:

- The outcome of external events when there is risk exposure (e.g. political developments in South Africa)
- The achievements of one or more individuals, such as members of a particular engineering project
- The internal operating process (e.g. attaining better quality or decreasing the default rate).

Thus, CSFs relate to the basic internal or external conditions for the firm's strategy (e.g. customer acceptance, competitive moves), or those competencies or resources (e.g. human, financial) it must attain.

Recent research has expanded this notion into a more comprehensive and strategic concept, suggesting that the definition and monitoring of critical success factors differs for various strategy types. A study of 128 firms in mature manufacturing industries found a number of interesting results (Jenster, 1984). In particular, this research indicates that the firms which had a higher return on equity:

1. Formally identified their CSFs
2. Used these factors to monitor their progress in the implementation of strategic changes
3. Benefited from formally integrated reporting and information systems.

Others have found that CSFs, when formally identified, implicitly communicate the top management's priorities and thereby direct organizational efforts in the desired direction (Millar, 1984). More specifically, the desired direction is attained through the motivation of the organization's employees. Provided with a framework against which they can make sense of priorities, assumptions and environmental conditions, the employees are then able to better contribute to the execution of long-range plans.

Consider a company which views the introduction of new products as one of its CSFs. Beyond communicating that top management views the organization's future as hinging upon being a product innovator, this clearly conveys to individuals where their most significant contribution can be made. Most members of management are strongly motivated to excel in relation to the expectations of corporate leadership. They will adapt to meet those expectations provided that top management's wishes are clearly and consistently communicated. Effective leadership necessitates the clear definition of success factors, the ideal organizational performance in relation to them, and the explicit communication of these factors to all appropriate levels of management in a structured manner.

In addition to providing a bridge between the firm's objectives and management's strategy, the isolation of critical factors also provides a vehicle for the design of an effective system of performance measurement and control. This way, the design of CSFs becomes more than just identifying the areas which "must go right", but assumes a powerful strategic role in which the specific efforts of top management and the employees are joined and aligned in a manner consistent with the firm's vision.

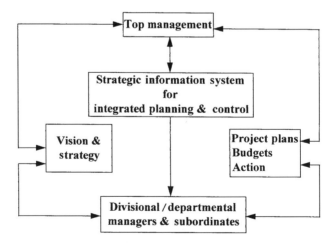

Figure 5.1 An information "bridge" for making strategy operational

In summary, the factors identified as essential to the organization's success serve as the primary integrating mechanism between management's long-range goals and the channelling of resources and executive attention. Explicit recognition and use of such CSFs provides, therefore, a planning process/system through which strategy formulation can be made operational and controlled within the firm, as depicted in Figure 5.1.

AN OVERVIEW OF THE DESIGN PROCESS

The design procedures for a strategic process and information system for integrating planning and control are shown in Figure 5.2 and discussed on the following pages. This approach is based on the idea that the executive must focus on factors most vital to the organization's success and then manage by creating a context within which others are able to align their efforts accordingly. The method incorporates nine steps:

1. Provide structure for the design process
2. Determine general elements which will influence success
3. Develop a strategic plan or review/modify the current plan
4. Identify a selected number of CSFs
5. Determine who is going to be responsible for what
6. Select the strategic performance indicators (SPIs)
7. Develop and enact appropriate reporting procedures
8. Initiate use of procedures by managerial personnel
9. Establish evaluation procedure.

```
Provide structure for design process
Determine general forces – audit of external and internal factors
Strategy formulation
Identify critical success factors
Determine who is responsible
Select strategic performance indicators
Develop and integrate reporting procedures for strategic monitoring
Implement and initiate system use
Evaluation of plans, process and system
```

Figure 5.2 Designing a strategic information system: procedural guide

The design method serves as the means for top management to create and identify essential strategic elements, make use of information relevant to success, align rewards and incentives, and reach strategic goals. More important, however, it is the means for creation of a *strategic context* for the firm.

On the surface, this design may not appear to be novel or unique. After all, planning and control system design has not undergone major changes in the last 15 years or so. It is argued, however, that the integration of the planning and control processes through the design of an information-based context can better aid managers in defining and interpreting environmental events and changes. In other words, we can say that this approach enables top managers to provide a setting in which others can interpret information and adapt their roles to meet the objectives of the firm. Thus, the design philosophy is that the strategy formulation and the plan execution cannot be treated as two separate issues. Modern strategic management must view the strategic planning process and the system facilitating implementation as interrelated.

DESIGNING A STRATEGIC INFORMATION SYSTEM

This section consists of a detailed discussion of each of the nine steps in the design and implementation process (see Figure 5.2).

Step 1: Structure the Design Process

Before engaging in the planning design process and the actual planning, it is important to determine who is responsible for overseeing the specific steps and the planning outcome. In most cases, it is recommended that the chairman/CEO designates a steering committee to oversee the whole process. This should include selected members of the board, the president, plus the vice-president of planning. This primary committee must articulate the firm's objectives and, in turn, oversee and receive reports from secondary committees consisting of lower-level employees. The secondary committees will be selected to tackle the specific steps and issues in the design process outlined below.

Step 2: Determine the Elements Influencing Success

The first step in the planning process is to audit the forces which are relevant to the firm's present and future position. Strategic areas may include:

- *General environment.* Factors which influence the firm and over which it has no control. Included here may be issues such as general socio-demographic trends, interest rates, exchange rate fluctuations, etc.
- *Industry characteristics.* Features of the firm's industry and related industries. In general, it appears that each industry has a set of common dimensions to which individual firms need to adhere. For example, supermarket chains will have one set of dynamic factors and banks another.
- *Competitive forces.* Postures of competitors, suppliers, customers, potential new entrants as well as those elements to which firms following similar strategies in related industries need to be alert. These may include certain quality standards, product mix, cost control, etc.
- *Company-specific characteristics.* Factors derived from the unique aspects of a particular firm's competitive position (i.e. its strengths and weaknesses as well as opportunities and threats), traits of the management team, and/or time elements.
- *Personal values of key players.* The demand, wishes, needs and capabilities of key players, executives and other personnel must be examined. For example, the personal preferences of the major stockholders should not be neglected.
- *Resource availability.* Availability of financial as well as physical and human resources will have an impact on the strategic success.

These strategic characteristics may form the basis for defining the firm's sensitivity to the influences or changes along the various dimensions. Figure 5.3 shows how the firm's sensitivity can be examined using a weighting scheme where 1 equals no effect, to 10, which implies substantial or critical impact. The Impact Grid can also be used in the design/review and integration of a firm's strategic plans, as well as to assess reversibility of resource commitments. Moreover, this evaluation is used to create the list of potential elements from which management selects the firm's five to ten

		Governmental issues (specific)	Competitor X (specific action)	Exchange rate	etc.
FUNCTIONS	Marketing				
	Personnel				
	Production				
PROJECTS	Project 1				
	Project 2				
PRODUCTS	Product 1				
	Product 2				
GOALS	Goal 1				
	Goal 2				

Figure 5.3 Assessing a firm's vulnerability to its environment – using an Impact Grid

critical success factors. The dimensions may also be used to develop alternative result scenarios and for the identification, achievement and evaluation of management's objectives, as well as in the subsequent transformation of ideas into action. This technical part of the strategy-formulation process has been described in numerous books and articles (see, for example, Grant and King, 1983).

Some of the identified factors affected by the various elements are *strategic* in nature, in that they relate directly to the way senior personnel interpret situations and carry out plans. Other success factors are *operational* and not necessarily directly useful to the tasks and activities of key personnel. While they are important to the way lower personnel define and integrate particular tasks, they may receive management attention on a less frequent, *ad hoc*, or by-exception basis.

Step 3: Develop or Review the Strategic Plan

The second step is the formulation of alternatives and the choice of a strategy, or a thorough review of the current strategic plan. This step is concerned with the evaluation of the firm's strategic ends and means. That is, this step must address the organization's mission by asking questions such as:

"What type of firm do we want the organization to be?"
"What type of activities do we want to engage in?"
"What markets do we want to pursue?"

Although these questions sound simple and straightforward, it is the author's observation that it can be a long and tedious affair which is validated by the experience of managers who have actually gone through this process. In addition, the associated objectives must be clearly defined, the goals relevant and attainable, and a set of alternatives must be identified. In this step, the firm's current plans may also be reviewed to ensure consistency among anticipated environmental threats and opportunities and the firm's internal capabilities.

Step 4: Identify CSFs

Critical success factors (CSFs) are those limited number of factors important to strategic success. They are the limited number of areas which must be monitored to ensure successful execution of the firm's strategic programmes. These factors can be used to guide and motivate key employees to perform in the desired manner, and in a way which will ensure successful performance throughout the strategy.

The use of these factors in discussions and planning within the firm will clearly and succinctly communicate critical elements of the strategy to members of the organization. More important, the CSFs direct the attention of key managers to focus on the basic premises of the firm's strategy. The selection of proper strategic dimensions is

Example 5.1   The Iowa Farmatics Inc.

Bill Sobek, founder of Iowa Farmatics Inc. (IFI), a distributor and manufacturer of fertilizer-spreading equipment, was proposing to withdraw from day-to-day management of the firm. The last 15 years had been marked by steady increases in sales averaging 23%. The success of the firm over the years had rested on a philosophy based on the primacy of customer service. Since the period for fertilizing fields is short, a disabled spreader can cost a customer a considerable amount of money. Although the firm inititially was a distributor and assembler of equipment, management realized that to ensure quick response to a customer's needs for spare parts, the firm had branched out into the manufacturing and extensive stocking of spare parts. In order to fully satisfy customer needs, the firm also began designing and manufacturing customized liquid sprayers. Unlike the standardized dry spreaders, these liquid spreaders are made to customer specification. Because of the unique nature of liquid spreaders, these units take considerable amounts of time to design and manufacture.

While most producers of farm machinery were hurting in 1984, the firm was straining capacity and planning for future growth became essential. The prospect of expanding sales of liquid sprayers into states outside the present market area looked very favourable. Although Bill Sobek desired growth for the firm, he recognized the need for any growth to be controlled. Additionally, he desired that even with future growth of the firm, his personal involvement would be significantly reduced. It was clear that the future growth strategy required an improved monitoring system and management structure.

The Impact Grid depicted in Table 5.1, exemplifies the relationships between developments in some of the critical success factors and elements of Sobek's strategy for IFI.

Table 5.1 An Impact Grid for Iowa Farmatics Inc.

CSF	Introduction of liquid spreader by competition	Disruption of parts supply	Securing distributors in new markets	Decentralization of management	Expansion of facilities
Marketing:					
Distribution	10	2	10	1	4
Promotion	10	8	2	1	1
Personnel:					
Design	10	2	1	1	5
Management	8	6	1	10	8
Production	8	4	1	1	8
Production:					
Assemble dry spreaders	1	10	1	1	10
Design liquid spreaders	10	1	1	1	10
Manufacture spare parts	1	10	6	1	10
Projects:					
Plant construction	7	1	6	1	10
Products:					
Dry spreaders	1	1	2	1	8
Liquid spreaders	10	1	8	1	8
Goals:					
Controlled growth	5	1	7	1	10
Reduced time commitment/CEO	1	2	3	10	2
Customer service	1	10	3	3	7

Key: 1 = Little or no impact … 10 = Substantial or critical impact.

essential, inasmuch as they will serve as motivation for those whose performance is being measured. Thus, the CSFs must:

1. Reflect the success of the defined strategy
2. Represent the foundation of this strategy
3. Be able to motivate and align the managers as well as other employees
4. Be very specific and/or measurable.

A manufacturer of cutting tools has as its major strategic theme "Shipping of orders within 24 hours". The board of directors identified timeliness of shipments, and industry market share as two of their CSFs.

Step 5: Determine Who is Responsible

Most organizations rely on the actions of a relatively small number of key people whose functions are vital to the strategic plan's implementation. It is important, once the critical success factors have been determined, that these individuals be identified and properly motivated to achieve the strategic ends.

The identification of key people is accomplished by analysing the critical success factors and selecting the individuals whose efforts apply to a particular factor. Key personnel include those employees ultimately responsible for achieving the particular strategic dimension or goal, plus other individuals designated to undertake specific major steps to deal with the critical dimension. The following simplified example illustrates how key personnel and CSFs were identified and matched by management of a manufacturing company attempting to implement a "low-cost strategy":

- *OSHA standard*
  Legal council
  Vice President of Operations
  Plant Superintendent
  Service Engineer
- *Customer Services*
  Vice President of Sales & Marketing
  Manager of Distribution
  Managers of Production Planning

Managers Service Department
- *Manufacturing costs – reduction by 22%*
Vice President of Operations
Chief Cost Accountant
Plant Superintendents
Managers of Production Planning
- *New "low-priced" products*
Vice President of Sales & Marketing
Senior Market Analyst
Manager of Products Development
- *Sales growth of 17%*
Vice President of Sales & Marketing
Manager of Advertising
Four Senior Salesmen
- *Work Force Development*
Vice President of Personnel
Manager of Training and Development
Two Foremen
Union Representative

It should be noted that because some critical factors are long range in nature, different key individuals may be identified over time as conditions change. While more than one individual may be designated as responsible for the achievement of a critical factor, each individual typically has appropriate strategic performance indicators or responsibilities assigned so that his or her performance can be monitored separately, as discussed in the following section.

This analysis of key individuals may also highlight certain organization problems. For example, the individuals selected to fulfil certain responsibilities must have authority and resources to take the necessary steps required for the successful implementation of the strategy. This authority should be clearly articulated to match accountability. Any organizational problems which exist should be explicitly addressed.

Step 6: Select Strategic Performance Indicators

CSFs are also the basis for identifying the Strategic Performance Indicators (SPIs) used in measuring the short-term progress toward the long-term objectives. The SPIs are the indicators specifically used to measure and monitor key individuals' short-term progress toward achieving good performance along a critical dimension. SPIs provide motivational information which must be explicit enough to allow managers to understand how their actions influence strategic success, even though they may not have a full understanding of the underlying strategy. The indicators must ultimately be approved by the steering committee and the board, but designed with significant input from subordinates.

SPIs must strive to satisfy six specifications. They should be:

1. *Operational.* They must focus on action and provide information which can be used for control.
2. *Indicative of desired performance.* Indicators must be measured against a desired level of performance.
3. *Acceptable to subordinates.* Subordinates should have significant input into determination of the indicators during the design/review process.
4. *Reliable.* Most phenomena cannot be measured with precision, but can be described only within a range or as a degree of magnitude. It is up to the steering committee to think through what kind of measurement is appropriate to the factor it is meant to measure.
5. *Timely.* This does not necessarily imply rapid reporting. The time dimension of controls should correspond to the "time span" of the event.
6. *Simple.* Complicated strategic performance measurement systems often do not work. They confuse the organization's members, and direct attention toward the mechanics and methods of control, rather that toward the targeted performance results.

After being selected, the indicators should be analysed in terms of the information required to measure their achievement. Performance indicators will generally require information from a wide variety of different sources, both internal and external, in order to enable management to monitor progress in the different functional areas of the organization.

Step 7: Development of Reporting Procedures

There are three basic steps for translating the information requirements of a modern business into a formalized reporting system:

1. *Strategic information planning.* This task addresses the development of an information plan for the management team. Remember that information can be a strategic resource to the firm. The first objective of the plan is to assess the gap between the available and required information to monitor the CSFs and measure actual performance. The second objective of the plan is to assess that availability of information related to the operating success factors (OSFs). The strategic information plan must develop an approach for obtaining the information which is not immediately available from existing sources. Since information systems are not created in one day, an interim system may be installed using some surrogate information until the sources called for in the information plan are established and procedures completed.

2. *Preliminary system design plan.* The functional and technical requirements of the reporting system and of the necessary hardware/software are identified during the preliminary design phase. The primary objective is to bring to the surface all associated design issues prior to the installation of systems and the establishment of procedures. For example, "What constraints do the firm's existing data systems impose? Can the barriers be overcome or do we have to undertake major redesign?"

3. *Procedure/systems installation plan.* This phase involves the detailed design, installation and testing of procedures and systems. The technical part of the process for computerized systems includes developing programming specification, developing logically structured programs and required procedures; training user personnel; and fully testing and converting the system. For manual procedures, it is worth while having the individuals involved in gathering and synthesizing information conduct a trial on old data. A simulation or case exercise can be successfully used.

In order for CSFs and SPIs to be of motivational as well as control value, they must be explicitly utilized by the senior managers. This makes subordinates aware that the measures are being used by management to track progress and performance. The competitive environment, the firm's size, the particular strategy – as well as the management style – will of course, determine when and how CSFs and SPIs are used.

For example, when Bob Russell of Golden Wheel Creations Inc. introduced the firm's new CSF-reporting system, he emphasized one-to-one meetings with subordinates. Moreover, the firm recognized high performance achievements on the bulletin board. Other executives went further and utilized a computerized information system that included a communication network for the management team, and direct information input from key customers. The system also allowed these customers limited access to the system.

Step 8: Implement System and Initiate System Use

Several criteria are important for successful implementation of plans and procedures. Top management support and involvement is essential. Lower-level employees may not take the plan or planning and control efforts seriously unless the firm's top management clearly demonstrates interest in the activity. Therefore, it is important that top management, whenever possible, actively guide and participate in the implementation. It is equally important to create commitment or a team spirit which will pull participants together.

A set of "implementation recommendations" is useful. These simple guidelines should be introduced by the CEO or the most senior manager at the "kick-off" meeting. The following recommendations are examples; others may be created to suit the particular situation:

1. This project and its success belong to all employees, with no one left out; thus, these game rules belong to all involved, let's all help to keep them.
2. Everyone involved must take responsibility and demonstrate team work.
3. Think positive – all negative and non-constructive statements undermine the project.
4. "Excuses" don't get the job done. If you can't complete a project assignment on time, the delay should be brought to the attention of the CEO/senior officer in *advance* of the due date.
5. Success is dependent on timely completion of all assignments. Any unsolved problems or emergencies must be reported to the

CEO or senior manager within 24 hours of discovery. All problems and emergencies are to receive immediate attention.

We recommend that these implementation recommendations be handed out to all participants. The implementation must be presented to support team spirit, not to alienate employees.

It is also vital that members of the organization have a firm understanding of the different steps. Thus it is necessary to involve the right people as early as possible in the process and to provide the necessary training and education. From time to time, managers expect that the benefits of plans and procedures will be realized with little effort. Adequate input of time and resources must be used in both plan development and execution.

Step 9: Establish Evaluation Procedures

It is important to establish a review schedule for the strategic plan as well as a re-evaluation of the procedures and information systems. This part is often forgotten. Procedures and managerial habits tend to live a life of their own. As the competitive and organization conditions change, it becomes necessary to re-evaluate the strategy, the CSFs, and SPIs, as well as the procedures and systems which generate the needed information.

CONCLUSION

Strategies are formulated based on a number of assumptions. During strategy execution, however, these premises and other factors are likely to change as time passes. Therefore, getting the right information on developments in critical issues and the firm's strategic progress is essential to the directors and managers of any business. Furthermore, this specifically identified information is used in communicating and monitoring strategic progress, and to measure key personnel on vital aspects of the firm's strategy and provide powerful motivators for the firm as a whole.

Research suggests that relatively few firms are engaged in systematic monitoring of factors critical to the firm's strategic success. However, the firms which have adopted these more sophisticated methods for strategy formulation and monitoring of strategic progress seem to achieve better performance. The planning process and procedures described in this chapter provide a framework which firms can use to bridge the gap between the vision of top management and successful strategy execution.

With the method presented here, the directors and the top management team are able to clearly communicate the firm's strategy to the organization. Moreover, they have a method for receiving the right information as well as for measuring performance and ensuring that appropriate actions are taken. In addition, individual responsibilities in relation to strategy implementation can be identified and monitored to reach the intended goals. Given appropriately tailored procedures, firms can attain higher levels of achievement and motivation among employees as they are helped to recognize top management's expectations and their own responsibilities in the execution of the firm's strategy.

ACKNOWLEDGEMENTS

The study conducted was by the author and partly sponsored by Arthur Andersen & Co., who share no responsibility in the conclusions of the research. The author acknowledges the valuable contributions made to this research by Harold Bott and John Rogan of Arthur Andersen & Co.

REFERENCES

Calingo, L., Camilus, J., Jenster, P. & Raghunathan T. (1983). Strategic management and organizational action: a conceptual synthesis, *43rd National Conference of the Academy of Management* .

Grant, J.H. & King, W.R. (1983). *Topics of Strategic Planning*, Little, Brown, Boston.

Hise R. & McDaniel, S. (1984). CEOs' views on strategy: a survey, *The Journal of Business Strategy*, Winter. See also Daniel, D. (1961). Management information crisis, *Harvard Business Review*, November-December; and Daniel, D. (1966). Reorganizing for results, *Harvard Business Review*, March-April.

Jenster, P. (1984). *Divisional monitoring of critical success factors during strategy implementation*, Doctoral dissertation, University of Pittsburgh.

Millar, V. (1984). Decision-oriented information, *Datamation*, January.

Rockart, J.F. (1979). Chief executives define their own data needs, *Harvard Business Review*, March-April.

6
Understanding Competitors: Methods of Analysis

THE NEED FOR METHOD

One of the pitfalls of competitor analysis is to arrive at a situation where there is a great deal of data but very little information. This happens more frequently than might be expected, and the end product of the competitor analysis effort is a cabinet of files of press clippings, often obtained at random, which may or may not have been circulated to managers in periodic bundles of cuttings. Every so often there is a splurge of interest in a particular competitor, followed by a scurry of activity as someone tries to makes sense of the heaps of data. Typically these files do not include very important information contained in documents like market research reports or internally generated information such as customer analyses. Sometimes the files may include snippets of information sent in by sales people, but unless the system is carefully designed, there is an initial burst of enthusiasm when the sales force is asked for its support which rapidly tails off over the next few months.

Of course, this bleak picture is not typical of every organization's competitor analysis activity, and there is no reason why it should remain typical of any. What requires careful thought is how competitor information will be collected, organized, analysed, and disseminated. There are elements of structure, system, process and culture to be considered. This chapter is about ways of using and presenting competitor information. It will be followed by an examination of sources, and in Chapter 10 we will return to the all-important aspect of organizing for competitor analysis.

WHAT DO WE WANT FROM COMPETITOR ANALYSIS?

Competitor analysis should deliver some specific advantages to the way strategic issues are considered, with possible side-benefits for shorter-term operational activity, such as being able to brief the sales force on the benefits of the company's product offerings compared to those of competitors. In order to achieve this, there is a need for up-to-date information that can be communicated and understood by those who are expected to use it. There may be several different requirements from competitor analysis. We suggest that these include:

1. *On-going knowledge of competitors.* This is to ensure that we are aware of what our competitors are doing that will affect us and what they might be considering doing. In addition, we need to turn the thinking around to how things we are doing will affect each of them and what the reactions of each competitor might be. Continuous knowledge of competitors calls for a method of recording information that is kept up to date, and which is always immediately accessible. The method we suggest is competitor profiling.

2. *Special studies.* From time to time every organization will need to produce a special report on a competitor which relates to a particular purpose. An obvious possibility is if a competitor is being considered as an acquisition candidate or as a partner in a strategic alliance. Another possibility is to answer a query that arises from an action observed from the on-going monitoring, such as what are they really doing in South-east Asia, or why have they started to recruit so many scientists. To answer this sort of question quickly requires organization of the competitor information so that what is available in the system can be rapidly identified and retrieved. It may also require a willingness to commit resources to special surveys and investigations, and the competence to undertake or commission these.

3. *Performance comparisons.* A third use of competitor information is for performance comparisons across as many parameters as possible. The aim is to be better than competitors in areas of performance which are critical, and knowing their performance is a first step to this. We enlarge on one tool for performance improvement (benchmarking) later in this chapter.

A trap to avoid is the writing of reports on competitors which resemble a corporate history book. We are interested only in those aspects of the past that have a bearing on the future, so what we choose to find out and analyse about competitors should be selective and relevant. Managers do not need all the atmosphere and character development that takes place in a great novel, so we should ensure that they are not swamped with a mass of detail that cannot be interpreted.

DEVELOPING COMPETITOR PROFILES

Just as we did with industry analysis, we recommend a method which shows the key information about each significant competitor on one A3 sheet of paper. This will not be all the information we keep about the competitor, but it is the shorthand version that managers should consult regularly, and which will be updated on a continuous basis. We should also explain the one piece of paper target, and in stating this we are thinking of a competitor who is in one of our industries and in one country. If we compete with the competitor in two industries, we will need one profile for each, although some of the information will be duplicated. Where we compete in more than one country, we will need a profile for each country, plus a global summary: how we might organize to achieve this is a matter for Chapter 10.

A second point is that we describe a generic profile based on a sort of average industry. Experience in applying this in a variety of industries and countries has shown that there is always a need to modify the format of the profile slightly to fit the real situation. Modification is always easier than developing the outline from a blank sheet, so we feel that the suggestions here are justified, even if in practice different needs mean that an exact copy is not workable in every situation. The outline given in Figure 6.1 is deliberately the same as that used in the case history in Chapter 8, where there is an example of what a completed profile might look like, but there have been very few examples in our experience where we have not found it necessary to adjust the outline to the specific situation. We probably do not need to add that the outline in this book is drawn to fit the page, and is not to scale. An A3 sheet gives scope for the boxes to be drawn to a size which allows space for information to be recorded.

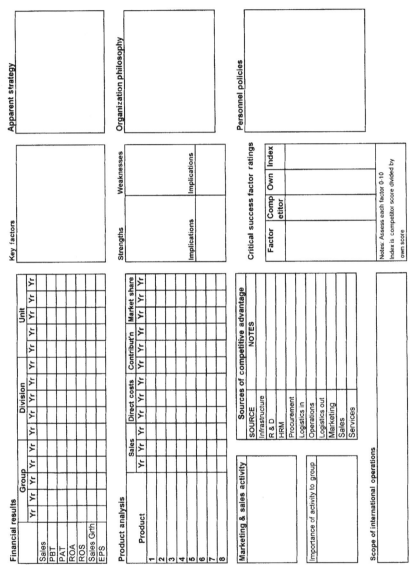

Figure 6.1   Outline competitor profile

Perhaps the best way is to think of the profile as a series of notepads on which information and assessments can be written. The headings, which are described below, sometimes cover hard fact, such as market share figures from an objective source. Often they are deduced from the evidence, such as the apparent strategy. Sometimes they are judgements, based on a mix of deduction and hard fact, such as the critical skills factor ratings.

- *Financial results.* The aim is to record a few meaningful figures that give a snapshot of the competitor's recent history. Unfortunately, few competitors are single-business companies and, even if they are, they may be multinational. The three sub-headings across the matrix reflect this. If the competitor were Otis Elevators, "group" would be changed to United Technologies, "division" to Otis' worldwide organization, and "unit" to the country company we were studying. In fact, in this example we may find it necessary to insert a sub-heading to cover the geographical region, or we may decide that the Otis organization is so big that we can miss out the parent company for our purposes. However, this would mean that some of the information suggested would not be appropriate, such as earnings per share (EPS). Let us also be clear that some of the information we need for the ideal profile may not be available, and cannot be reasonably estimated. The next chapter deals with the sources of information, and although there is frequently more available than may be believed at first, sometimes nothing can be entered in some of the boxes.

- *Product analysis.* Companies compete at the level of products and services. It is possible to argue that there is competition at the unit level for scarce resources, but for the most part we are concerned with product competition in relation to our industry. Thornton, for example, is a British manufacturer of chocolates. Among its competitors are Nestlé and Cadbury-Schweppes. The resources that these giants can command, and the synergy between their activities, are of concern to Thornton because they affect how these competitors may behave. However, Thornton competes only with the chocolate confectionery activities, and would have no interest in the wide range of other products the other companies produce. And even within the chocolate confectionery market, Thornton has a niche position and would be more interested in the boxed chocolates products than chocolate bars.

As designed, the outline suggests analysis of up to eight products, although this can be extended, and records information under the headings sales, direct costs, contribution, and market share. In many cases what is recorded here will be estimates, based on evidence from sources such as market research and reverse engineering. For some types of product an additional column showing advertising expenditure may be of value, and there is also the option of a column showing growth trends.

- *Marketing and sales activity.* This notes key information about how the competitor influences the market. It may include information about the size and organization of the sales force, and note promotional activities and their duration. Information about discounting may be of value. Other relevant information might be the number of outlets operated. For example, this would be important if Nestlé were studying Thornton, because a feature of the latter organization is a network of tied retail outlets trading under the Thornton name. If analysing a professional services firm, it might be relevant to include the number of major organizations they serve, information which often appears in their marketing literature and some journal surveys.

- *Sources of competitive advantage.* The thinking behind this box is derived from the value chain approach (Porter, 1985), which will be discussed later in this chapter. It is an attempt to identify which of the particular activities of the competitor provide value to the customer, and are therefore a source of competitive advantage. The headings here are the generic descriptions used by Porter, and are useful as a reminder to the analysts, but are jargon to most managers. Replace them with a tighter everyday description of the actual source of advantage.

- *Importance of the activity to the whole group.* Our argument here is that a competitor is likely to be more aggressive, and to respond more fiercely to attack, if the activity is of importance to its overall results. This means it is of value to try to establish just how important it is. There is no need to be pedantic. It does not need very much analysis to determine that the activities of the training department of a large multinational, which sells its services to other companies, are not particularly important to the overall strategy of the company, and would probably be abandoned if put under severe pressure. A division which has lost money over several years may not receive the same support as if it were a major contributor, and may be vulnerable in that it may not be able to match your modernization programme, and so will fall further behind. However, a division which contributes most of the profits and cash to a multinational might be considered to carry an invisible sign: "don't tread on me – I bite".

- *Scope of international operations.* At first sight this may not seem to be important to anyone studying competitors within a particular country. This would probably be a correct assumption if all that was recorded was the number of countries in which the competitor operates. There are two more important aspects. First, there is the competitive advantage given by multi-country operations, which may be economies in production because factories produce on a larger scale, the bigger base of revenue to support R&D, and in certain cases the ability to offer advantages that cannot be matched by all competitors. An example of the last is the business travel agency competitors, where only those that have established a global network can gain the volume business of global customers. Second, the way in which a competitor organizes its international operations will have a considerable impact on how it takes decisions. Hussey (1998) states "The competitive reactions to your strategy will be very different if the competitor operates on an individual country basis, what has been termed 'multi-local', than if it manages globally through an integrated strategy. One Europe-wide grocery products company I studied operated at a disadvantage because each country's operation was treated as a separate business, and had to achieve its return on investment targets as its main priority. Its main competitor, who was winning all the battles in every country, treated Europe as one strategic area and would put resources into any country to beat off a competitive threat, regardless of the short-term impact on that subsidiary's bottom line. The virtually uncoordinated country strategies of my client meant that it could rarely win against the superior strategy of the competitor. Knowing how your competitor views global operations is a critical first step to understanding and predicting how it will behave in different circumstances" (p. 179).
- *Key factors.* There are always a number of facts about a competitor which help understanding, and which are either a manifestation of its strategy or suggests that a new strategy may emerge. Under this heading we would record facts such as the

location and number of factories, where R&D is undertaken, changes to the top management team, and any recent change in ownership. It is a notepad for whatever is important and what is worth noting will vary with the industry and the type of competitor.

- *Apparent strategy.*   This is the heart of the profile and also the most difficult box to complete. The word "apparent" is used deliberately: it is what can be deduced about what the competitor is trying to do. Although a useful picture can be developed, it should never be forgotten that there is uncertainty, both in whether the deductions are correct and for how long they will remain correct. Continuous monitoring and analysis of the competitor is the best way of confirming the deductions, spotting inconsistencies, and observing when new strategies appear to be being implemented.

- *Strengths and weaknesses.*   This box does not need explanation but it does require a caution. Although the assessments of your own managers may be valid, where possible they should be backed up by an analysis of the hard evidence. There may be a temptation to mix wishful thinking about weaknesses you would like the competitor to have, with an overestimation of its strengths and infallibility. One American client had undertaken regular assessments of its competitors, and concluded that a number of them were on the verge of financial collapse. This assessment lost some of its impact when it was realized that identical conclusions had been reached every year over the previous five to ten years, and the competitors were still alive and kicking. Customer surveys can be used to reveal some strengths and weaknesses which might otherwise be seen only from an internal, and biased, perspective.

- *Organization philosophy.*   How an organization runs itself will have an impact on its strategies and many operational issues. What role does its head office play in the running of the organization? Is the competitor a pawn in a much larger strategic game that the head office is playing? How is performance of the competitor judged by its head office? How do its accounting principles affect how it views its costs at the product level? Such questions are not only matters for competitors who are subsidiaries of larger organizations, and even single-industry companies are affected by the structure and management style.

- *Personnel policies.* The personnel policies of an organization have an impact on its strategies and performance. A low reward policy may make it difficult for a competitor to attract and retain staff, affecting operational performance and the longer-term success. The quality and qualifications of its employees, the career development opportunities open to them, and the training that is provided are matters which may have strategic importance and are worth recording.
- *Critical success factor ratings.* The concept and use of critical success factors need no further explanation, and what is suggested here is a development from the previous discussion. The first task is to assess the critical success factors for the industry and to rate your own company against them (a 0–10 rating is suggested). This element would be a constant on the profile of each competitor. Next, rate the competitor in the same manner. The index is created by dividing the competitor's score for each factor by your score. Making such judgements about a competitor forces deep consideration, and experience shows that it is best undertaken by a panel of knowledgeable managers rather than by an individual acting alone.

Before moving on, we should spend a little time on the use of the profiles. First, they present a good way of ensuring that all information is analysed and recorded, so that the assessment is always up to date. Ideally they should be discussed regularly by a panel of interested managers, a matter we will return to in Chapter 10. When strategies are considered, they are an essential tool to use in conjunction with the industry charts discussed earlier. Finally, they enable comparisons to be made of what competitors actually do against what you thought they would do, so that there can be immediate reporting to management that something needs consideration. Essentially they are a tool for senior managers and analysts who are involved in strategic decisions. Because they show what you think a competitor is doing, they should be treated as confidential, as if they moved into the hands of the competitors they could become a target for misinformation. For dissemination of regular competitor news across a wide number of people we recommend another approach, which will be discussed at the end of this chapter.

MARKETING DIAGRAMS

It is possible to be more imaginative in the way information is displayed on the profile, to substitute graphs for tables, and to include diagrams such as the three-dimensional approach of Abell (1980) discussed in Chapter 4. Such diagrams can give a visual indication of the differences between competitors which can save lengthy narrative explanations. Market positioning diagrams have a much older pedigree than most of the techniques discussed so far, and offer another way of comparing competitors in a diagrammatic way. The concept is simple, and is not very different from the method used by Porter (1980) to map strategic groupings.

Again the idea is to create a matrix with two axes which show a view of how the competitor is positioned. A possible matrix might be constructed with axes for price (low to high) and perceived quality (low to high). Competitors offering a food product might be compared using convenience and nutritional value as the factors. For a car polish the factors might be speed of application and life of each application. A number of such diagrams, with all competitors plotted, can aid understanding of the market, and each individual competitor. The technique has been used in other marketing situations, such as a comparison of advertising campaigns. We have used it to look for gaps in a market, for example to identify possible journals that might be launched to meet the needs of specific segments of the market.

PORTFOLIO ANALYSIS

Another diagrammatic technique which has value in the examination of competitors is portfolio analysis. Like the market positioning diagrams, portfolio analysis was designed for a different purpose. A full description of the technique and its origins is beyond the scope of this book, but for those who want to probe deeper we recommend Hussey (1998), which provides scoring rules for one variant of the technique, and Segev (1995a, b). The Segev books cover a wide range of variants in detail, one giving conceptual descriptions, and the other is in effect a detailed manual, including computer software to enable application of the various methods.

Here we will restrict ourselves to the bare bones of the technique, and then draw attention to the two ways in which it might be useful in competitor analysis. Figure 6.2 illustrates a typical portfolio chart onto which it is possible to plot strategic business units, or with some adaptation to the scoring rules, major product groupings. Each business activity plotted is typically represented by a circle, the area of which is proportionate to the importance to the company of that activity. There are several different ways of measuring this, and one which is the easiest to use in competitor analysis is revenue.

The basic purpose of portfolio analysis is to enable an organization to look at all its business activities in relation to each other, to help determine which to invest in, which to manage for cash, and which should be sold or closed down. In the example, the probability is that an activity with weak market prospects but a high market share should be run to generate as much cash as possible, with just enough investment to maintain the business. A weak share in a poor prospect market raises the question of whether the business can ever become successful, and, even if it could, whether this would be the optimum use of scarce resources of talent and money. The indicative

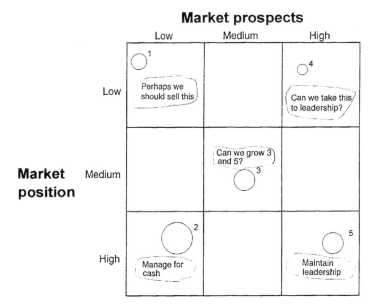

Figure 6.2 Example of portfolio chart. Each circle is one SBU, area is proportionate to revenue and comments are indications derived from the chart: more analysis is needed to reach a decision

answer from the analysis is to consider disposal. At the other extreme, a high market share in a high prospect market implies a cash-hungry business that needs to invest to stay ahead and which should yield good returns. A weak share in a high prospect market is something the organization should either try to develop or drop altogether if it does not want to do this. Without a commitment to driving for a much higher market share, activities in this box will tend to get weaker over the long term as the leading contenders strive for more market share and market growth.

The remaining positions on the chart are interpreted as various degrees of intensity of the same three broad strategies. All indications are indicative, and other evidence should be examined before decisions are made. The main value of the portfolio chart is not to give dogmatic answers but to help the organization to choose between its activities, if it does not have the resources to back them all, to examine how a strategy such as acquisition or strategic alliance might change the position on the matrix, and to ensure that the number of cash-hungry activities chosen does not exceed the cash-generating/raising ability of the organization.

The chart also helps a consideration of timing. In a fast-growing, emerging industry, where a company has a strong position in one or two countries, it is tempting to think of an expansion plan that rolls out across the world, building on success and reducing apparent risk. However, the analysis behind the portfolio chart might show that this would be disastrous as it would allow other competitors to get ahead in the race, after which it may become impossible to catch up again. If the investment required is too great or too risky for the company, the indication would be either to sell the business now, while there are potential buyers, or to expand by other means such as strategic alliances.

One use of portfolio analysis in competitor analysis arises from this sort of situation. If we plot competitors on the company portfolio chart we can see which are better placed than we are to win such a global race. This may be most useful when we are looking at a global opportunity, at a stage when every competitor has a regional strength but no one has yet gained a truly global position, as there may not be a full awareness of the other competitors who have not yet been encountered in the marketplace.

A second use of the portfolio approach in competitor analysis is to try to think like the competitor when it is a multi-activity organization. We may compete with only one of its activities, but what it does in our industry is partly affected by the relative position of the activity in the competitor's portfolio. If they have an activity in the central box of the matrix, which has to operate as a cash generator to provide resources for more promising cash-hungry elements of the portfolio, while our choice is to develop that business because it is one of the best on our own portfolio, we may well have an advantage in that they may not wish to match our investment. The disadvantage of using portfolio analysis in this way is that it requires the collection of information on other industries in which the competitor operates but in which we have no direct interest. It is thus a tool to be used sparingly, but is nonetheless valuable when justified by the situation.

SOURCES OF CUSTOMER VALUE: THE VALUE CHAIN

In our discussion of the competitor profiles we touched on a list of headings which aimed to show how the competitor was delivering value to the customers. This was inspired by the value chain concept originated by Porter (1985). He argued "To diagnose competitive advantage, it is necessary to define a firm's value chain for competing in a particular industry" (p. 45). He also maintained that "Competitive advantage cannot be understood by looking at a firm as a whole. It stems from the many discrete activities a firm performs in designing, producing, marketing, delivering, and supporting its product. Each of these activities can contribute to a firm's relative cost position and create a basis for differentiation" (p. 33).

Porter envisages an organization as having five broad operational areas: inbound logistics, operations, outbound logistics, marketing and sales, and service. Each and all of these is potentially capable of delivering unique value to the customer which, provided the economic equation is satisfactory, can create competitive advantage. So the first step is to examine the processes which cluster under these broad headings, to establish where the costs are incurred, and which produce value to the customer.

Supporting these operational activities are procurement, technology, human resource management departments, and the infrastructure of the firm. These may not be visible to the customer, but nevertheless can create or destroy value. For example, the comprehensive training given by an airline to its cabin staff may create value not through the training but through what the customer experiences, the behaviour of the in-flight staff.

The idea is that a chain of value exists inside every organization, and understanding this and building on it is one way to build a strong competitive position. It follows that understanding a competitor's value chain, to the degree that it is possible to do this from outside, is a useful step in determining an appropriate strategy.

Value is created, according to Johansson et al (1993), in four broad ways, alone or in combination: improved quality, service, reduced cost to customer and reduced cycle time. The starting point for an assessment of the value chain may be to establish what the *organization* believes are the processes which deliver value to the customer, but by itself this may be dangerous and inadequate. It is the customer that is the key, and to make any sense of the value chain there is a need to establish what the customer is looking for. However, there are limitations to this when the company is considering an innovation that has never been done before, and therefore customers may have no experience or even understanding of it.

So although much of value chain analysis is about self-inspection, it may be meaningless unless it has customer inputs. Market surveys may yield some of this information but greater depth may come from focus groups of current and potential customers. Such marketing research methods can also yield valuable information about the value chains of competitors. A focus on these formal ways of obtaining information should not obscure the important information that is gained when the organization is always in close contact with its customers, enjoys good relations with them, and discusses their needs with them almost continuously. Unfortunately, comparatively few companies are close enough to their customers so that they are really in each others' confidence, and in any case knowing a customer well may not help you understand why its competitors do not buy from you.

Porter's thinking goes beyond the boundaries of the firm, and argues that the industry company is only one series of links in a much larger chain which stretches from the raw materials to the ultimate buyer. Many of the value improvements lie at the interfaces between the organizations which make up this chain. Therefore there is considerable merit in working closely with suppliers, customers and through them the customer's customers, to seek areas of overall improvement. Collaborative work of this kind is, of course, now a feature of modern approaches to quality management, and appears in much of the literature on business process re-engineering, and it is no longer considered stupid to give up an activity which is not performed as well as it could be and to transfer it to a supplier.

BENCHMARKING

Using competitor analysis for performance improvement takes us to the topic of benchmarking. There is often confusion about what benchmarking really is, and some consider that they are benchmarking when they compare performance ratios. Although it is an important first step to use such ratios when they can be obtained, benchmarking is about understanding the processes through which someone else is achieving performance which is better than yours, and comparing them with your own. It follows that the elements in benchmarking are:

1. Decide *what* to benchmark, which may come about from a comparison of performance ratios of competitors or from a less specific indication that performance could be improved.
2. Decide *who* to benchmark against. This, of course, requires their agreement, and normally benchmarking is a reciprocal process.
3. Study your *own* processes in the area which is causing you concern.
4. Study the equivalent processes of your *benchmarking partner(s)*.
5. Compare the results with what *you* are doing.
6. Develop an *action plan* to improve.

It follows that benchmarking as a whole has only limited use in competitor analysis, since it is unlikely that the necessary cooperation can be obtained. In any case, the normal code of practice in benchmarking is that information obtained from a reciprocal process is only used for the purpose agreed at the outset, which would make it unethical to use such information for a wider purpose Only the first step, comparing as many aspects of performance as possible against competitors, is often all that is possible, although this, of course, is very valuable. Performance indicators may be collected by trade associations and other external organizations. Although the names of the competitor are usually replaced by a code number, it is possible to compare your performance against others, even if you are not quite sure who has the best performance in that area. Other indicators can be developed from marketing research. It is possible, for example, to obtain information on how long it takes various competitors to deliver the goods from the time a customer makes an order, or to compare the performance of service engineers when called into a customer's premises. When a process is carried out in full view on premises which are open to the public it is possible to observe and record it. Things such as the length of customer queues at supermarket checkouts or bank counters and waiting times at peak periods could be obtained, although loitering too long in a bank may result in the attentions of the security staff!

Benchmarking can be a very useful tool in building competitive advantage, and is one of the tools that might be used to help achieve world-class performance. Xerox is recognized as being among the leaders in the use of benchmarking, and the methods this organization uses are described in Watson (1993). Bounds and Hewitt (1995) give a case history of Xerox's overall performance improvement activities over several years.

If you cannot easily benchmark yourself against a competitor, what can you do? There are two options.

• In many industries it is possible to find a firm in the same line of business with whom you do not compete. So an electricity-generating firm in Holland should be able to benchmark against a similar firm in Japan or the USA, or a chain of health shops in Hungary might find cooperation from a similar chain in the UK.
• As the interest is in processes, and these are common across wide swathes of economic activity, we may learn most from benchmarking against firms that are not in our industry but which operate the particular process. Once this expansion of thinking takes place, it becomes possible to see that we may actually gain more through doing this than if we restricted the study to our own industry, because members of our industry may include the best in the world in one process but be well below world-class with another.

Benchmarking can be used totally internally where, for example, an organization has operations in several countries or has numerous branches which undertake the same tasks. Here it is possible to benchmark against the best with relative ease. This may bring an overall improvement, and build confidence in the process before going outside, but it is unlikely to help the organization jump ahead of the competition.

Finally we would add that the last stage of the process, developing and implementing the improvement, does not mean that the aim is just to copy someone else. Other people's solutions may have to be adapted to fit the circumstances of your organization, and in any case it may be possible to spot how those solutions can be improved to take you even further ahead.

COMPETITOR NEWSLETTERS

Although it moves us from methods of analysis, we should like to suggest a way of disseminating information about competitors which can be used more widely than the profiles. This is a development from the common practice of sending out files of press articles, which has value but tends to be repetitive, and what is passed out is not validated. Instead, it is worth considering the production of a periodic competitor newsletter, which can be produced in confidential and non-confidential versions. In this way a summary can be provided of the facts gleaned from the various sources, so that there is an awareness of what the competitors are doing. The ideal would be to have only one version which incorporates information from various sources, and this is particularly motivating when it can acknowledge the contribution of pieces of information provided by the sales force and others with their ears close to the industry gossip. However, this depends on the trust management has in its employees, as the newsletter should not reach competitors. In any case, the newsletter should avoid any statements which are based on unsubstantiated rumour, which could cause problems if repeated to customers or if they became known to competitors.

Like so much in competitor analysis, the right answer requires a healthy dose of common sense, and, given this, sensible decisions can be made.

REFERENCES

Abell, D.F. (1980). *Defining the Business*, Prentice Hall, Englewood Cliffs, NJ.
Bounds, G. & Hewitt, F. (1995) Xerox: Envisioning a corporate transformation,

Strategic Change, **4**, No. 1. (This appears also in Hussey, D.E. (ed.) (1996). *The Implementation Challenge*, Wiley, Chichester.)

Hussey, D.E. (1998). *Strategic Management: From Theory to Implementation*, 4th edition, Butterworth-Heinemann, Oxford.

Johansson, H.J., McHugh, P., Pendlebury, A.J. & Wheeler, W.A. (1993). *Business Process Reengineering: Break point Strategies for Market Dominance*, Wiley, Chichester.

Porter, M.E. (1980). *Competitive Strategy*, The Free Press, New York.

Porter, M.E. (1985). *Competitive Advantage*, The Free Press, New York.

Segev, E. (1995a). *Corporate Strategy, Portfolio Models*, International Thomson, London.

Segev, E. (1995b). *Navigating by Compass*, International Thomson, London.

Watson, G.H. (1993). *Strategic Benchmarking*, Wiley, New York.

7
Sources of Information for Competitor Analysis

LEGALITY AND ETHICS

Competitor intelligence is legal: industrial espionage is not. This chapter is only about activities which are legitimate, and do not involve theft, trespass, electronic bugging, or the bribery of a competitor's employees. Nor do we want to be drawn into an argument over whether documents in a dustbin outside a competitor's offices have been abandoned and can therefore be taken, because even if this were not theft, taking these documents would not appear to us to be ethical.

Ethics are personal, and our views may not be the same as those of all readers. One test is whether you would be happy for your competitor and all your customers to know how you obtained a piece of information: if you feel that your methods should be hidden, they are probably not as ethical as they should be. In our code we would rule out lying to a competitor when making a direct approach for information. Thus we might employ a student to visit competitors to obtain information, but would not allow the request to be disguised as an academic project. Our involvement would be declared at the outset, and this includes not hiding behind a partial truth (the academic assignment is genuine, but the information is for us as well as the project). Similarly we believe it to be unethical to press an employee who joins us from a competitor to reveal confidential information about that competitor, to have someone apply for a job advertised by a competitor to obtain information about the company, or any of the similar dubious activities which we are often expected to applaud in private detective novels and television series. The end does not justify the means.

HOW COMPETITOR INFORMATION ARISES

Competitor information arises in four different ways:

1. The evidence left by its activities
2. The organization's own need to communicate with actual and potential stakeholders
3. Legal or association obligations, which make certain information public
4. Activities of outsiders, which may not be welcomed by the organization.

None of the information that can be gathered as a result of this activity should be treated in isolation. The same facts may appear under more than one heading, and even an apparently trivial snippet of information can sometimes provide the key which enables another piece of information to be interpreted more accurately. This means that all four of the broad sources should be examined in detail.

One of the best examples that has been published of a comprehensive competitor analysis appears in Gulliver (1990). The motivation was acquisition, and the study was of Distillers by the Argyll Group. Guinness became notorious for the way they won control of Distillers against Argyll (those who do not know the background will find a brief summary in another part of the quoted article):

> My team went back 15 years with the Distillers accounts and up to 10 years with their principal trading subsidiaries. With a total of about 80 trading subsidiaries we were able to prepare a group consolidation which gave us a good feel for the contribution of individual profit centres. In addition we scrutinized analysts' reports and trade and financial press cuttings back to the 1960s. Drinks industry reports were obtained, and independent market research on Distillers' products and markets were commissioned... We also looked at its industrial relations.
>
> Finally we made a pavement inspection of Distillers' properties. After checking trade directories and *Yellow Pages*, a small team photographed and produced a report on every Distillers' property we could find...
>
> The bid for Distillers by Argyll was an enormously complex exercise in research, analysis, and the development of a strategy for the bid, and post the merger.

EVIDENCE LEFT BY A COMPANY'S ACTIVITIES

Much of a company's commercial activity leaves some trace or is observed in some way: what we might term the forensics and witness statements. Products offered for sale may be capable of being observed, the sales measured, and market shares established. Buyers may be asked to give their opinion of a product or organization. Aerial photographs may be taken of an extensive plant. Lorries may be counted in and out of a warehouse. The only questions are whether your activity is legal and ethical, and whether the likely costs exceed the expected benefits.

Imagine that you are standing on the bank of the river Zambezi in Zimbabwe, facing upstream. On your right-hand side the Devil's Cataract tumbles noisily into the gorge below. On your left hand there is a statue of David Livingstone. You start to walk upstream, and soon the made-up tourist path stops, although it continues as a narrow, winding path, made by people or game. You notice some elephant droppings. A little further on you realize that the droppings look very fresh. As someone with no expertise in animal tracking you can make one deduction. An elephant has passed this way recently, but you do not know its direction of travel, or how long ago. As a sensible person you turn back, hoping that the elephant was going in the other direction.

If you had a tracker with you with the required expertise, you might increase the amount of information that you could gain. First, the tracker would be able to judge when the elephant passed from an expert assessment of the droppings; second, the direction of travel could be ascertained from the signs on the ground; third, the tracker would establish whether more than one elephant has just walked this path.

If you persuaded the tracker to put in additional effort even more may be discovered. By moving around the area it may be possible to establish whether the path is frequently used by elephants, and whether others were travelling through the bush on a parallel route.

It is a similar combination of observation, expertise, and effort which can be used to discover what is probably the most valuable information you can gain about a competitor. It is often also the most relevant, since companies compete at the level of products and services, and may not be directly interested in non-competing activities of a competitor.

Information from the Market

As all businesses succeed or fail in the marketplace, this is where we should start. The richness of the seam of information that can be mined here varies with the market and the measurement services that have been established by market research organizations. These tend to be strongest for fast-moving grocery products and weakest for professional services and industrial capital products and consumables.

- *Market-measurement services.* There are organizations in many countries, such as A.C. Nielsen, which offer an accurate way of measuring sales of all the competitors through various types of outlet. This is achieved through regular "audits" of a sample of retail outlets, which records sales over the period, quantities in the retail area and in the stock room, and prices. From this information it is possible to calculate the total sales in each measured product category passing through this type of outlet and the brand shares. In some countries organizations such as Nielsen and SAMI/Burke offer data collected from supermarket scanners at checkouts. Other providers operate in other industries, such as the firms who analyse doctors' prescriptions to provide information on the market size and brand shares of various ethical pharmaceuticals. It is also possible to measure market movements and brand shares at the level of the consumer. The most consistent information comes from carefully controlled panels of consumers who keep diaries of their purchases in the product areas being measured. These are aggregated to produce comprehensive reports, which, although they may have more opportunity for error than the audit approaches, have the immense advantage that they cover all purchases from all types of retail audit. There may be published or syndicated surveys of various types which estimate market size and brand shares. These may be available from a variety of sources, covering a large range of consumer and industrial products, and, it has to be said, with varying degrees of efficiency and effectiveness.
- *Market Surveys.* As we all know, thousands of market surveys are undertaken every year. Many of these are specifically related to a product that a company either has on the market or hopes

to launch, or to the advertising that promotes it. Consumers are asked what they think of a product, why they buy it, where they buy, if they buy, how often, who makes the buying decision, what newspapers they read ... the list is almost endless. Surveys can be a very useful tool for probing a competitor's strengths and weaknesses.

Such surveys have to be related to the perceptions of the customer. A shopper may have views about certain retail companies, but these will be related to the outlets he or she deals with. Few consumers will have a view about Unilever, but they may have a very clear appreciation of the strengths of a particular detergent against others they have tried. The retail buyers, who deal with all the competitors, have a more complete view of a supplier, although their views relate to the subsidiary or division which they deal with, and not usually to the entire organization.

Where the survey method really comes into its own in helping to assess strengths and weaknesses is with industrial goods and services, where the respondents should be well informed, may deal frequently with competing companies, and are exposed to an entire unit of a supplier organization. Often their experience is based on a close relationship with the whole supplier organization, and their views of the various suppliers may have great usefulness. The patterns that emerge of who each buying organization in the sample knows of, and deals with, can give insight into the segmentation strategy of a supplier. When the market is fragmented, and has many niches, as in the provision of management training, surveys can help to establish which of the firms in the market are real competitors of each other.

Although many organizations undertake regular surveys of their markets, these are not always designed to answer the questions that increase understanding of competitors. Additional surveys may be an option which should be considered by any organization that is serious about competitor analysis.

- *Bid analysis.* There are some industries where competitive bids are very common. Examples include civil engineering, building, some plant and machinery, lifts and escalators, and professional services such as management consulting, engineering consulting, and management training. The proportion of work that is subject to such bids varies with industries, and is higher with construction-related products like lifts than it is with a professional service such as management consulting, where buyers do not always solicit bids from competitors.

Wherever there is a competitive bid situation, there is information to be gained, whether the contract is won or lost. To obtain this information means contacting the buyer to ask for information. This should be done in a tactful way, whatever the outcome. It is just as important to know why your organization won a contract as why they lost it. Our experience of this sort of follow-up is that buyers are usually cooperative, and in some cases have prepared an analysis of the strengths and weaknesses of the various bids which they are willing to share with all the bidders. An example can be found in Hussey (1988, Chapter 9), which shows part of the analysis which Coopers & Lybrand were willing to share when seven proposals were considered for a new management development programme. The published reference hides the individual details of bidders, but in the actual situation full information was disclosed by agreement with the bidders.

Where competitors in an industry bid for a high proportion of all contracts, post-bid intelligence can provide extensive and accurate information about competitors. From your own proposal you know the technical specifications, the geographical details, the buyer, the purpose, and other information such as, in the case of lifts or air conditioning, the size and nature of the building. If you win the bid you know the price. If you lose, you only need to ask the buyer for the name of the winning firm and the price to have all the information you need to complete the picture. The name of the successful competitor is unlikely to be withheld, although some buyers may not give out the price of the winning bid. However, in these cases it may be possible to estimate the winning bid price from your own price and what the buyer tells you about the reason you lost. Put all this together in a database, and you have the ability to look at your strengths and weaknesses against each competitor. Overall market shares may hide the fact that competitors do better in certain segments, geographical areas, or with certain buyers.

For the appropriate types of business, a systematic and continuous follow-up of all competitive bids can be very rewarding. The key words are systematic and continuous.

Product Analysis

Once a product is out in the market it can be purchased by a competitor and examined. This may not be a practical proposition for a multi-million-pound paper-making machine, and, of course, only applies to products and not services, but this still leaves numerous products where this action can be taken.

Examination of a competitor's product can be a valuable source of information. For an engineered product, like a photocopier or video recorder, it provides an opportunity for the company to compare performance with its own similar product. It enables reverse engineering to take place to see how particular functions of the product are arrived at.

Both of these were used to good competitive effect by Ashbrook Simon Hartley (ASH), a US manufacturer of belt presses. For the uninitiated, a belt press is a machine for squeezing out liquids, and may have a number of purposes. With this company it was in sewage treatment, and the separation of liquids and solids for processing. ASH had found that winning competitive bids from the municipal buyers was a matter of chance, since the order always went to the lowest-priced bid that met the minimum specifications. They examined their competitor's machines and were convinced that their product offered superior operating performance. In order to convince buyers of this, they persuaded them to arrange side-by-side tests on-site before a vendor was chosen. This was achieved by each supplier bringing a truck-mounted machine to the site and coupling it up alongside the competitors' machines and processing sewage under controlled conditions. ASH always outperformed the competitors, which not only increased its proportion of wins but also led to a gradual increase in the performance requirements specified for the machines in future invitations to propose. A side-benefit was that the need to maintain a number of truck-mounted machines, and have trained teams to operate them, raised the entry barriers for newcomers. Much more had to be invested before a sale could be made.

The ability to analyse a product such as canned dog food, or to reverse engineer a computer, in many cases will enable an estimate to be made of the costs of production. This requires considerable effort and expertise, and is likely to be more accurate if there is an awareness of the manufacturing processes used by the competitor, and if the market information enables good estimates to be made of the volume of product the competitor makes. It is unlikely that accuracy could be achieved without combining product analysis with other competitive information. In combination with market audit or other information on a competitor's sales volumes, and other information from annual reports and other sources, it may be possible to estimate the sources of a competitor's profits in fine detail.

Although it is not difficult to see that Argyll, in the example given earlier, might be able to estimate Distillers' costs of a bottle of whisky, as one of the elements in a detailed product contribution summary, there can be a danger in assuming that competitors follow the same production methods as your own company. This was one of the factors that led the British motorcycle companies to misread the situation when Honda made its first attacks on the British market.

When it is not possible to buy a competitor's product it may be possible to arrange to see it on the premises of a buyer. Although this does not give an opportunity to see how it is made, it will provide opportunities to see it working and to obtain information from the buying organization of its performance capabilities.

Sometimes detailed knowledge of the competitor's product is needed to avoid patent infringements (patents are discussed briefly under another heading). Canon successfully developed a copier that did not infringe Xerox's 600 patents. It is hard to see how this could be done without comprehensive knowledge of the Xerox products.

Other Types of Survey

In addition to market surveys there are other types of data collected by survey techniques on certain industries which provide capacity or sales information that is not otherwise published. Journals and specialized economic monitoring services tend to be the major source. It is, for example, possible to obtain regular information on the revenue of many consulting firms, the number of partners they have, and the number of other employees, and sometimes similar information on specific segments from the pages of *Management Consulting*. Capacity information is available on a large part of the petrochemical industry from regular reports by journals such as *European Chemical News*.

Other Information from Observation

The Argyll example quoted earlier shows how information on properties was gained from a pavement inspection. Although the amount
of effort spent should be related to the use to which the information
will be put, particularly as many of the possible approaches are
expensive, there are situations where direct observation can be
extremely useful:

- The best way for one supermarket to monitor its competitors is
  for regular visits to be paid on a controlled basis to a sample of
  their stores, to observe prices, new products, and layout changes.
- Where dealers store equipment such as excavators and similar
  mobile plant in open yards, a regular observation on a controlled basis will allow stock levels to be observed. This method is
  used regularly by one manufacturer of such products in the USA,
  the information being used to predict changes in discounting
  and other promotional actions.
- Market Planning Systems Inc. of Phoenix, Arizona offers a
  sophisticated approach to modelling area demand for retail
  petrol, which enables the total distribution system of a local area
  to be modelled and the sales volumes of every retail outlet in the
  system to be estimated in what they call "tactics" – what – if
  questions which enable the impact of competitor actions such as
  price change, promotions or modernization to be studied. The
  data sources for these models which are built for specific clients
  include: the client's own statistics; observations taken of all
  competitor sites either to read the meters on the pumps or, if
  these are not accessible, to estimate the number of customers;
  aerial photographs which enable traffic volumes to be estimated
  around each filling station; and maps.
- There are usually opportunities to visit the factories of competitors, which can give clues to processes, the age of plant, efficiency, and the culture.

THE ORGANIZATION'S OWN NEED TO COMMUNICATE

Much information which is useful in competitor analysis is not
considered by the competitor to be confidential and may be made

widely available. This is because the modern company, particularly the quoted company, has a need to communicate with its current and potential stakeholders, and sometimes even with its competitors. The latter is a rather special case and we do not mean illegal actions such as price collusion. Porter (1980, 1985) discusses market signalling, and shows how a company may wish to signal to competitors that it either will or will not take a particular action, or to indicate that an apparent opportunity is not likely to be viable. This may be a very good reason why chemical companies frequently disclose plant capacities or announce plans to expand capacity. Signalling is normally done through company press statements, speeches, and interviews with journalists that the company has engineered. There is also a school of thought that argues that all competitors will make fewer decisions which damage the whole industry if good market information is available to all, and that there is value in sharing certain information about the market.

But the main bulk of information that a company issues of its own volition is intended to inform and/or influence stakeholders or those who may become stakeholders. The company's own publications and circulars may be targeted at particular groups, like investors, customers or employees, but few can be contained within those groups, and some are multi-purpose. Much of this material goes into very wide circulation, and will yield useful and accurate information. Statements to the media, and interviews by journalists, result in articles and broadcasts that are available to all who seek them out.

Investors: Present and Potential Shareholders

Private companies and partnerships may not have much motivation to ensure that investors are aware of the reasons for actions, the strengths of the organization, its values, and its vision, and may be able to treat anything that they do produce as secret. This is not so with public companies, or those that need the support of the financial institutions, or believe that they will need such support in the future. For these organizations the annual report is expanded beyond the minimum legal requirements, and is made available to shareholders, stockbrokers, customers, candidates for employment, and anyone else who cares to ask. In most countries it is lodged with the annual return and is open for inspection by the public. The quickest way to obtain this is to get on the competitor's mailing list, which can be done by a straightforward request, and if this is denied, by right through the purchase of a single share.

Because the annual report is a focused document, within a legal framework, some companies also produce company brochures and annual fact books, which are available to anyone with a legitimate interest in the organization, and which are often available on a help-yourself basis in company offices and other places. The 1996 fact book of ICI is used as an example, and our copy was picked up in the careers centre of a British university, although it is not a recruitment brochure.

The ICI fact book consists of 51 pages of factual information, some of which might have been obtainable from press cuttings, statistical publications, and the annual report, but much would otherwise have been difficult to discover. The fact book "explains what the ICI Group does, how it is organized, who runs it, where it operates, and what its major products are", and it does this very well. It describes the overall organization in terms of the financials, vision, structure, and the pattern of share ownership. Each business sector is described, with financials, much capacity information, summaries of recent acquisitions and alliances, and a great deal more. There is a listing of worldwide locations and their activities.

ICI is not the only organization that issues regular fact books or similar publications. However, it is true to say that most public companies do not go into this amount of detail. For them, a main way of reaching the investors is either through the media or meetings with investment analysts who write briefings for investors and may publish assessments of the prospects of all players in an industry. It is possible, but may be difficult, to research newspaper articles more than a few months in arrears, and although possible for journal articles which are retained in libraries for longer periods, it is generally more effective to organize collection of cuttings and articles on a continuous basis. There are organizations which can provide such a service, in the form of either copies or abstracts: the latter may be particularly helpful for items that are in foreign languages, since the abstracts may be provided in your own language. Database services may be useful, particularly those which include stockbroker reports. The great source of information through the Internet is taken up later in this chapter.

However, it is worth stressing that abstract and cutting services and database services only go to some of the sources, and it should not be assumed that there is total global coverage of all media. Check that the service is looking in the places you wish searched (this issue will come up again later in the context of case histories).

So far much of the discussion has taken single-country views of competitors, which may be relevant for some things but not for others. If you want to understand the local subsidiary of a multi-national company it is really necessary to study the parent as well. And if you are interested in a multinational, it is worth remembering that what the chairman says about the global strategy when opening a new complex in South Africa, and which is only reported in that country, may include information that would be invaluable if only you had known about it.

Customers

The type of communication a competitor produces will vary with the industry, and any product which flows through a distribution channel may require different communication media to the inter-mediary than to the end user:

- *Advertising.*   An analysis of advertising may be useful for two purposes. First, it may help you to see how the competitor is trying to differentiate the product. Second, it may enable you to establish which market segments the competitor is targeting. The task may be relatively easy for industrial products, where advertising is not usually the key element of the marketing mix. It may be very complex with fast-moving consumer goods, where the media may extend from press and direct mail to television, radio, and cinema. The size of advertising spend may be critical to success.
- *Product brochures.*   Product brochures may be produced for persuasive purposes or to convey complex technical informa-tion. Both can provide useful information, and this source of information may be particularly important for industrial plant and machinery or for major consumer products like motor cars or computers. The brochures can give a better understanding of the competitor's product range, identify what the competitor feels are the strong points of the product, and may also yield

price information. It is easier to pick up brochures for consumer products, which are often in the retail outlets for the taking, but it is not difficult to find ways of obtaining brochures for industrial products: sometimes the easiest way is the most successful – just telephone the competitor and ask for a copy.

- *Company brochures.* Not all industries produce company brochures aimed at customers, although the fact books described earlier may also be used for this purpose. However, for professional service companies, such as engineering consultants, market research agencies, management consultants, management training colleges and the like, the brochure may be the key document in the promotional armoury. Such firms sell intangibles, and usually concentrate on approaches, values, philosophies and skills, rather than specific products. Analysis of these brochures will often reveal what the competitor believes to be its strengths, details of its main area of focus, and the type of market it is aiming for. The cynic might argue that relative fee rates can be judged by the relative thickness and quality of the paper, and the brochures struggle to build an image to counteract the basic problems of marketing intangible products.
- *Customer newsletters, journals, and related material.* These take many forms. The nature and style of the publication may sometimes reveal more than its content. Contrast, for example, the regular publications of various management consultancies. McKinsey produces a quarterly journal, of very high quality papers, which helps to sustain an image of quality and relevance. Harbridge Consulting Group published a brief article nine times a year in its *Management Development Update*, which brought new ideas, case histories, and research findings to the attention of clients. The purpose was image building, establishing the expert nature of the firm, a soft sell of capability, and to give something of interest and professional value to the market. Other firms issue a newsletter, which describes their recent activities. Not all such publications are useful in competitor analysis. It is doubtful that much could be gained from some of the magazines issued by life insurance companies to their clients.
- *Public relations.* PR activity may take a variety of forms, but the most obvious are press statements and interviews which are designed to speak to customers. The trade or specialist consumer press is often the target, although when the issue is important

enough it will make the main newspapers and other journals, and may lead to broadcast material on television or radio. Such material may announce new products, give notice of price changes, discuss new distribution arrangements, describe a plant expansion, stress a commitment to quality, or show how a problem has been overcome. And these are just a few of the things that may be learnt about competitors in this way. Journalists may initiate interviews and company statements, and may undertake surveys which provide statistical information about the firms in an industry. Accounting and management consultancy journals may be among the few sources that reveal turnover and levels of employment of partnerships. We discussed earlier how to monitor the media for competitor information.

- *Directories.* Some information appears in directories, although often these reveal less than is obtainable from other sources. In a fragmented market directories may help to establish the number of competitors. Occasionally a directory is published which incorporates some form of survey, giving information not easily available from other sources. However, it should be remembered that numerical information provided to directories is not subject to audit and may be optimistically rounded upwards. The best place to consult directories is often a specialist library, where many can be accessed at the same time.

Employees and Potential Employees

Communication with employees is seen as critical for effective management, particularly in times of change. This means making much more information available to employees, to explain what the company is doing and where it is trying to go to. Some of this information will appear in shareholder and customer publications; much will be additional to these.

We have already mentioned that ideas of what information should be kept confidential have changed, and in this section we are discussing information that is freely given and widely disseminated. We do not include confidential discussions which take place inside a company and which can only be discovered by illegal or unethical methods.

Employee Newspapers and Journals

Although intended for employees, these are often made much more widely available, and may be sent to pensioners, suppliers and customers, as well as interested parties like competitors. They are often exchanged between company HR departments. Some libraries maintain collections of them.

Anyone with experience of several companies will know that there are great differences between employee publications of companies. Some are mainly concerned with social news about employees, and are almost neutral about anything the company is doing. Others contain information about company successes, which may or may not be interesting to a competitor. The real value comes when the journal explains something the company is doing and the direction it is taking. One of our clients obtained considerable information on a competitor's information systems strategy by reading copies of the competitor's internal journal, which had been lodged with a London library. This caused it to examine what a competitor might have gleaned from its own journal, also in the library, and they were surprised to find that most of their Asia-Pacific strategy could have been deduced from a series of articles they had published.

Case Histories and Case Studies

A company may cooperate with an author or academic to enable a case history article about the company to be written, or to allow an academic case study to be written for use in a university, and which may be available through the case clearing house or in an academic textbook. Managers inside a company may find it of value to write a case history themselves for publication in a book or journal. All will disclose information about the subject organization, which may not otherwise have become available. This may appear as written, video or audio material.

The reasons for doing this are varied and are generally in the company's interest. Generally it fits with the need to communicate to employees and customers, and gives reinforcement to the things the company is trying to achieve. British Petroleum went as far as to invite a journalist to attend some of its board meetings and to write up some articles based on the decisions taken to implement its Project 1990, a major business process re-engineering initiative. This action helped pass the change message to employees, and showed customers that the company was in the forefront of good management practice. In addition to helping to put over a message or a particular aspect of the corporate image, such material is also useful internally to confirm the quality of managers and management actions, and as materials in internal training activities. Undoubtedly, some companies also feel that by cooperating with universities they are establishing goodwill with potential graduate recruits, and giving something back to the community.

Such case studies and case history articles are unlikely to disclose a competitor's strategic plan but they may provide many facts and figures about aspects of the competitor's business, an indication of problems the competitor is grappling with, and some of the actions being implemented which will have an effect on the competitiveness of the competitor. They may give insight into the way the competitor "thinks" and behaves.

Surprisingly this is one of the sources of potential information that we have found is often overlooked. Undoubtedly it is a matter of luck whether a case study or case history has been written about your competitor, but as several thousand are published in the world every year it is at least worth looking. Second, not everyone is aware that academic case studies can be accessed at the universities, or often in the case clearing house (which in the UK is in the Business School at Cranfield). Harvard has its directory of case studies on CD-ROM to facilitate searching. Articles appear in many different journals and newspapers, many of which may be outside the normal press scanning activity. For example, the journals *Long Range Planning* and *Strategic Change* both publish some six to eight case history articles every year, and there are many management and functional journals that have similar philosophies.

It is one of the many sources which becomes more accessible as more contents pages and abstracts of journals are published on the Internet.

Recruitment Advertisements as a Source of Competitive Information

One potential source of information about competitors is the advertisements they place to recruit employees. More is likely to be learned from the display advertisements for senior managers and specialist staff than those for more junior people which appear in the small advertisement sections of newspapers and journals, partly because there is more space in the display advertisements, and partly because more of these jobs reveal something about the strategic direction of the advertiser.

Of course, many advertisements are placed by consultants without revealing the client's name, although sometimes those in the industry can make a shrewd guess about who is advertising, and the most senior jobs of all may never be advertised and may be filled instead by headhunters. Many advertisements which do appear will not yield anything of value, and sometimes those that do provide information only repeat things that are already known. For these reasons, ploughing through pages of advertisements in journals and newspapers may not be the most exciting activity in competitor research, and the ratio of valuable information to the number read may be quite low.

Nevertheless the source should not be ignored, as information does appear that may fill in a piece of the jigsaw puzzle or confirm something already expected. The value may come from the fact of the advertisement: a batch of new jobs in a particular area of research and development may give a strong clue to the competitor's strategic thinking, for example. It may be useful to know the rates at which jobs are being advertised, although the salaries quoted are not a perfect indication of what is actually paid to the successful applicant. Information about the organization's strategy or operations may be included, and sometimes this may be the only source of such information: but be aware that figures in advertisements are probably and legitimately rounded.

The best way to illustrate the sort of information that can be gained is to look at the strategic information we found in the recruitment pages of one issue of a major British Sunday newspaper. The date 12 January 1997 was selected for one reason only. It was the day we thought of doing the exercise. Of course, we do not know all the industries in which the advertisers operate, nor do we have any interest in what the particular companies are doing, so we cannot evaluate whether any competitor of theirs might already know what the advertisements reveal. What is clear is that the information from the revealing advertisements we found among the many that gave little strategic insight would have been of interest to a competitor if not already known. We look first at two advertisements which would have provided a competitor with significant strategic insight. Table 7.1 (on pages 132–3) summarizes a number of other advertisements, where useful strategic information is given.

1. The healthcare company Pfizer placed a revealing advertisement. After a preamble about aiming to be number 1 in the world by 2000, the focus is put on a "recent announcement" of a major nationwide expansion of the field sales force. Competitors may have been already aware of this announcement from other sources, but what the advertisement begins to show is the extent of the expansion, and the fact that any previous announcement was serious and not just puffing. Area business managers were sought for 12 locations, hospital specialists for 15, and medical representatives for 20. This seems to me to be a valuable piece of information that any competitor might wish to put alongside the other information available on this company. As the locations of all the new positions are listed, the advertisement gives at least partial information on how the field force is deployed.

2. Prudential advertised for a number of positions for its new retail banking subsidiary. It would be very surprising if any competitor in the financial services industry were unaware of the plan to move into banking. The recruitment advertisements gave some idea of the speed at which things are moving.

Of course, information obtained from advertisements has to be compared with what has been found out from other sources. You will rarely find all the crown jewels on display in an advertisement, but you may gain knowledge which helps you to understand more about a competitor and make sense of some of the other things they appear to be doing. And you may find nothing of value at all, which would have been the case in most of the other advertisements in this particular Sunday newspaper.

Graduate Recruitment Activity

Many companies have a focused recruitment activity aimed at newly qualified graduates, working directly with the universities. The visible output of this, as far as competitor information is concerned, is in details/advertisements in specialist recruitment directories and in company recruitment brochures. The crown jewels are not left carelessly around in either of these activities either but, as with advertising for specific jobs, some information may be gained that contributes to the big picture. These sources may be of particular value when the competitor is a partnership which does not lodge annual reports with the registrar of companies, or for limited companies which have opted to restrict their annual returns to the legal minimum.

- *Company brochures.* Many of these give background about the company, and may include details of internal organization which is not always easily available from other sources, although, of course, it may be. A typical example of what may be in a recruitment brochure is provided by that published in 1997 by Cegelec Projects Ltd. The brochure explains that this is a subsidiary of the global company Alcatel Alsthom, information which a competitor should already know. After this, the brochure concentrates on the Cegelec Projects, giving a description of the activities and the number of employees. This is followed by a two-page spread describing the activities of the eight trading divisions of the company. The rest of the brochure deals with what the graduate can expect from the company. Brochures of this type frequently reflect the culture of the organization, although some companies may say only what the potential recruit is expected to want to hear and not what the true situation is. We have never seen a brochure that states that the company is run by an arrogant autocrat, although some such organizations recruit graduates!

- *Recruitment directory entries.* An example comes from *Prospects Directory, 1997*, published by CSU Publications. The proportion of entries that reveal competitor information of possible value compared to those that do not, is low. However, this is a feature of many sources of competitor information, and the source is worth checking. The entry for Smurfit UK is one example of hard information that may expand what can be discovered from other sources. The size of the Irish parent company is given in turnover and employment, and in the number of countries in which it operates. It also states that growth has been obtained by acquisition. Within the overall company, Smurfit UK is part of the UK and Ireland region. Details are

Table 7.1 Examples of information gleaned from recruitment advertisements

Company	Hard facts	Soft facts	Other
Altran, consultancy & technological support – advanced technologies	European growth rate 39% pa, turnover £165 million, 250 clients	Claims European market leadership	Expanding in the UK
APS Berk	Plant at Eastbourne produces 2 billion units in solid dose form	A leader in UK generic pharmaceuticals	Employs 200 (manufacture, packing, warehousing and support).
Crosby Valve and Engineering, division of FMC Corp. UK	Sales of about £17 million, 80% of which is exported		
Golden Wonder Crisps	Turnover £200 million, 2000 employees. Largest plant, Widnes, with 550 people, producing branded and own-label crisps, runs a three-shift operation	Claims brand leadership in the own-label market, relaunched key brands, restructured the sales force	Over £50 million has been invested in plant in the 1990s. Market share claimed to be growing in its branded products
Jarvis Facilities Ltd, a specialist railway and facilities management arm of Jarvis plc	A £120 million company	Intends to become the market leader in the UK in railway renewals, electrification and maintenance	Three new engineering posts were advertised in support of its strategy

Vertex	Turnover of £200 million and a workforce of 2500	Claims to be a leading technology outsourcing business	Seeks two people to help it implement a programme of cultural change
Rosti UK, technical division (injection moulding)	£78 million turnover, four UK manufacturing plants		Vacancies are at the Peter Tilling plant in West London which runs on a 4-day continental-shift basis.
UK-NSI, owned by Seiki of Japan, develops and manufactures automotive instrumentation			Have invested in systems for stores, production and material control. Are in the process of implementing computerized warehouse and MRP systems
UK subsidiary of *Mitras Industries Holdings Gmbh* (glass reinforced moulded products to the automotive industry)	£7 million business, which has a unionized workforce of 100		Seeking a managing director and a technical manager

given of the three operating divisions of the UK company:
Paper, Board and Reclamation operates 18 sites with sales of
£150 million; Print and Carton has sales of £45 million per year;
Corrugated has 23 plants with an annual turnover of £200
million. Summary descriptions of the activities of each division
are given.

Unfocused Communication

Some organizations also communicate in a less focused way, either
because they have a feeling of social duty or sometimes as a matter
of management egotism. Books have been written about many of
the major organizations, sometimes as a corporate venture and
sometimes giving cooperation to the author. As with some of the
royal biographies, this cooperation is regretted from time to time
when the resultant publication does not please the management.
Such books may contain information that helps one understand the
ethos of a competitor, but are often of limited value in competitor
analysis. But sometimes there are nuggets of information to be
found.

LEGAL OR ASSOCIATION OBLIGATIONS

All organizations face legal requirements to provide information,
and many have similar obligations through membership of a trade
or other association. Although much of what is disclosed remains
confidential, as indeed it should do, there may also be requirements
to disclose information to the public. Some examples of sources
arising through legal requirements are given below.

- *Annual returns of limited companies.* We have already mentioned that in many countries limited liability companies are
  required by law to make an annual return in a specified form,
  and this document is available for public consultation. In the
  UK the return is lodged with the Registrar of Companies, and
  the disclosure requirement is most stringent for public limited
  companies (PLCs). The annual report, which forms part of the
  return, is, as we have seen, a vehicle of communication to stakeholders, and often contains more information than the minimum
  legal requirement. It is an obvious first piece of information to

obtain when the competitor is a PLC. If the company is not a PLC, the annual report may give no more than the minimum legal requirement. For a company with many subsidiary companies it is often possible to obtain extra information, which does not appear in the annual report of the holding company, by turning up the records of each subsidiary in each country of operation. An illustration of this activity was given in the Argyll example discussed earlier. In the USA, a useful source for listed companies is the 10K form which has to be filed with the Securities and Exchange Commission. In the UK registered charities have to make similar returns to the Charity Commissioners. While this may be of little interest to most industries, there are a few where competitors are charities (see Chapter 8 for an example). There are no requirements in the UK for disclosure on partnerships and organizations which do not have limited liability.

- *Monopolies and mergers.* Many countries have anti-monopoly legislation which will put into the public domain information that would not otherwise be disclosed. Enquiries are initiated by the relevant government body from time to time. In addition, an intention of an organization to acquire another can be referred for investigation when this might lead to an uncompetitive situation. Member countries of the European Union are also subject to EC rules on monopolies.

- *Court cases and legal enquiries.* Information may come into the public domain through court cases, such as prosecutions for infringements of health and safety legislation, or claims for compensation for injury, or discrimination in employment. There may be conflicts over a contract, which results in one or other party taking action against the other. Industrial tribunal hearings may cover a variety of employment law issues. These are only a few examples of many situations that can arise. Enquiries of various sorts may be initiated by governments, and the results usually enter the public domain.

- *Patents.* If an organization wishes to protect its inventions it has to apply for patent protection in its home country and in others where it wants the protection to apply. A study of the patent documentation of a competitor may reveal useful information about products (although remember that not all patents may be used by the owner), and give some clues to new product strategies. The Canon example given earlier would have involved a detailed study of all the Xerox patents.

- *Freedom of information Acts.* In some countries, notably the USA but including others, there are freedom of information Acts, which mean that much information which would have remained confidential moves into the public domain and can be accessed.

ACTIVITIES OF OUTSIDERS

Not every piece of information available about a competitor comes from voluntary or legally driven causes. There are sources which come from organizations and sources who obtain and disclose information that might otherwise have remained hidden. Investigative journalists are one example, although more does not need to be said about this, as the sources have already been covered. Similarly disclosures by lobbyists or disgruntled employees which find their way into the media will also be found along with other articles on the competitor.

Not everything is reported in this way, and various web sites on the Internet may be the only source of such information. Some is published in books and reports assembled by a pressure group. For example, organizations appear from time to time, such as Counter Information Services, which in the late 1970s produced critical reports on industries and companies, and Social Audit Ltd, which used unofficial sources to compile a social audit on a number of organizations. Remember that any pressure group, or organization with a particular social or political bias, may not always be completely objective.

The international trades unions have also sometimes used their members to compile detailed reports on the activities of selected companies, and sometimes these can be purchased.

COMPETITOR ANALYSIS ON THE INTERNET

The Internet was born during the cold war, nearly fifty years ago, as a conduit for communication in the event of attack from the enemy. In the private domain, the Internet has become one of the most significant mechanisms for information search and retrieval in competitor analysis, and it has forever changed marketing intelligence. Today, a single analyst equipped with a computer and a modem can accomplish more than a large planning department could achieve just ten years ago. The enlargement of the Internet has meant the immediate availability of information stored on data-bases thousands of miles away. Whether the analyst is pursuing a one-time project or intended to establish on-going monitoring of a competitor or an industry sector, the Internet provides important efficiency gains.

The so-called search engines, software programs, such as Yahoo, designed to allow the user to specify a word or string of words of interest (for example, "enzymes and animal and feed"), will generate a list of possibly relevant databases where the word(s) appear in documents. The single biggest challenge for the analyst is the over-abundance of information, which means that several screenings must be performed. One-time searches usually end the investigation with a number of documents which can be downloaded on to the investigator's own computer.

On-going surveillance of a particular competitor or industry sector often combines the above type of enquiry on a regular basis with the use of automated procedures which consistently scan various sources for information about the target. This can, at the simplest level, be a personalized information gathering using free services such as Pointcast (http:www.pointcast.com), which allows the user to have updates every 20 minutes on issues related to a listed US company or news release on a specific industry. More sophisticated services are provided by firms such as Reuters or Bloomberg's, which can be tailored to a company's specific needs. For example, Reuters provide a product with access to thousands of databases and fast network services for around £400 per month. A large European firm working in the highly fragmented market for flavours and fragrances receives over 3000 pieces of information per day about competitors and customers, which the market research department distribute through its internal network to the relevant decision makers in the firm. The head of the firm's market research department commented: "We are increasingly seeing a parallel between our task and that of a CNN newsroom."

Other sources of information gained from the Internet include scanning the competitor's own Internet sites, including so-called

---

Essential rules of web searching

1. *Specify the purpose of the search.* The best way to start any search is to define the scope of the enquiry. This can be helped if hypotheses are generated to help define the research questions to be examined.
2. *Think small.* General databases are useful, but it is often from smaller databases that the golden nuggets can be obtained.
3. *Avoid fluff.* You will achieve the best results when you use specific terms, names and phrases: stay away from common words like "market price".
4. *Learn the language.* When you make searches on the Internet you need to make use of the particular words and marks needed for a proper search. Words like "and", "not" and "or" let you combine various combinations of concepts or names. In addition, the rules for different search engines may vary.
5. *Use multiple search engines.* You will find that different search engines lead you to different information sources. Multiple search engines will therefore expand the number of sources which you reach.
6. *Note where you have gone.* Intensive searches can often make you forget which sites you have visited. Add a bookmark, or print the first page as a reminder.

"chat forums" where customers discuss applications or problems related to the competitor's products or the firm's job listings on the Internet. It should be emphasized that we are advocating that analysts should stay within legal and ethical limits. Break-ins by hired computer hackers, whose only limit is the bounds of their creativity can get into even the most highly guarded computer system, and thus to the innermost secrets of organizations, are not part of our recommendations.

There are, however, several areas of legitimate Internet usage which have value for competitor analysis:

- Regular Internet searches can be made on the names, products/ services and markets relevant to the firm's competitors.
- Publicly listed competitors have to file documents containing high levels of detail. In the USA, the Securities and Exchange Commission's database "Edgar" holds for many US or internationally operating firms a goldmine of information about competitors. US and international firms must, among others, submit forms such as 10K and 20F, which often have surprisingly detailed information about many aspects of organization, strategy and performance.
- On-going subscriptions to services (some are free) which keep you abreast of news releases about the competitor and its activities. Pointcast has already been mentioned, but new services are emerging almost daily. Such services include at the low-end Microsoft Investor, or IBM's Infomarket where detailed information can be acquired for immediate use.
- More general studies can often be retrieved from various investment bankers, such as Lehman Brother's web site, or public sites, such as the US Department of Commerce, the Swedish Trade Council, or various trade associations.

As part of a recent investigation of a telecommunications firm in Thailand, a search through the web site of the Stock Exchange of Thailand yielded up-to-the-minute information. This search took place from a small winter cottage in Sweden: time and space seems to be undergoing a contraction.

Finally, you may want to outsource your Internet search to one of the many firms which offer this service, such as ARDAK Corporation of Virginia, which offers a host of services to track competitor and market information on the Internet.

REFERENCES

Gulliver J. (1990). How Scotland lost out to back street Hammersmith. *The Times*, 31 August.
Hussey, D.E. (1988). *Management Training and Corporate Strategy*, Pergamon, Oxford.
Porter, M.E. (1980). *Competitive Strategy*, The Free Press, New York.
Porter, M.E. (1985). *Competitive Advantage*, The Free Press, New York.

8
Competitor Analysis in Practice: A Case History

SCOPE OF CHAPTER

Case histories of industry and competitor analysis are difficult to obtain because of their confidential nature and because it is not always ethical to make public one's value judgements of competitors. In this chapter we have tried to demonstrate the results of the practical application of competitor analysis techniques, using mainly real information to illustrate the methods. However, we have used simplified examples in some of the analytical displays, and where necessary for ethical reasons have used fictitious exhibits rather than disclosing our opinions of real competitors. Such exhibits have been reduced to a minimum, and are only included where necessary to ensure understanding of the methods actually applied. The chapter describes experience while developing a strategy as managing director of Harbridge Consulting Group Ltd, and is written from the viewpoint of that firm.

One of the difficulties of competitor analysis is knowing what information to obtain. The problem often varies between the extremes of having too few data for meaningful analysis and having so much that it becomes difficult to make sense of it. Once a decision has been taken on the information needed, the problem shifts to one of how to obtain it, using legitimate and ethical methods. Finally, we reach the crunch issue of what to do with what we have collected.

The industry is one of two overlapping industries in which we operate. It is typical of many industries in that definition is difficult and there are hazy borders with related industries. It is also subject to certain international forces for change, although it is by no means a global industry. It is fragmented in all senses, and is unusual in having a mix of private and public sector competitors. Within the private sector there are organizations which gain tax advantages from being registered as charities, although this means that they have to operate under certain rules. Among the other private sector businesses are a mix of one-person businesses, partnerships, and limited companies. And like so many other industries, many competitors have operations in other industries, making it difficult to interpret their results. Indeed, most aspects of the situation have echoes in other industries.

It is a professional services business, although there is some competition from "products" such as videos. Many of its characteristics would be recognized by other professional services businesses, such as solicitors, accountants, and surveyors. All the methodologies illustrated have relevance in other industries, and we have used them in client situations that collectively span almost the whole spectrum of business activity.

THE OUTLINE APPROACH

Figure 8.1 shows the outline approach which we have been using continuously on this and other industries since the early 1980s, although some elements of our approach are even older. In our own case the analysis of information went through only the four linked stages shown on the outer ring of the diagram in the thick boxes. The thin outlined boxes are not appropriate in every situation. Our four stages helped to identify what information was required to enable meaningful analysis to take place.

All the information sources shown in the figure have been used to a greater or lesser extent in applying these methods to various situations. In our own industry databases are less helpful than other sources of information, which is a reflection of the structure of the industry, the few quoted companies in the industry, the lack of published statistics, and the relatively small size of most of the players.

Before going deeper into the methods used, we should like to

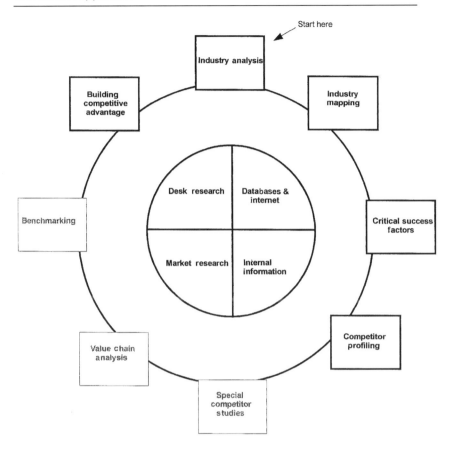

Figure 8.1 Approach to competitor analysis

explain the reasons for starting what became an increasingly detailed competitor analysis system. In early 1980 we had virtually no information about our market in the UK, or our competitors, which made strategic planning a hit-or-miss affair. The UK side of the firm had shown little or no growth for many years. It was also in a classic consultant's situation of basing a business on the skills of its professional staff, and changing emphasis with the departure or engagement of every key employee. What we wanted to do was to position the firm in areas where we could build and sustain competitive advantage, to properly understand the pressures on the industry, and to identify our real competitors from the 600 or so businesses which operate in the UK management training market. We wanted to improve our ability to plan, so that we could do at least as well as the best in growth years, and better than most in the lean years. We wanted to acquire a depth of information that would enable us to speak authoritatively about all aspects of management develop-ment.

We had one additional reason, which is probably the only one not similar to any firm in any other industry that contemplates competi-tor analysis. We needed a "laboratory" in which we could try out some of the concepts we were developing for use with clients. What better laboratory was there than our own business, where we could be freed from the restrictions of client confidentiality, and develop examples which could be shared with others?

Our advice to anyone starting competitor analysis is to think through the aims of the exercise first. Competitor analysis may be undertaken for many reasons, and that for purely tactical purposes may take a different form from that for strategic reasons. Our intentions were mainly strategic, although, as we will show later, we did gain some tactical benefit.

INDUSTRY MAPPING

A journey around the thick outlined boxes of Figure 8.1 begins with what we see as the essential first step in competitor analysis: obtain-ing a detailed understanding of the competitive arena. To do this we used the principles of Porter (1980). For our total strategic analysis we set industry analysis within the context of the outside environ-ment, as in Figure 3.2, which appeared in Chapter 3 (page 53), although for the purpose of this chapter I will not discuss environ-mental issues.

Our method explodes the supplier/competitor/buyer boxes of the "Five Forces" model to mirror the total channel from the first link in the supply chain to the final consumer. The first task is to develop this in block diagram form, using knowledge of managers, logic, and available market information. We tend to incorporate substitutes into this diagram, if they are already significant or appear likely to become so. In addition, we analyse influencers of a buying action (influencers were described in Chapter 3). In some industries the influencers may do more to shape the competitive forces than the competitors themselves.

In theory the development of such a block diagram should be easy. In practice we find that many of our clients face difficulty, tending to draw diagrams that reflect their preconceived ideas, or the elements of a channel which they themselves use. When we began our journey towards useful competitor analysis, we found similar problems. We knew what we did, and who some of our competitors were, but surprisingly little about buying decisions, substitute products, or the overall structure of the industry. How we began to collect this information will be discussed later, but the example which appears in Figure 8.2 is the result of several rounds of analysis and is not the original.

As we began to develop our understanding we were able to use the block diagram to record the key information about the industry. Figure 8.2 gives a simplified view of our industry map. The main difference is that the real map contains more competitor assessments, uses a personal system of abbreviations, and includes more analysis of the buying decision. Tables 8.1 and 8.2 show our assessment of the evolution of the market for the type of service we provide. These three diagrams, supported by the additional information which we have omitted for simplification or sensitivity reasons, provide the basis for a detailed strategic evaluation using Porter's (1980) principles. Before we discuss a few of these findings, we should like to mention two decisions that we had to make about the arena we were charting.

There were good reasons for studying the UK as the geographical area, and much of the market is still local to the UK. However, like most industries there is an international dimension. In more recent years we have explored this in more detail, in particular researching other countries in Europe, and, of course, we had access to information about the USA through our parent company. These findings have had a profound influence on our strategy, although including the detail of the analysis would expand this chapter to book length.

The second decision was around the problem of industry definition. Figure 8.3 (page 148) highlights some of the issues. The provision and delivery of management training and development services sounds like a neat industry. However, the suppliers to it, of which a few are illustrated in the figure, are frequently engaged also in related businesses. This has at least two implications: how statistical information is collated; and the gradual merging of some of the activities outside the circle with those inside it.

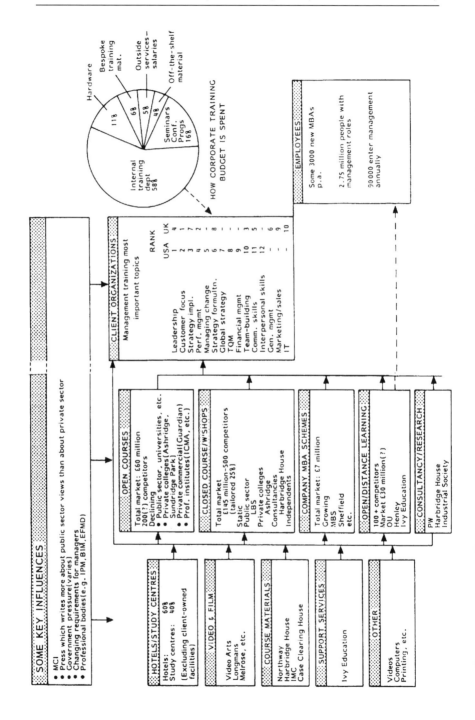

Figure 8.2 (*opposite*) Industry map – management training and development.
Notes: (1) Market estimates are aproximate. (2) Market is fragmented (many
suppliers, many buyers, multiple buying points in many companies, priority of
management development low but higher than in early 1980s). (3) No one
supplier dominates (e.g. largest has £12 million turnover). (4) Few suppliers or
clients take an international view. (5) High growth 1987–9: now static and
some sectors declining. (6) Company names given as examples

Table 8.1 Management training and development market: market sectors (£
million)

	1990	1991	1992	1993
Open public subscription	57	52	46	
Closed (seen as tailored)	25	30	26	
Closed other	133	137	130	
Distance learning and other	44	70	70	
Management consultancy	55	52	48	
Totals	314	341	320	288

© Harbridge Consulting Group Ltd: used with permission.

Table 8.2 Market for management training and management development
consultancy (%)

Year	Index 1987 = 100	Growth over prior year	Market 1 (£ million)	Market 2 (£ million)
1987	100		169	209
1988	130	30	220	272
1989	153	18	259	320
1990	186	21	314	389
1991	202	9	341	422
1992	189	(6)	320	395
1993	170	(10)	288	356

Notes to tables:
Market 1 is an estimate based on the survey undertaken by the Osbaldeston working party
for the CBI/BIM study *The Making of British Managers*, supplemented by Harbridge
Consulting Group research. This provided a basis for estimating 1985. The study collected
information from suppliers of company training.

Market 2 is an estimate based on the survey undertaken for the Department of
Employment by Deloittes. This provided a means of calculating the management training
market for 1987, but was based on employers' expenditure. One reason for the difference is
that these figures would include sponsored academic courses, which were excluded from the
supplier survey, and are excluded from our definitions of the market. The correct figure
probably lies between these extremes.

Growth has been estimated from an index calculated from the annual revenue of the
major competitors over the period 1987–92. The competitors for whom such figures could
be obtained covered some 16% of the total market. This is not an ideal way to calculate
growth, but was subjected to sanity tests based on the firm's own research, and is believed to
be as accurate as was needed for the analysis. No better figures are available: 1993 was
based on conversations with suppliers and buyers in February 1994.

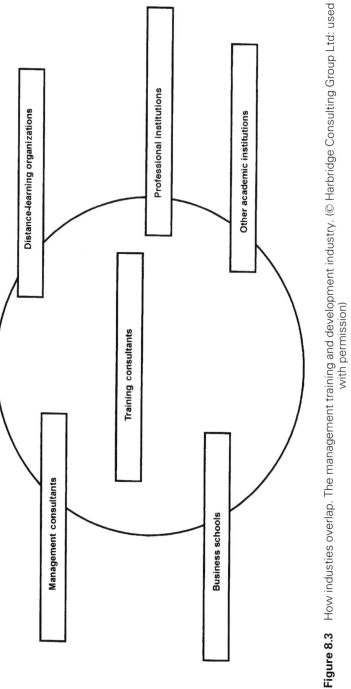

Figure 8.3   How industies overlap. The management training and development industry. (© Harbridge Consulting Group Ltd: used with permission)

For example, the Management Consultancies Association publishes statistics on the consultancy industry and included in their figures is a sector that covers management training. Users of these statistics might be tempted to think that this covers the output of the management training industry. Not so: it excludes the activities of the other providers as not only are they not members of the Association but most of them are not eligible to be members. Similarly, government frequently looks at the industry as if it were supplied only by the academic institutions (which in the UK are mainly public sector), and often speaks of total UK training when it actually means non-managerial training. The private sector holds a larger market share of the management training market than the public sector, even before we count the in-house training activities of the "buyers".

The related activities of providers change the dimensions of the circle. Three examples clarify this statement:

- As management consultants we frequently combine consultancy and training skills to produce a solution for clients which broadens the traditional use of training, and lies both inside and outside the circle. It is indeed one of the areas of differentiation which we seek.
- Academic qualifications moved into the industry when business schools began to offer tailored MBA degrees to individual companies and consortia of companies. An additional twist is that we run courses for two clients which are accredited by two different business schools towards their MBA degrees.
- Distance learning has been a growth sector of the industry. Not surprisingly, some of the traditional correspondence schools have developed products which compete in the industry, and organizations such as the Open University offer their products to corporate customers as well as to private individuals.

From what we have said it is apparent that the boundary of the industry, even as defined, is constantly changing. It is also apparent that different views could be taken quite logically on what the boundaries of the industry actually are. This suggests a need for careful study of some of the key competitors, including some with whom we do not compete directly, to identify the directions in which they could move and which would change the shape of the market in which we compete. Technological development alone will change the market, and thereby ensure that segment boundaries and competitive positions also change in the future.

INTERPRETING THE INDUSTRY ANALYSIS

It would be boring to most readers if we offered a full interpretation of the industry map. What we should like to give is enough of a description of some of the findings to carry the case study along, to help later when we look at how the information was obtained, and to make the value of such industry maps a little clearer. All the points we mention are strategically important to us, and have been used in formulating our own strategies.

- The industry is fragmented. There are numerous competitors, no one organization has more than a 10% market share (although shares are higher in specific segments), and there are numerous buyers.
- There are no universal patterns by which the buyers organize their management training activity. It is not possible to look at an organization from the outside and predict whether management training is centralized, decentralized, or a mix of both; or identify the level at which management development decisions are taken, how much training is performed, or what proportion is undertaken by the organization's own staff.
- Entry barriers to the industry in general are low, but few new entrants are able to grow into significant competitors, although an exception is when the new entrant is a spin-off from an existing competitor. It is probable that there will be a future shift to more outsourcing of training by large organizations, and that this may reduce entry barriers as management buy-outs of training activities establish new competitors.
- Not only do most buyers undertake a proportion of their management training with their own resources, but a number effectively become competitors by offering their services to other organizations.
- In addition to the sectors shown on the map there are numerous segments. Competitors can be grouped roughly into those who

offer a "commodity" product and those who are highly differentiated, and who support their activities with proprietary approaches. For example, we do not compete with most of the 600 organizations, and the number of competitors in our chosen segments usually varies between one and twenty. The story would be very different if we were at the commodity end of the spectrum, and I suspect that we would be a much smaller firm.

- There are "switching" costs, although they are not large enough to hold a dissatisfied buyer. The nature of these costs is that only differentiated competitors are likely to benefit from them. The product is perishable, in that much of what is offered is time based. Yesterday's unused consultancy time has no resale value.
- There are interesting issues around the way most buyers make their buying decisions. Management development/training departments are controlled through budgets which measure the costs of training rather than the benefits. Not surprisingly, actions follow what the system appears to demand, and most buyers would rather save £500 in the costs of an initiative (on which they are measured) than spend an extra £500 in order to gain an additional £10,000 of benefit from the training (on which they are not measured).
- Many relationships between competitor and client exist at the personal level, with the advantages and disadvantages this suggests. The key for an organization which wishes to grow is to add a parallel relationship between the consultancy and client organizations, while not destroying personal relationships. Because the range of subjects and methods within management training is so great, there is always an opportunity to innovate. The cost of concept development is a growth barrier to the independent one-person business.

All this can be summed up in the statement that 600 competitors are not frightening if you can take strategic actions which result in your competing with a manageable number. The opportunities to add value are very great, and the more this is done, the greater the distance the differentiated firm can gain over the bulk of the competitors.

The purists could fairly query whether all these conclusions could have been read from the example of the industry map presented here. Because it is abridged, some could not have been read off this map, although more can be seen from the originals which we use ourselves. However, all conclusions could have been reached through the exercise of completing the map, while the mapping process itself throws up areas where the "facts" do not make sense, shows clearly where there is a lack of knowledge, and often helps missing information to be arrived at by logical deduction.

PROFILING COMPETITORS

From what has been said so far, it is clear that we do not have to study 600 competitors in detail. Many can be grouped, since they behave in roughly the same way. Figure 8.4 shows some of our thinking on competitor groupings in this industry. This diagram could be expanded by adding the dimension of type of ownership, since public sector organizations, for example, have very different ways of operating to private sector firms. More ideas on competitor

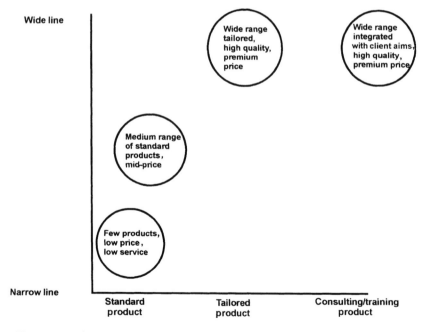

Figure 8.4   Strategic groupings: a hypothetical example from the training industry. The terms low and high quality are relative to each other and do not imply that one is "better" than another. (© Harbridge Consulting Group Ltd: used with permission)

groupings are given in McGee and Thomas (1992), McNamee (1990), and Porter (1980).

Currently we keep tabs on about 120 competitors. This includes the twenty or so that are the most significant to us, a number which have the capability of becoming more significant, and enough of the others so that we have a feel for the total situation. We do not keep information on any sole practitioners. When we started the exercise, we had very little idea of who our competitors were. This may sound surprising to someone used to a typical industry structure where there are clear market leaders, but less so we suspect to someone from a similar fragmented professional services market. The steps we took to find out will be discussed later. It took two to three years from our first researches to developing profiles in the form illustrated in Figure 8.5 (pages 154–5).

The profile illustrated is a fictitious example, but we have tried to make it realistic by not completing every information cell. Complete information on any competitor is very rare. What the profile shows is where the competitor gains its revenue, and a series of notepads for recording strategic information, focusing on what really matters when we formulate our own strategies. Most of the notepad items are self-explanatory, although two deserve further comment:

1. *Sources of competitive advantage.* This is the first step towards a value chain analysis, and moves on a little from where we are in our own situation towards ideas we are beginning to develop. Porter (1985) discusses value chains. In our own business we are still some way from having the information that makes their use possible.
2. *CSF ratings.* This is an abbreviation for critical success factors, and is a useful standard for competitive comparisons. CSFs are those factors which are essential to success in an industry. They are not necessarily the same across all segments. For example, the "commodity" competitors require different CSFs to those which are essential for us to compete at the differentiated end of the market. An example from the detergents industry may be clearer. The CSFs of a brand operator like Unilever, part of whose success comes from identifying new demand and creating a market image, are not the same as those needed for success in contract manufacture, where the task is to supply own-label products to retailers. The contract manufac-

Key factors

1 Own training college
2 Offers training (Management) in all European languages
3 Ties into world network
4 New CEOs in parent and SuperConsult. Watch for changes
5 Clients from bottom half of Times 1000 and similar European companies
6 Prices at high end of their sectors

Apparent strategy

1 Targeting tailored training market
2 Developing new products
  (recent advert for development personnel)
3 Will not expand UK college
4 Expected to open French college next year
5 Major expansion of Continental client base

Organization philosophy

Historically country companies have all reported to US parent

Recent announcements suggest a change to a more global approach

Do not use external associates – employees only

Personnel policies

Professional staff have degrees or professional qualifications Recent adverts seek postgraduate degrees

Salaries at academic scales plus profit sharing. Some difficulty recruiting

No equity participation – a quoted US company

Strengths	Weaknesses
1 Reputation in standardized training and open courses 2 Strong financial backing but parent co. wants dividend growth	1 Not well known among larger cos who buy tailored programmes 2 Employs the wrong people for tailored work 3 High staff turnover
Implications	Implications
Could solve all problems but corporate cash only available for quick-return projects	Strategy may be defeated by HR issues

Critical success factor ratings

Factor	Competitor ratings	Own ratings	Index
Quality image	6	9	67
Degree known	8	6	133
Quality of staff	6	9	67
Proprietary concepts	5	5	100
Financial resources	8	4	200

Notes: Assess each factor on a scale of 0-10
The index is COMPETITOR SCORE divided by OWN SCORE

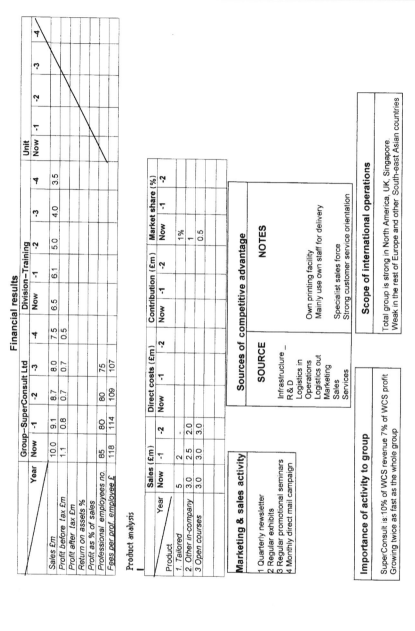

Figure 8.5 Competitor profile: SuperConsult Ltd (a subsidiary of World Consulting Services). (© Harbridge Consulting Group Ltd: used with permission)

turer has to be able to produce low-cost products which are similar to the brand leaders, and has to react very quickly to new opportunities. However, this type of business needs no understanding of consumer marketing, since it does not own any brands of its own.

What this profiling has done for us is to provide more discipline to our collection of information. It has given us the opportunity to deduce missing parts of the jigsaw puzzle, provided a means of storing information in an easily retrievable way, and given us a series of documents that, with the industry map, allow us to survey a vast array of information painlessly when making our own plans. It has become easier for us to identify firms in the industry where collaboration is possible, and to pinpoint appropriate competitors whom we would recommend to clients (strange as it might seem, this happens, and if we are making a recommendation we like to be sure that we are pointing the client to the right people).

While we have by no means reached perfection in our profiling, and still tend to update records in blitzes rather than as a continuous process, we have been able to develop a much better understanding of our industry map through this additional work. We have also been able to draw up some very useful generic comparisons of strengths and weaknesses between ourselves and different competitor groups (for example, business schools), while understanding the individual differences within each competitor group. In a fragmented market, it is more useful to find a strategy that builds advantages over the majority of competitors, rather than trying to beat each one singly. Products, image, and philosophies that result from this sort of exercise have to stand the test of the market.

DEFINING A COMPETITOR'S BUSINESS

Some of the original thinking about business definition comes from Abell (1980), who suggested plotting businesses on a three-dimensional chart showing customer functions, customer groups, and alternative technologies. Several variations on these themes are possible, and indeed one could delve much deeper into the literature on segmentation to develop the ideas further.

We used simpler matrix displays, which helped us to show the

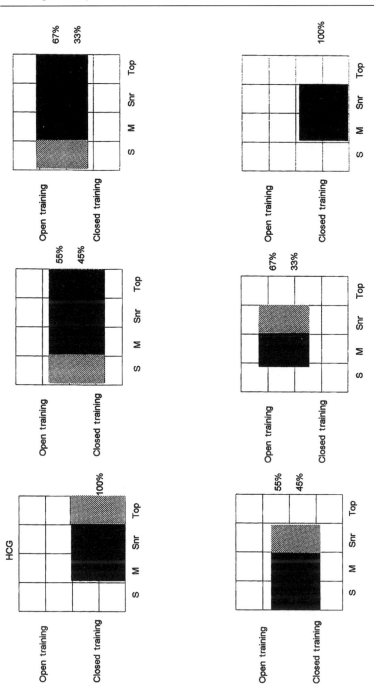

Figure 8.6 Management training activities: a sample of competitors. White = no activity, black = heavy activity, grey = some activity

difference between ourselves and other organizations in a diagrammatic way. Figure 8.6 shows some of the actual charts we made, although we have taken off the names. What these did for us was to make us realize the considerable difference in focus of businesses which we had seen as roughly comparable to ourselves. Some, although of high standing and quality, do not really compete with us at all, although we still monitor them because they may change!

In a less fragmented industry, we should have spent more time on this more detailed type of analysis. The number of competitors, and their low market shares, means that the value of going deeper than we have is questionable.

OBTAINING THE INFORMATION

None of this analysis would have been possible if we had been unable to obtain any information. In the beginning the task was somewhat daunting and it would have been easy to decide that nothing could be done as the information was too sparse. In the early years desk research yielded very little, because little was published at that time. This meant that we had to consider primary research if we were to obtain any information at all. Our first major competitor study was undertaken in 1985, and this set a foundation which helped us make sense of information from other sources. After that time there was an increase in the number of published research studies, which meant that our information was becoming more complete.

Our first piece of research into the market was completed in 1983. This was not at that time intended to help us follow the sort of competitor analysis described in this chapter, but was the first of a series of reports that we have carried out into management development and training to increase our knowledge of the "state of the art" and to gain marketing information. Most of these reports are published, so that they can be shared with other interested parties, and although they have contributed greatly to our understanding of buyer behaviour, and awareness of changing needs and responses, they are not primarily market research reports.

In 1985 we undertook two interrelated pieces of research. We wanted to find out whether the market for our type of training was expanding. Were we getting our fair share of the growth? What were the factors that the buyers considered when choosing a supplier?

We knew many of our competitors, but did we know them all? There was a great gap between the ones we could list and the columns of names shown in directories. Who were the competitors who might be considered most critical to our future? Who did the buyers think were our competitors, and who did our competitors think were their most serious rivals? We wanted to know if we were competitive in price, quality, speed of response to the client, and in our overall philosophies; and we wanted to answer the same questions for each major competitor. From this, our first intention was to prepare a market-related assessment of our strengths and weaknesses, relative to those of competitors.

A sample survey was conducted by telephone of 43 buyers of our type of training service, exploring aspects of all the research objectives. We interviewed on a personal visit nine major competitors, building up our list of real competitors from information supplied by buyers and competitors. We were able to check much of the information provided by competitors from the interviews with buyers. All this research was done honestly and openly by one of our consultants.

The information from this survey provided the base from which we could build, and develop on the lines already discussed, and led to immediate tactical and strategic decisions. Meanwhile, we continued to add more valuable data from our research for publication, and focused some of this on areas of the industry map which were hitherto blank. We published a report on distance learning, for example, in 1986, and another in late 1989 on consortium and company MBAs. Although not part of the published report, this survey enabled us to quantify the size of this sector of the market. As Table 8.3 shows, many of the earlier studies have been regularly updated and expanded, so that we are able to note trends and changes in the market.

In 1987 we used an MBA student to build up the files of competitor information which we had started to compile. This involved collecting brochures from competitors, annual reports (where available), and press cuttings. In addition, we established our first database, using an earlier format of competitor profile. We did the usual searches at Companies House, and probably bored the Charity Commissioners with our complaints about competitors who

Table 8.3 Primary research undertaken by us for the analysis

Date	Published	Unpublished
1983	Management training in UK companies	
1984	MBA and UK industry	
1985		Competitor study
1986	Tailored management education	
1986	Distance learning	
1987		Competitor information project
1988		Innovation training
1988		Management skills
1989	Consortium/company MBAs	
1989		Management training Europe part 1
1989		Management training Europe part 2
1989		Hotels/study centres
1990		Competitor update
1991	Management training in UK companies	
1992	Competency assessment	
1993	Company MBA	
1993	Management training in UK businesses	
1993		Competitor update

were registered as charities and who had not lodged their returns for several years.

Most of this activity is typical of competitor analysis generally. Three activities which yielded useful information were:

- Continued direct contact with competitors, including the exchange of the sort of information which would be in the annual report had we all been private limited companies. The competitor analysis system we have built up means that there is somewhere to put the results of all these formal and informal comments, as well as information that comes to us about a competitor from elsewhere in the industry.
- Obtaining feedback from clients when there is a pre-qualifying exercise or a competitive bid (whether we win or lose). This has been an invaluable source of information. On occasion, buyers have prepared an analysis of all the bidders which they have been willing to share.
- Helping journalists to write about the industry, and suggesting

who to approach for the collection of data for league tables. In this way we filled in a number of *gaps* in our own information, especially as a few firms who had refused to exchange information with us on grounds of confidentiality did not feel the same inhibitions when it was a question of gaining publicity.

Published information and market intelligence have become more important since 1987. A number of studies have been completed which when supplemented by our own studies have enabled us to quantify the sectors on our industry map. There is still no sound statistical base for the industry, but the combination of all our sources means that we believe that our estimates are as accurate as they need to be for the type of decisions that have to be made.

In 1989 we reworked our competitor database, and now store information in a form similar to the profiles in this chapter. We had hopes of creating a dynamic database that enabled us to update the industry map automatically every time a competitor profile was updated. This is not economic at present. The main conclusion that can be reached from our work is that a competitor analysis system will improve over time if continuous effort is applied, that even small pieces of information can be coordinated and used if there is a mechanism to handle them, and that lack of published information about an industry and competitors may make analysis harder, but need not prevent it.

We have begun to extend the scope of our study to other countries in Europe, and have spent more effort on identifying organizations with whom we can build alliances rather than undertaking a complete competitor analysis.

BUILDING COMPETITIVE ADVANTAGE

None of this analysis is worth while unless it leads to actions. The sort of strategic and tactical actions which we took may give an indication to readers of benefits they might obtain from competitor analysis:

- We identified much more clearly where we could gain differentiation, and where there were market segments where we could gain clear advantage.
- As a result, one of the things we did was to build our geographic

and language capability, so that through our own resources or alliances with other organizations we are able to run the same course for a multinational company in every West European language. This is especially important when the course is intended to support a Europe-wide strategy by the client. We started many new initiatives to build image and awareness, including our regular publication *Management Update* (10 issues per year, free to management development and human resources personnel). We redesigned all our stationery and literature to achieve a common image.

- A strategy was developed for operations in other countries in Europe.

- A number of different products and concepts were developed. The growth of in-company MBA schemes made us seek to become better informed about what was happening, and to find ways in which our work could gain academic accreditation in certain circumstances, without in any way losing our commercial image for that of a pseudo-business school.

- We identified private sector competitors who operated in our sector of the market, and began moves to establish a trade association among those with whom we shared common concerns.

At the tactical level we are now able to identify more accurately which competitors are significant for different types of assignment and their respective strengths and weaknesses. Even when we do not know who else has been asked to bid, this helps us plan our own proposals and presentation in a way that emphasizes our advantages.

We redesigned our basic approach to proposal writing, so that our strengths insofar as they were appropriate to the assignment were presented in such a way as to invite the client to probe to see whether other bidders also possessed them. Our research had shown significant areas where we knew that many of the competitors likely to be asked to bid did not possess similar strengths. Almost immediately after completing our 1985 competitor study we had opportunities to apply these tactical concepts, and won two major assignments on competitive bids in quick succession. We developed strong long-term relationships with both clients.

Our strategy has helped us to grow faster than the market since the mid-1980s, and our concepts of industry and competitor analysis have helped us to develop these strategies. Add this to the benefits which we have observed our clients gain from similar approaches, and the value of competitor analysis becomes clear. However, it is not without cost, and anyone thinking of undertaking it needs to decide whether they are looking for a one-off injection of competitor data into their strategy formulation or wish to set up a continuing system. Either needs a dedication of effort, and the continuing system needs some attention to organization and resources.

In either case, and whether the aim of competitor analysis is tactical or strategic, the only justification for the costs and effort is the action that results from the new knowledge. We hope that this case history has given some indication of the benefits, as well as a methodology, and that it shows that an initial lack of competitor information can sometimes be overcome.

REFERENCES

Abell, D. (1980). *Defining the Business*, Prentice Hall, Englewood Cliffs, N.J.

McGee, J. & Thomas, H. (1992). Strategic groups and intra-industry competition. In Hussey, D.E. (ed.), *International Review of Strategic Management*, Vol. 3, Wiley, Chichester.

McNamee, P. (1990). The group competitive intensity map: a means of displaying competitive position. In Hussey, D.E. (ed.), *International Review of Strategic Management*, Vol. 1, Wiley, Chichester.

Porter, M. (1980). *Competitive Strategy*, The Free Press, New York.

Porter, M. (1985). *Competitive Advantage*, The Free Press, New York.

9
Assessment of National Competitiveness: A European Example

This chapter presents and demonstrates a practical methodology for assessing *national competitiveness*, the impact of national economic, political, and social structures on business vitality. Databases containing a wide array of national data, such as the World Competitiveness Report employed here, are especially suited to the multi-dimensional nature of competitive analysis. Denmark's competitiveness in attracting foreign industrial capital is appraised alongside the full methodological exposition. Denmark's dependence on foreign input and product markets is among the important competitive features identified.

Revived by a wave of neo-mercantilist theory and popularized during a period of economic stagnancy in the industrialized nations, national competitiveness is again a hot buzz-phrase in business and policy circles. Images of economic efficacy and operating advantage conjured by the phrase have strong appeal at a time when most Western economies face disappointing export realities. Despite its popularity, national competitiveness is difficult to define and ever tougher to quantify. Nations do not compete in marketplaces, organizations do. At most, organizations bear the imprimatur of their home nation while striving for marketplace success. National competitiveness thus reflects the ability of organizations to prosper in various operating environments and is best defined as the impact of national economic, political, and social structures on business vital-

This paper was prepared by Professor Per V. Jenster and Dr Geoffrey M. Rubin.

Box 9.1	Framework for depicting national competitiveness		
Current and future prospects of national competitiveness	Multiple data sources	Model and measurement construct	Descriptive positioning of national competitiveness

ity. To this end, it is worthwhile understanding the analytical efforts which can help us comprehend current and future prospects of national competitiveness, as depicted in Box 9.1.

The aim of this chapter is to construct a concise, objective, and meaningful measure of national competitiveness. By definition, national competitiveness is the sum of many environmental features. This conceptualization is sustained in the proposed measure by utilizing a wide variety of national data. The pragmatic structure of the test promotes objectivity and replicability of results. In addition, this measure gauges national competitiveness without complex analytical or computing tools. The measure of national competitiveness demonstrated in this chapter provides policy makers, business executives, and investors with an inexpensive and reliable gauge of national business environments.

BACKGROUND

National competitiveness has only recently evolved into a broadly defined concept of business environments. Initial formulations of national competitiveness cited *comparative advantage*, or national specialization of production in relatively low-cost techniques. Seminal work by Smith (1776) and Ricardo (1817) shaped academic thought on this topic for nearly 200 years. Profitable activities of a nation, this theory holds, are determined by endowments of labour and natural resources. This resource-based view of competitiveness adequately explained trade patterns of the unfinished goods and simple manufactures of the nineteenth and early twentieth centuries. The unprecedented post-Second World War trade boom showed that more complex forces determined national industrial prominence. In the past decade, more broadly conceived notions of international business success have coalesced into a new treatment of national competitiveness.

Scott (1982) and Rugman (1985) were among the first to criticize one- or two-dimensional measures of competitiveness that require "synthesis of the concepts and analytical methods of economics, political science, and sociology." Fagerberg (1988) considers technology, price, and delivery capacity the hallmarks of the competitive nation. Austin (1989) identifies a host of national characteristics relevant to business success, including economic, political, institutional, and social attributes. New definitions of national competitiveness generally regard a nation's ability to successfully support business organizations. Krugman (1991) feels that the word "competitiveness", when applied to nations, is "so misleading as to be essentially meaningless." Scott and Cherington (1989) and Porter (1990) discuss various definitions of national competitiveness. A nation is "competitive" in the industries best supported by its operating environment. As the national political, economic, and social fabric ultimately determines the appeal of business environments, realistic measures of national competitiveness must consider a rich set of environmental features.

Theoretical advances have outpaced methodological treatment because the diverse nature of national competitiveness resists rigorous mathematical modelling. Many past measures of national competitiveness are limited by reliance on only a handful of factors. The OECD (1987) measure of competitiveness, for example, uses price and export share data to assess the standing of its members. Vihriala and Viren (1987) consider exchange rate movements as indicators of competitiveness, while Lundberg (1988) uses net export data. These narrow interpretations do not accurately represent the current theoretical conception of competitiveness. (Porter, 1990, reviews and critiques past measures of competitiveness.) A useful measure of national competitiveness should incorporate a wide range of national factors and indictors of performance.

Porter's (1990) book represents an important step in the development of national competitiveness measures. With the aid of a large team of researchers, Porter paints vivid details of ten national business environments. As he notes in the Preface, "one outcome of both the nature of [the multi-factor] theory and the approach I have taken is a very long book. It is something I could not avoid if I were to test the theory against sufficient evidence and develop its implications for business practitioners and policy makers." This comprehensive approach adeptly characterizes the complexities of national competitiveness, but less costly methodologies might have more relevance in certain applications. (Scott, 1982, also advocates this holistic – and expensive – methodology.) A concise, affordable, and easily executed statistical test seems more appropriate for initial inquiries into national competitiveness. The remainder of this chapter develops and demonstrate a practical methodology for assessing national competitiveness.

MEASURING NATIONAL COMPETITIVENESS

A multi-step, systematic analytical structure facilitates measurement of national competitiveness. In fact, the systematic methodology sharpens conceptual focus by forcing the analyst to explicitly interpret the theory of competitiveness for each application. This methodology proceeds as follows:

- *Defining the audience and scope of the report.*   Implications of national competitiveness differ among decision makers. Analysis must be tailored to the needs of the audience. Similarly, composition of the nation sample is contingent upon the audience's agenda.
- *Choosing the data source.*   Data sources must reflect the need for information on a range of economic, political, and social factors. Data must also be available for each of the nations in the chosen sample.
- *Identifying components of competitiveness.*   Which aspects of the national environment (government fiscal policy, national infrastructure, workforce skills, etc.) are of particular interest? Again, the perspective of the report is crucial.
- *Matching the data source with the components of competitiveness.*   Database variables which help explain performance in the various categories are grouped.
- *Computing relative national standings in each component of competitiveness.*   Raw data is converted into a single measure of performance in each competitive category.
- *Interpreting results.* Assimilation of individual analytical results brings the entire competitive picture into focus.

Important aspects of this methodology are detailed in the following sections. In addition, an authentic application of national competitiveness assessment is presented.

Defining the Audience and Scope of the Report

Properly identifying the analytical perspective is crucial because operational "competitiveness" is unique to each organization. An essential component of the national environment for one enterprise might be meaningless to another. For example, corporate leaders examining potential plant sites have different agendas than national policy makers seeking to appraise the relative strengths of their economies. Analysis must focus on the competitive aspects of nations of interest to the audience. In fact, audience perspective is the most important guide to selecting relevant data points and forming a conceptual framework of competitiveness.

The audience for our example is the Danish Ministry of Finance. In the spring of 1991, the ministry sought to assess the overall vigour of Denmark's investment environment. Of specific interest to the ministry was Denmark's ability to attract foreign industrial capital. Analysis thus considers a general array of characteristics that might influence plant location of a typical manufacturer. The wide scope of our ensuing analysis reflects the ministry's broadly defined field of interest. This interpretation might have little meaning to organizations with different agendas.

An established analytical perspective helps to resolve the associated issue of defining the relevant population of competing nations. National competitiveness is not an absolute concept; a nation's appeal depends upon the characteristic of its realistic competitors. The audience agenda determines the scope of national coverage. For example, a pharmaceutical manufacturer has many more plant sites to consider than an aluminium producer. In selecting the population of competitor nations, the trade-off between small-sample precision and large-sample coverage must be considered. In general, the population sample should encompass all nations of realistic import to the audience.

In our example, Denmark's ability to attract foreign industrial capital was the chief concern of the Ministry of Finance. The competitor population is thus the set of likely substitutes for investment

Table 9.1   Nation sample for
competitiveness analysis

Belgium	Netherlands
Denmark	Norway
Finland	Sweden
France	UK
Germany	

in Denmark. Table 9.1 lists the nine nations included in the competitor population. Although this list might be too large for some industries and too small for others, geographic and economic realities might confine the investment activity of many enterprises to these nations. By focusing attention on this group, our analysis implicitly investigates national competitiveness within this set of nine nations. For the Ministry of Finance, Denmark's standing in this group is a sufficient indicator of competitiveness.

Choosing the Data Source

Data sets employed for national competitiveness assessment should share a few characteristics. First, they must contain a wide array of data on the economic, political, and social institutions of nations. Second, individual data points should be of fundamental interest to the audience, even if the data initially seem unrelated. Third, the data must be reliable. Fourth, the data should be available for all nations in the chosen sample of competitor nations. As a practical matter, the data need only be assembled in spreadsheet format, as more powerful statistical software is unnecessary.

Data for our case example are from the 1991 *World Competitiveness Report* (WCR), a publication of the World Economic Forum and IMD, the International Institute for Management Development. The WCR contains two types of data on more than 300 economic, political, and social variables for 34 nations. About 200 variables are from publicly available sources such as the OECD, the World Bank, the IMF, and GATT. The remaining WCR data are collected from a survey of more than 10,000 business executives worldwide. The survey data are qualitative and characterize the "current wisdom" of business leaders. Importantly, this database complements objective measures of national condition with a survey of managerial perceptions, thus providing a window onto the business activities of tomorrow. The WCR contains robust indicators of the economic, political, and social status of nations and additionally satisfies the other three criteria of analysis – relevance, reliability, and coverage.

Identifying Components of Competitiveness

In this step of analysis, the breadth of national competitiveness is delineated into a set of distinct categories. This reduces the task of national appraisal to a series of factor analyses. Audience perspective determines the composition of competitive categories. Categories should be precise, fairly uniform, and logically related to the particular agenda of the audience. For example, competitive categories for high-tech industries might include education, human skills, and technical support, while heavy industry might focus on the labour resources and capital markets of the competitor nations. The simplest method for selecting competitive categories is determining the components of success relevant to the audience. Nations which best provide crucial resources are the ones most competitive for that organization.

Table 9.2 lists relevant competitive categories for the Danish study. In keeping with the intent of discerning a general ability to attract European investment, these 16 categories comprise a portfolio of activities of interest to most industries (although different industries will emphasize different categories). One group of categories describes the natural resources of the competing nations. The paramount importance of energy sources in some industries merits an individual category. Human Resources, which include characteristics of the general, technical, and managerial workforces, has differing degrees of influence on all conceivable industries. The Public Priorities group of competitive categories measures the government's influence on business vitality. The Social Support category, for example, gauges the social, political, and economic harmony of the nation, the extent of worker motivation and security, and the protection of the environment. The Industrial Environment group of categories describes the operating environment new firms might expect in the nine nations. Current Standing categories relate

Table 9.2   Danish study: competitive categories

Natural Resources:
  Energy
  Materials
	Public Priorities:
	  Free Market Commitment
	  Social Support
	  Infrastructure

Human Resources:
  General Workforce
  Technical Workforce
  Management
	Industrial Environment:
	  International Focus
	  Domestic Demand
	  Support Industries
	  Firm Structure

Technology	

Finance	Current Standing:
	  Productivity
	  Export Performance

the operating success of existing businesses. Taken together, these 16 categories form a working guide to national competitiveness for the Danish Ministry of Finance.

Note that competitive categories change with the perspective of analysis. For some decision makers, only a handful of categories might be relevant; for others, the list might be expanded. The exercise of defining competitive categories is significant in that it forces the analyst to identify factors of success for the organization. In fact, it seems impossible to predict organizational success in various national operating environments without having a firm idea of what that organization needs to succeed.

Matching the Data Source with Components of Competitiveness

At this juncture, the analyst possesses, on the one hand, a data set containing economic, social, and political variables, and, on the other, a list of the various categories which comprise competitiveness. The next step is coupling database variables with competitive categories. There is no formal guide to this matching process; intuition reveals which database variables substantially describe each competitive category. For each category, the analyst simply lists the database variables which might explain category performance. These lists can be of any length, and individual variables may be used for more than one category. A meaningful link between the variables and competitive categories is the only requirement. Variable selection is undeniably subjective, but, as discussed later, methods exist for promoting robust conclusions.

Variable lists for the Danish study range in length from 28 explanatory variables for the Natural Resources–Materials category to only four for Human Resources–Management. Variable lists for the Technology and Industrial Environment–International Focus categories are reproduced in the Appendix. Note the logical link of each variable to its respective category. Variables measuring energy efficiency, telecommunications infrastructure, information technology utilization, R&D funding trends, and patent success reflect national competitiveness in the Technology category. National performance in each of these criteria would certainly interest a technology-minded firm examining new plant locales. For the Industrial International Focus category – a category measuring industrial integration with foreign firms and markets – trade legislation, exchange rate performance, managerial export mentality, and public promotion of exports explain competitiveness. The proposed variable lists are certainly not unique. The analyst need only ensure that each variable represents a characteristic ultimately important to the decision maker.

Within each category, some variables might have more significance to the decision maker than others. The criteria can be weighted in a fashion that reflects their importance. In the Technology competitive category, for example, "Total R&D Expenditure" and "Total R&D Personnel" were given twice the analytical weight of variables such as "Energy Consumption per GNP" and "Adequacy of Telecommunications Infrastructure", which in turn are twice as important as "Number of Facsimile Machines in Use" and "Size of Domestic Electronic Data Processing Market". Criteria weighted in this manner preserve the integrity of results by allowing "marginal" criteria to enter analysis with less weight. The three-interval weighting scheme was chosen for analytical clarity, but in practice any relevant weighting scheme can be employed. If, in any category, one or two criteria are deemed to be of paramount importance, their weights should reflect this position.

One should not let the taxonomy of competing nations, competitive categories, explanatory variables, and variable weights confuse the core issues of this methodology. Within the multi-factor view of competitiveness, organizations must assimilate dozens or even hundreds of individual facts about each nation. When analysis covers a number of nations – as it must, if a robust inventory of competitiveness is desired – the sheer magnitude of information begs for a statistical methodology. The paradigm presented here provides a simple method for extracting useful information from an abundance of important facts. Categorical division is done for ease of exposition. If the chosen variables reflect the national characteristics of consequence to the audience, this methodology provides a valuable – and concise – commentary on the nature of national environments.

Computing Relative National Standings in Each Component of Competitiveness

Within each competitiveness category, variable values and weights are consolidated into a single measure of competitiveness. Table 9.3 demonstrates the calculation methodology for a hypothetical competitive category. Competitive standings for three nations – labelled A, B, and C – are computed in this example. Variables 5.12, 5.17, and 5.18, all from the *World Competitiveness Report*, explain category performance; 5.12 and 5.17 are hard statistical criteria taken from an OECD database or similar source; 5.18 is a question from the WCR survey. The Raw Data section transcribes the source data and calculates a sample average and standard deviation across nations. Variable weights previously chosen by the analyst are also listed. In this example, 5.17 is given twice the weight of 5.12 (4 to −2), which in turn is given twice the weight of 5.18 (−2 to 1). (Negative variable weights denote those variables in which lower raw values imply stronger competitive performance. In our example, a low score for variable 5.12 – the amount of energy consumed for each dollar of GNP – suggests superior energy efficiency.)

Raw data is transformed by substracting the sample mean and dividing the resulting quantity by the sample standard deviation. This transformation gives the number of standard deviations a nation's score is above or below the sample mean, providing a consistent and unitless method of comparison across nations. Country A, for example, consumes 5641 kilojoules of commercial energy per dollar of GDP (variable 5.12). Substracting the three-country mean of 4817 and dividing by the sample standard deviation of 624 yields a score of 1.32. Similarly, country A's relative scores in vari-

Table 9.3 Competitive category calculations

No.	Variable Weight	Definition	Country A	Raw data Country B	Country C	Avg.	Std dev.
5.12	– 2	Kilojoules commercial energy per $US of GDP, 1988	5641	4130	4680	4817	624
5.17	4	Per capita trade balance in non-energy raw materials, $US, 1988	2.8	13.8	– 4.2	4.13	7.41
5.18	1	S: Adequacy of domestic natural resources; 0 = low, 100 = high	81.87	74.96	83.12	79.9	83.59

Variable number	Transformed data Country A	Country B	Country C
5.12	1.32	– 1.10	– 0.22
5.17	– 0.18	1.30	– 1.12
5.18	0.53	– 1.40	0.87
Weighted average:	– 0.94	2.00	– 1.06

Note: S denotes a survey question from the *World Competitiveness Report*.

Table 9.4 Competitive category scores

Competitive category	Belg.	Denm.	Finl.	Fran.	Germ.	Neth.	Norw.	Swed.	UK
NR: Energy	− 1.10	0.04	− 0.99	0.99	− 0.36	− 1.90	4.08	0.38	− 0.24
NR: Material	− 0.23	− 0.91	0.06	− 0.29	− 0.29	− 0.42	1.04	1.47	− 0.43
HR: General Workforce	− 0.53	0.19	0.31	0.19	0.48	− 0.40	0.01	− 0.48	0.22
HR: Technical Workforce	− 0.26	0.76	0.80	− 0.94	0.94	− 0.09	0.86	0.20	− 2.26
HR: Management	− 0.34	0.68	− 0.18	− 0.84	3.50	0.62	− 0.37	0.33	− 3.39
Technology	− 1.12	− 0.42	0.82	− 0.24	1.76	− 0.17	− 0.67	1.15	− 1.11
Finance	0.22	0.71	− 0.56	− 1.11	0.76	0.68	− 1.55	− 0.13	0.97
PP: Free Markets	0.22	0.15	− 0.57	− 0.76	1.44	0.30	− 1.07	− 0.86	1.17
PP: Social Support	− 1.83	0.91	0.94	− 1.29	0.47	− 0.07	1.44	0.96	− 1.52
PP: Infrastructure	1.22	1.70	0.31	− 0.79	1.04	0.75	− 1.06	− 0.72	− 2.46
IE: International Focus	0.10	1.53	− 0.42	− 1.86	2.17	1.22	− 1.25	0.01	− 1.49
IE: Domestic Demand	− 0.85	− 0.96	2.45	− 0.36	0.84	− 3.18	0.30	1.24	0.52
IE: Support Industries	− 0.17	− 0.27	− 0.06	0.15	1.09	− 0.25	0.03	− 0.41	− 0.10
IE: Firm Structure	− 0.96	1.87	− 0.36	− 1.50	1.29	1.59	− 2.31	0.31	0.08
CS: Productivity	− 0.73	− 0.83	2.22	− 0.83	0.41	0.21	1.26	0.04	− 1.76
CS: Exports	1.77	0.42	− 1.09	0.28	1.21	0.56	− 1.94	− 0.45	− 0.76

ables 5.17 and 5.18 are −0.18 and 0.53, respectively. Variable scores are written by multiplying the transformed data with its given weight. A nation's average weighted score is a measure of aggregate performance in the category. Country B has the highest average weighted score, calculated as:

$$-1.10 \times -2 = 2.20$$
$$1.30 \times 4 = 5.20$$
$$-1.40 \times 1 = -1.40$$
Average: 2.00

This analytical method yields a quantitative measure of national performance in each category. Quantitative methodologies of this nature are essential when dealing with large data sets and nation samples. Both ordinal (relative rankings among nations) and cardinal (absolute scores for each nation) comparisons among nations are easily made. By incorporating many data points, the undue influence of single variables on the category scores is limited and subjective bias prevented. Overall, this analytical method presents an opportunity for gleaning robust, concise measures of competitiveness from large data sets.

Table 9.4 lists category scores for the nine sample nations of the Danish study. Again, these scores reflect both the direction and magnitude of relative performance in each of the competitive categories. A score near zero implies average performance against the group. Large positive scores denote superior performance in the competitive category, negative scores inferior performance. With these scores, the overall picture of competitiveness begins to unfold from the mass of unorganized but important data.

INTERPRETING RESULTS

Category scores appraise performance in each of the unified, tightly defined competitive groups. Further assessment of "overall competitiveness" requires interpretative analysis rather than formal numerical manipulation. The following examination of Denmark's competitiveness heuristically demonstrates some of the devices needed to form the final link between numerical analysis and operational conclusions.

Figure 9.1 graphically displays Denmark's scores in each of the

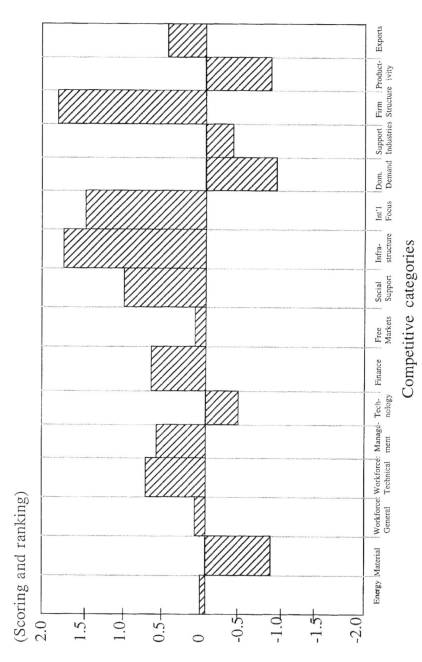

Figure 9.1   Danish competitive performance – competitive category scores

competitive categories. Additionally, the rank position of Denmark's score within the group of nine is listed. Inspection of the figure shows a rough trichotomy in Denmark's categorical competitiveness. Denmark has a solid competitive advantage in three of the 16 categories: Firm Structure, Infrastructure, and International Focus. In four categories – Material Resources, Technology, Domestic Demand, and Productivity – Denmark performs poorly. In the remaining nine categories, its competitive performance is mixed. This rough categorical partition provides important insight into Denmark's competitive strengths and weaknesses.

The Firm Structure competitively gauges the social responsiveness and operational freedom of firms in each nation. High scores reflect a flexible – and mutually beneficial – relationship between firms and society. Denmark scores particularly well because its firms have wide discretion to set prices (3.39), distribute profits (3.44), allocate corporate assets (3.45), and reorganize when in financial trouble (3.47). (Numbers in parentheses refer to WCR variable numbers.) Equally important, Danish firms enjoy the highest degree of public trust in the sample (6.07). In Finland, Norway, and Sweden, the balance between public and private interests is skewed towards the former, while poor corporate images persist in Belgium, France, and the UK. In Denmark, the mutually beneficial pact between the public and business community, guaranteeing both operational freedom and social awareness, affords a significant competitive edge.

Denmark also leads all sample nations in the Infrastructure competitive category. Survey respondents gave Denmark's rail (5.29), air (5.30), and sea (5.31) access especially high marks, with the road system (5.28) only slightly behind. The impending series of bridges linking the Continent and Scandinavian peninsula via Denmark should further enhance Denmark's competitive advantage in this category. In fact, the four highest scores in this category are posted by Denmark, Belgium, Germany, and the Netherlands, which together form an infrastructure "super-region", efficiently linking the Northern Continent. Denmark offers a prosperous environment to firms which can capitalize on the excellent physical access and geographic location.

Denmark also achieved high marks in International Focus, a competitive category which relates a nation's integration into the international economy. Respondents were most satisfied with

Danish policies concerning the exchange rate (2.10), international partnerships (2.38), and export credits (2.42). Only concerning trade legislation (2.07) were Danish respondents bearish. The huge difference in scores between Denmark, Germany, and the Netherlands at the top of the scale and France, the UK, and Norway at the bottom implies significant competitive advantages for nations in the former group. A strong Danish score in the Export Performance category testifies to the international emphasis of the Danish business environment. The volatile political and financial environment across Europe promises to make this competitive category of continued importance to firms. In particular, Denmark can enhance its position in this category by further promoting its strong links to both the EU and the Nordic Council. Implications of Denmark's Maastricht No vote are discussed later.

Denmark's greatest competitive weakness is in the Material Resources competitive category. Denmark is resource-poor on nearly all accounts, especially compared to its Scandinavian neighbours. On the bright side, Denmark's competitive position in Energy Resources is not bad, primarily due to strong conservation programmes (5.10, 5.11, and 5.12) and low dependency on oil (5.15 and 5.16). Still, Denmark is an unattractive choice for resource-dependent enterprises.

Domestic Demand, an indicator of economic size and activity, represents another competitive weakness for Denmark. First, Denmark's economy (1.01) is simply smaller than that of its neighbours. On a per capita basis, Denmark does perform well on one account – GDP (1.04) – but meagre per capita retail sales (1.34) suggest a Domestic Demand weakness even after adjusting for size. Most troubling are demand growth statistics. Denmark's GDP (1.07), per capita GDP (1.08), and per capita retail sales (1.35) are growing more slowly than in most other sample nations. Denmark's poor score in the Current Productivity category, which incorporates many of the same criteria, is further evidence of a small and slowly growing economy. Although weak domestic demand is certainly a drawback, European market unification, coupled with Denmark's superb infrastructure and location, might minimize the negative effects on Danish firms of a small local market.

Denmark's low score in the Technology competitive category is particularly intriguing. This category incorporates a wide range of data on R&D expenditure, patent development, and telecommunications capability. Poor performance in the most fundamental measures of R&D commitment – total R&D expenditure (7.01), total R&D personnel (7.14), business expenditure on R&D (7.05), and perceived research effectiveness (7.35) – overwhelms the belated growth in this area (7.15, 7.23). Of interest, the low Technology score comes despite a strong score in the Technical Human Resources category. Danish managers feel the quality of their technically skilled workforce (8.29, 8.30) is the best in the sample. Denmark also leads all sample nations in spending on secondary education (8.11, 8.12). So why is the significant Danish investment in technical skills failing to translate into a strong technology sector? Part of the reason lies in Denmark's low Support Industries category score. The Danish economy is more service-oriented than some of its manufacturing-oriented counterparts. With less manufacturing, R&D spending suffers accordingly. A more subtle, yet related, basis for the low Technology score is an acute "brain drain" (8.40), reflecting better opportunities abroad for many of the well educated. Overall, Denmark has failed to fully reap the benefits of strong educational investment. Despite the necessary human resources, Denmark does not offer a particularly strong technological environment.

Constructing a "competitive check list" is one means of assimilating information from the categorical analyses and couching the results in a form of value to the audience. Table 9.5 shows the competitive check list for the Danish study. On opposing sides, Denmark's competitive strengths and weaknesses are listed. Each of these characteristics were identified from the categorical analyses described above.

Currently, the Danish industrial environment is not well suited to supporting traditional manufacturing concerns. The lack of natural resources and small population size and growth certainly discourage a Danish location for many primary producers, although an advanced infrastructure and the possibility of a mobile labour market help to minimize these adverse characteristics. A stunted industrial support system and weak domestic demand also seem unattractive to large manufacturers. A natural response to this portfolio of characteristics might be to shore up the high-technology sector. To date, however, the Danish experience in technology fields is, at best, mixed. Although some of the essential human and capital commitments are either in place or improving, Denmark cannot lay

Table 9.5 Competitive check list: Denmark

Strengths	Weaknesses
Social Accord	Natural Resources
Managerial Freedom	Population Size and Growth
Geographical Location	R&D Expenditure and Performance
Political Affiliations	Managerial Initiative
Infrastructure	Domestic Demand
International Focus	Industrial Support
Capital Markets	Productivity
Conservation/Recycling	
Education	
Technical Workforce	

claim to having an environment entirely beneficial to technologically oriented manufacturers.

Ironically, the very competitive characteristic which helps Denmark to surmount these obstacles – international orientation – was recently jeopardized in the Danish Maastricht referendum. Denmark has an excellent infrastructure, a prime geographical location, and, as of 1990–91 (the period of WCR data collection), an internationally integrated business environment. Intact, these attributes ease many of the faults outlined above. Other nations can supply the raw materials, labour, and product markets which Denmark lacks. The solid infrastructure and central locale helps to limit the cost of international transactions. Political unity with the EU would have reduced costs even further. Once the small Danish supply and demand markets are supplemented by foreign markets and a strong domestic financial sector, Denmark possesses many of the qualities a pan-European producer might desire. Overall, two facts seem clear. First, Denmark is poorly equipped to support industrial investment in isolation. Second, Denmark has – or, rather, had – the international perspective needed to overcome many domestic shortcomings. In light of this, the Maastricht No vote is puzzling.

Another notable feature of the strategic check list is the disparity between managerial freedom and managerial initiative. Danish corporations are afforded wide latitude in running and organizing existing operations. Venture opportunities seem more limited in respect to both managerial and capital resources. This general bias towards low-risk investment makes Denmark better suited to supporting mature industries than venture firms. Further, strong accord among the business, public, and social sectors makes Denmark an attractive home to stable, image-conscious organizations. One "venture" field to which the Danish operating climate seems amenable is conservation/recycling technology. Denmark has the deepest conservation and recycling experience in the sample, and society supports an environmentally aware agenda.

The competitive check list is useful for assembling the relevant results from competitive analyses. Although this methodology lacks the depth to pinpoint exactly which industries will thrive in a particular business environment, it does help the analyst to establish a reasonable characterization of national competitive strengths and weaknesses.

SUMMARY AND CONCLUSION

Corporate officers, public leaders, and business investors are alike in their need for a reliable gauge of national competitiveness. Appraisals of national operating environments and identification of compatible activities can be a valuable first step in a variety of endeavours such as determining plant location, targeting growth industries, and construction portfolios. The methodology presented in this chapter helps to assess the complex economic, political, and social phenomena which, together, comprise the relevant operating environment for most enterprises. With the advent of multi-dimensional databases such as the WCR, this methodology can be cheaply and easily utilized in a number of similar applications.

Pedagogical examination of Denmark's competitiveness in attracting industrial capital yielded a number of important insights. The Danish operating environment is too small, on its own, to support a variety of potential industries. An internationally integrated economy overcomes many of these problems, but the Danish Maastricht No vote jeopardizes this crucial aspect of Denmark's operating environment. In fact, cross-border trade in both inputs and output is essential to the Danish competitive position. Analysis also highlights some of the problems Denmark has encountered in establishing its technology sector and promoting venture capitalism. Overall, the Danish study demonstrates how appraisals of national competitiveness can be synthesized from a large set of important yet unorganized data.

APPENDIX: EXAMPLES OF COMPETITIVE CATEGORY VARIABLE LISTS

Variable No.	Weight	Variable name and description
Category: Technology		
5.12	−2	Energy Consumption Kilojoules per constant 1980 $US of GDP, 1988
5.25	1	Facsimile Machines Number of facsimile machines per 100,000 inhabitants exported by Japan in 1990
5.27	1	Electronic Data Processing Equipment Production and purchases of EDP equipment in $US million, 1989
5.32	2	Telecommunications Infrastructure S: Extent to which telecommunications meet the requirements of companies competing internationally; 0 = inadequate, 100 = adequate
6.37	2	Information Technology S: Extent to which computer-based information technology is effectively used; 0 = insufficiently, 100 = sufficiently
6.38	1	Electronic Data Interchange S: Effective use of EDI, or connecting a company's system to those of other enterprises; 0 = low, 100 = high
6.40	2	Labour-saving Technology S: Extent to which labour force willingly accepts introduction of labour-saving technology; 0 = not at all, 100 = very willingly
7.01	4	Total Expenditure on R&D As a percentage of GDP, 1989
7.02	2	Growth in Total Expenditure on R&D Annual compound growth, 1983–8
7.05	2	Business Expenditure on R&D As a percentage of total R&D expenditure, 1989
7.07	1	Real Growth in Business R&D Expenditure Annual real compound percentage change, 1984–9

7.08	1	Future R&D Spending S: Expected increase in R&D spending over the next five years; 0 = will just cover inflation, 100 = will grow much faster
7.14	4	Total R&D Personnel Nationwide Per 10,000 of the labour force, 1988
7.15	2	Growth of R&D Personnel Nationwide Annual compound percentage rate, 1983–8
7.22	2	Patents Average annual number of patents granted to residents per 100,000 inhabitants, 1986–8
7.23	2	Change in Patents Granted Annual compound percentage change in patents granted to residents, 1982–8
7.27	2	Securing Patents Abroad Number of patents secured abroad by residents, 1982–8
7.28	2	Change in Securing Patents Abroad Annual compound percentage change in the number of patents secured abroad by residents, 1985–9
7.30	2	Protection of Intellectual Property S: Effectiveness of intellectual property legislation; 0 = low, 100 = high
7.31	2	Search for Technology S: Effectiveness of companies in seeking new technologies and commercially exploiting them; 0 = ineffective, 100 = effective
7.34	1	Linking R&D Efforts S: Extent to which synergies are developed between state and private R&D efforts; 0 = not actively, 100 = to a great extent
7.35	2	Basic Research S: Effectiveness of basic research in meeting the long-term needs of the economy; 0 = low, 100 = high
7.36	1	University Research Programmes S: Access business has to university R&D programmes; 0 = low, 100 = high

8.30   2   Quantity of Skilled Labour
             S: 0 = not available, 100 = readily available

Category: Industrial Environment – International Focus

2.07   2   Trade Legislation
             S: Extent to which trade legislation and trade
             practices are conducive to long-term
             competitiveness; 0 = not at all, 100 = very
             conducive

2.08   2   Exchange Rate Index
             Average trade-weighted real value of each
             currency (1971 = 100), 1990

2.09   −2   Exchange Rate Stability
             Parity change from national currency to SDR,
             1989 over 1982; 100 = no change

2.10   4   Exchange Rate Policy
             S: The country's exchange rate policy;
             0 = discourages, 100 = encourages international
             competitiveness

2.21   2   Export Flexibility
             S: Extent to which producers are prepared to
             modify products to suit foreign markets; 0 = not
             at all, 100 = to a great extent

2.38   2   Partnership With Foreign Firms
             S: Extent to which government allows
             enterprises to freely negotiate ventures; 0 = not
             allowed, 100 = freely

2.42   1   Exports Credits and Insurance
             S: Availability of reasonably priced export
             credits and insurance; 0 = limited availability,
             100 = easily obtainable

Note: S denotes a survey question from the *World Competitiveness Report*.

REFERENCES

Austin, J.E. (1989). Country analysis framework, HBS Case Services 9-389-080.
Fagerberg, J. (1988). International competitiveness, *Economic Journal*, **98**, No. 391, 355–74.
Krugman, P. (1991). Myths and realities of US competitiveness, *Science*, **254**, 8 November, 811–15.

Lundberg, L. (1988). Technology, factor proportions and competitiveness, *Scandinavian Journal of Economics*, **90**, No. 2, 173–88.

OECD (1987). *Economic Studies*, No. 9 (Autumn), 146–82.

Porter, M.E. (1990). *The Competitive Advantage of Nations*, The Free Press, New York.

Ricardo, D. (1817). *Principles of Political Economy and Taxation*, third edition, 1821. Reprinted 1971, Penguin Books, Harmondsworth.

Rugman, A. (1985). National strategies for international competitiveness, *Multinational Business*, No. 3.

Scott, B.R. (1982). Country analysis, HBS Case Services 382–105.

Scott, B.R. & Cherington, P.W. (1989). US Competitiveness in the world economy in the 1990s, HBS Case Services 9-389-058.

Smith, A. (1776). *An Inquiry into the Nature and Causes of the Wealth of Nations*, edited by E. Cannan, University of Chicago Press, Chicago. 1976.

Vihriala, V. & Viren, M. (1987). Finland's competitiveness at the long-term average level, *Kansallis Osake Pankki Economic Review*, No. 2, 7–10.

World Competitiveness Report (1991). International Institute of Management Development, Lausanne, Switzerland.

10
Organizing for Competitor Analysis

As we have shown in earlier chapters, most organizations will give some thought to competitors, although this may be a piecemeal, functional approach. In almost every organization there will be some people who obtain information about one or more aspects of the activities of the main competitors. To move from a piecemeal approach to something that is more systematic, thorough, and continuous requires a dedication of corporate effort. Therefore it should begin with a top-level decision that this is the way the organization wishes to go, and a recognition that such an effort will require some expenditure, and a commitment of management time. Without high-level commitment, competitor analysis will become little more than files of unassessed snippets of information, the dust on which is disturbed periodically when something happens that calls for urgent analysis.

There are several elements to consider once the question "Do we want to do this?" has been given a yes answer. Figure 8.1 summarized the elements of an approach to competitor analysis which have been described in this book. The centre of the diagram is a reminder of the sources of information, and the thick boxes on the outer ring show the essential elements. The thinner, grey boxes illustrate approaches which may be important for some organizations, or for any organization at some time, but will be less universally used at any one time.

Using this figure as a guide, it is possible to distinguish a number of tasks which need to be undertaken to ensure that competitor analysis is useful and effective, and that these require a number of different skills and expertise. So starting from the centre of the figure, and working outwards, we can identify the following:

- Collection, assessment and storage of regular external sources of information: databases, press clippings, abstract services, company annual reports, directories, competitors' literature and the like
- Marketing research, covering primary sources, and numerous secondary sources additional to those mentioned above
- Collation and coordination of internal sources of information, which will vary from information from formal company records, such as sales analysis, to the harnessing of informal sources which may be tapped by many levels in the organization
- The task of regular analysis of the information
- Decisions and strategies which arise from the analysis
- Overall coordination of the competitor analysis activity, including determination, with the specialists, of sources that should be tapped, and the organizing of special external studies, such as additional marketing research to that coming from normal requirements.

One difficulty in describing how to organize for competitor analysis is that it is easier to identify what needs doing than how to ensure it gets done. This is because organizations are of different shapes and sizes, may span several industries, and may be local, global, or something in between. In this first part of our discussion we are assuming that the organization is a local business, of sufficient size to already have the various specialist functions we mention, and with a focused business, even though this may span more than one industry. Later, we will look at the complexities of the organization with many SBUs and operating in many countries. However, it will be obvious that all the initial discussion will be relevant to the more complex companies, and the issue is how to deal with their additional complexities.

However, none of this means that smaller organizations cannot undertake competitor analysis. It just indicates that the specialist support functions will not exist to the same extent, and that the tasks will have to be divided differently. In the case history in Chapter 8, the management of the competitor analysis activity was undertaken by the managing director as part of the strategic planning activity, and various people in the organization were involved in the special studies mentioned. At the time the case history was written, the firm also employed a research assistant, who collected much of the intelligence, helped with some of the studies, and also fulfilled a general library and desk research role in support of client work. Because good employees are ambitious, and might be expected to seek promotion which the organization could not provide at this level, an arrangement was made with a university that the organization would recruit annually one business student for the industrial placement year of the degree. Although this meant regular replacement of the assistant, it did mean that a high-calibre person was always available, and as it was the most popular placement in the university, there was no difficulty in ensuring that the person recruited was appropriate for the task. At no time did the organization in the case history employ more than 20 full-time people in its UK office, which demonstrates that lack of size is not a barrier, provided the organization believes that seeking competitive advantage is important.

THE COORDINATOR

Because of its importance, we will start with the last task on the list, and discuss the others in order. Typically this task requires a person of considerable seniority. Frequently the activity is part of the strategic management directorate, with the ultimate responsibility falling on the director in charge. This fits well with the overall strategic planning responsibilities, and ensures a measure of integration with strategic thinking. Sometimes there is a designated competitor analysis unit within this directorate, although this does not necessarily imply a large staff, or even full-time commitment of one person.

It would be a mistake to try to centralize every one of the tasks on the list, but the role is more than one of coordinating the work of other departments and functions of the organization. There has to be a proactive element, with adequate authority to be able to insist that certain things are done, such as the press clippings service being extended to take in new sources, or regular estimates of competitor product costs being made by a cross-functional team from research and development, manufacturing, purchasing, and accounts. If value chain analysis is to be undertaken, the coordinator has to have the power to be able to pull together a multi-functional team to undertake the work. The role should also become a centre where all sources are pulled together, and cross-validation is undertaken of one source against another.

One task when establishing a competitor analysis unit should be an audit of the information that currently comes into the organization and the analysis currently undertaken. This should be compared to the needs of the organization, as discussed in earlier chapters. One suggested questionnaire for a strategic information unit will be found in Stanat (1990). This book also contains helpful advice on managing a strategic information unit.

REGULAR EXTERNAL INFORMATION

Many organizations have an information department, which frequently has grown out of the old corporate library. Where this exists, it is not sensible to establish a duplicate organization to access similar sources. Such departments are frequently very competent at accessing and distributing information, but comparatively few deliver intelligence rather than data. It is, of course, possible to give this function more responsibility for evaluating information, and producing summarized reports, but this depends on the capabilities and ambitions of the people staffing the unit. It may be better to use the unit as a first point of contact for regular information, and for periodic scans of databases, and to leave the evaluation to the analytical stage.

However, as implied earlier, it is vital to ensure that the sources taken are adequate, and reflect what is needed for competitor analysis. There are now numerous clipping, briefing and abstract services, but the scope of these should be carefully studied and the gaps filled. A quick look back to Chapter 7 on information sources will remind you of the wide variety of journals and newspapers and other sources which should be covered, and it is unlikely that the normal services cover them all. Unless special arrangements are made, the usual clippings service would be most unlikely to cover recruitment advertisements. A balance must be determined between reliance on external services, periodic searches of library sources, and in-house scanning of journals and other material.

MARKETING RESEARCH

Much marketing research will take place at the brand and product levels, as surveys, subscriptions to marketing audit services, the purchase of published reports, and similar matter. Other research may be carried out at the instigation of the public affairs department, usually to provide data on the image of the organization compared with other organizations. The majority of organizations have specialist staff in the area of marketing research.

For competitor analysis purposes, there is a need to have access to all such research. Costs may be reduced if there is an opportunity to add questions which are needed for competitor intelligence purposes to a survey which is planned to meet a marketing need.

It would be sensible to use the skills of any specialist market research staff if there is a need to undertake particular surveys of customers or suppliers to provide information for competitor analysis purposes. Although it may be undesirable to use any in-house unit to actually undertake research into the strengths and weaknesses of the various players in the market, because of the danger of creating a biased response, the unit's experience of commissioning research can reduce costs and improve the survey.

INTERNAL INFORMATION

The mobilization of internal information presents one of the biggest organizational problems, because it needs to tap into every area of the organization and to access both formal and informal systems. Information which comes out of the internal routine management information system, such as sales analysis, usually presents few problems, as it is produced to a routine and can easily be accessed by the appropriate managers. As with the external information, it is prudent to audit what is available, because the priorities of competitor analysis may indicate a requirement to change the internal data that is collected. It would be wrong to assume that only that which is currently produced is available.

Accessing informal knowledge is much harder. For example, sales personnel often obtain useful information from customers about the activities of competitors. They may be the first to know that a competitor has launched a new product, that special deals are being offered, or that some aspect of customer service has been dramatically improved by a competitor. This information may come from clients and customers, and even from conversations with the sales people from other organizations. What typically happens when competitor analysis starts is an appeal to the sales people to pass on the snippets of information they pick up, and in the first few weeks a flood of useful information may result. Very soon this becomes a trickle, and then runs dry. To ensure a continued flow means establishing the importance of this source, and making it easy for information to be passed upwards.

This requires that managers down the line make competitor information a part of the agenda of the meetings they have with their subordinates, both asking for information and passing on relevant information from other sources. What is passed on should be tailored to the interests of the recipients, which in most cases will be tactical and related to their jobs. Although it is possible to use these meetings to pass information upwards, their main purposes is to help create a culture of competitive awareness. E-mail and voicemail systems are a more immediate way of reaching the competitor analysis unit. Mention was made in a previous chapter of the competitor newsletter that some organizations use to disseminate information. This has the advantage of passing back something to those who provide information, although the emphasis is again more likely to be tactical than strategic.

The above example was chosen because the sales force is one of the units of an organization that has regular contact with customers. However, it is not the only part of the company that can pick up competitor information. Many functions also have such opportunities. Manufacturing personnel may meet competitors at conferences, local business association meetings or may hear gossip from suppliers. Service engineers may note customer comments on the reliability and quality of competitors' products. Research and development may hear papers delivered by employees of competitors, or may note changes in the disciplines of a competitor's R&D personnel. The method for mobilizing these opportunities for competitor information are the same: through the management structure, easy ways of passing on information, and feedback through the line, and/or by direct communication. All this has the advantage that all parts of the organization use the information as well as contribute to its collection.

REGULAR ANALYSIS OF THE INFORMATION

Here we are concerned with strategic analysis, the regular updating of the industry and competitor analysis through the methods emphasized in this book and in Figure 8.1, and any additional special studies which may be required. Analysis covers the task of industry mapping, competitor profiling, and the initial interpretation of this. So it is a question of turning information into various forms of useable intelligence, evaluating that information, initiating action to validate suspect data, or to plug essential gaps of information, interpreting this and ensuring that the results are in a form which can be easily communicated to those involved in the strategic decision process. It should not be a passive activity, merely dealing with what comes through the door, but a very active process which seeks to provide information and interpretation which is of strategic value to the organization. It is possible for this role to be fulfilled by the coordinator, and certainly he or she should have responsibility for it, but the scale of the task may require the establishment of a competitor analysis unit, of one or more people, within the coordinator's department.

The end products of the analysis stage should be something more than clever interpretation. If the results are to be used, there must be corporate ownership of them. Although part of this comes through the strategic decision process, the way in which the competitor analysis unit works can help to build this ownership and improve the validity of the interpretation of the figures. For example, regular discussions with key functional managers with emphasis on those parts of the analysis that relate to their areas, or to knowledge they have provided, may both avoid misinterpretation and make the whole process more participative.

DECISIONS AND STRATEGIES

None of this effort will have much value to the organization unless the information is used to build competitive advantage, to seek out new opportunities, or to lead to ways of changing the structure of the industry. In most organizations strategy is not something that happens once a year when a strategic plan is prepared, however helpful such a plan may be. Strategic management is a continuing process, which should react to and anticipate the various changes taking place and the opportunities which emerge, and the more turbulent the business environment, the more need there is for rapid strategic response methods.

Organizations vary in the processes by which strategic decisions are taken. Our assumption here is that the chief executive exercises strategic leadership, but that his top executives, as a minimum, are heavily involved in the process. This is not a universal pattern, nor is it the only route to a successful strategy, but it is common enough to make it a reasonable assumption. Many of the top executives will be responsible for a function, and will bring to the table their views of the issues and opportunities faced by the organization. Corporate strategy should be more dynamic than merely adding up what everyone wants to do, although the functional insight may be important. It is not our task to debate the entire process of strategic management, so we have limited ourselves to four suggestions for ensuring that industry analysis and competitor information are properly considered in the decision process:

- *Dissemination of hard information.* The obvious task is to ensure that the industry maps and profiles and the results of other analyses reach the decision makers at times when strategy is being considered, and that they are updated when significant changes are observed. This gives a sound foundation, and the shape of such a reporting service might well be an annual "book" containing up-to-date versions of the various analyses, regular information on major matters of importance as they occur, and updates of individual pages of the reports when this is worthwhile (as, for example, when there is another year of data to add to a competitor profile). Additional consolidated updates might be provided for any special needs that might emerge during the year. This assumes a paper-based system, and it is, of course, possible to go one better and always to be up to date if an online competitor information system is set up and significant specific information is passed on by e-mail.

  Unfortunately this does no more than provide the opportunity for managers to use the information. It may not ensure that they do use it, nor will it be enough to create a culture which makes everyone in the organization relate to the importance of competitor analysis. So we need something like the next actions as well.

- *Strategy workshops.* At least once a year it is worth holding a strategy workshop as part of the strategy process. We have used this term instead of "meeting" because it implies a less formal, very participative approach. Competitors would be a key part of this workshop, which among other things should encourage discussion of the implications of the competitive environment, ways of changing it, the strategies that competitors appear to be pursuing, and the likely reactions of competitors to the strategic options that are on the agenda. Of course, there is much more to strategy than just competitor analysis, and the workshop should cover all elements. The process should be designed to improve the quality of strategic thinking by getting top managers to internalize and use competitor and other relevant data, and to facilitate creative thinking.
- *Regular management meetings.* Time should be allowed on every regular executive management meeting to review the competitive arena and the actions of competitors. The reasons for this are to ensure that key information is shared, and to help create a situation where strategies are regularly reviewed in the context of competitor behaviour. Such a discussion should be seen as important as the discussion of results against budget which is normally a feature of such meetings.
- *Periodic meetings to discuss competitors.* At periodic intervals it is worth holding meetings to discuss competitors. One way this has been done in some companies has been to allocate a competitor to each member of the team, with a view to becoming expert on that competitor. Each manager would role-play a competitor at that meeting, with the aim of building a better understanding of the competitor and its strategic behaviour.

These methods can be modified and carried down to levels of management below the top group.

MORE COMPLEX ORGANIZATIONS

We mentioned earlier that our description was based on a relatively simple organization in terms of industry and geographical spread.

Now is the time to discuss some of the complications that must be considered in organizations with more geographical or industry complexities. We will first change our basic assumption somewhat, and assume that our organization is not operating in only one country and operates in many countries but still in related industries. What was described above would be appropriate for each country operation, particularly if the business were run as a multi-local operation, but the terms chief executive and top management group would mean "of the subsidiary".

This leads us to a consideration of the role of the centre. This is a very important role, because even if country strategy is largely delegated to the country level, the group chief executive has an overall responsibility, should be concerned about the overall shaping of the industry, and has to balance risk and investments, and make decisions about entering areas of the world where the organization does not currently operate. In addition, many of the competitors might be expected to be multinational, and can only be fully understood when all their operations are studied. In these circumstances there is a role for a central competitor analysis unit, to ensure that competitor analysis does take place across the whole organization, to coordinate information on multinational competitors, and to ensure that they are considered in the overall corporate strategy.

Much of the collection of information, and the analysis of local competitors would take place at local level, so the corporate role would be somewhat different from our first example. Coordination, and making sure competitor analysis took place, would require multinational meetings to share methods and information. If our organization took a global view, with more of the strategic task centralized, there would be some further modification of the roles of the central and subsidiary competitor analysis units. Under any organizational concept, it would be criminal not to use the local operations as a source of information about competitor activity.

The role of the centre changes somewhat when the organization is a conglomerate, because although each business unit has industry competitors, customers and suppliers, the corporate office does not. Who were the competitors of Hanson, for example, before the decision was taken to focus down to a core of activities? At this time the company activities included tobacco, bricks, and batteries, as well as many other unrelated products. The corporate office of such an organization could have little direct interest in any competitors, except as an acquisition strategy, but might have a very deep interest in ensuring that each business studied their own competitors and were taken into consideration in strategic decisions.

This different role of the head office applies when activities are in totally unrelated activities, which can never become related. No stretch of the imagination could envisage the merging of markets of cigarettes and dry cell batteries. Not so with the various components of the financial service industries, where industries are merging, and a company in insurance may be of considerable strategic interest to an organization in banking. So it is not just the number of industries which dictates whether there are corporate-level competitors, but the degree to which they are related or have the potential to become related in the future.

BUILDING COMPETENCE IN COMPETITOR ANALYSIS

No organization will become effective in competitor analysis just because top management says it is a good thing to do. Something more than an initiating memo is needed, and this chapter has already dealt with some of the things that will help create the right climate for competitor analysis within an organization. (Hussey, 1998, provides a basic guide to the management of change, much of which would be relevant if competitor analysis is being introduced to an organization.)

One assumption that is often made is that managers and their staff will immediately be competent at competitor analysis once the organization has decided to undertake it. This is by no means a safe assumption, and a manager who fails to understand the reasons for and concepts of the approach may not only make poor decisions but may also demonstrate an attitude which makes it harder to gain the support of his or her subordinates.

Our suggestion is that appropriate training be arranged. An example of the scale of effort made by one organization is given in Hussey (1985):

> One of the world's largest multinational companies, always seen as one of the best managed, identified that more attention had to be placed on competitor analysis both at top level and in the development of marketing plans by each operating unit. This was after careful self-analysis had

revealed that much of the company's growth was without profit, because of weaknesses in the market place where competitors were proving more aggressive than the assumptions on which past plans had been based. Many companies would have issued an edict that in future strategies were to be formulated after more competitor analysis, and many would have failed to cause any changes whatsoever. In this company the chief executive personally directed a world-wide educational initiative to bring the new thinking into life. He led top managers in a week long introduction to the theme of "what about competition?", and insisted that several hundred senior managers should spend two weeks on a strategic planning workshop. He also introduced an 8-hour audio-visual presentation to thousands more managers as a basis for discussion of and commitment to real strategic thinking. Many implementation workshops have been held throughout the world with practical training in competitor analysis, leading to the implementation of more realistic strategies.

The precise training solutions should be tailored to suit the organization, but a workshop mode, which includes the analysis of the participants' own industries and actual competitors, can be very effective. All the case studies in this book have been found to be very effective in providing training in industry analysis.

Competitor analysis can take strategic thinking a long way forward, but making it happen in an organization requires thought, and effort. Our own experiences have convinced us of the value of thinking in this way. Although the concepts described here are comparatively recent, and much of the methodology for applying the concepts has been developed from experience, the basic idea that, in any conflict situation, the protagonist who has most intelligence about the competitors and is able to use this in strategic thinking is not new. It should give much comfort that the idea has stood the test of time. All we in management have to do is to make it work.

REFERENCES

Hussey, D.E. (1985). Implementing corporate strategy: using management education and training, *Long Range Planning*, **18**, 5.
Hussey, D.E. (1998). *How to be Better at Managing Change*, Kogan Page, London.
Stanat, R. (1990). *The Intelligent Corporation*, American Management Association, New York.

11

The European Wine Industry

In 1991 the wine industry still continued to be a big business in Europe in terms of consumption, production and employment. Of an estimated 1991 worldwide wine production of 340 million hectolitres, the European Economic Community (EEC) accounted for 65% of production and annually consumed more than 180 million hectolitres. With more than 5 million people employed in wine-related jobs (2 million full-time, or 15% of the total European agricultural workforce), the EEC was predicted to retain its pre-eminence within the international wine industry for years to come. This primacy did not mean, however, that the industry was not subject to change, even a dramatic one.

MARKET OVERVIEW

Traditionally, wine was the beverage of choice, both as an accompaniment to fine cuisine and as an everyday part of European family life. In 1989, the European wine industry represented a US$ 30 billion retail value, corresponding to 14.5 billion litres and 41.5% of world wine consumption (Tables 11.1, 11.2, and Figure 11.1). After many years of decline, the European market showed emerging signs

This chapter was prepared by Professor Per V. Jenster and Lars Jenster, Diploma d' Oenologie, as a basis for class discussion rather than to illustrate either effective or ineffective handling of a situation. The case is based on an MBA Consulting case by Pierre Brault, Jim Dickson, Roy Frey, and Eugene Kopp.

Table 11.1 Consumption in Western Europe (million litres)

	1985	1986	1987	1988	1989
France	4287	4235	4139	4150	4160
Italy	4610	4510	4400	4138	4138
Spain	1803	1843	1786	1788	1850
Portugal	891	840	658	536	578
Greece	330	310	303	303	249
Austria	276	285	295	25	268
Switzerland	320	315	320	318	316
Germany	1550	1424	1584	1578	1588
Luxembourg	20	21	22	22	23
UK	618	643	684	642	683
Ireland	36	33	35	36	38
Belgium	201	204	208	209	209
Netherlands	202	202	214	203	200
Denmark	105	101	106	111	122
Sweden	98	101	102	103	107
Norway	21	22	25	27	27
Finland	22	24	25	27	30
Total	15,390	15,113	14,906	14,450	14,536

Source: OIV (Office International du Vin), Euromonitor.

Table 11.2 Market value in national currencies

	1985	1986	1987	1988	−1989	1989 US $ million
France	38,900	40,249	41,262	43,203	44,759	7016
Italy[a]	5643	5812	6468	6653	7040	5131
Spain	48,800	50,100	50,500	50,350	50,250	424
Portugal	13,110	15,700	14,020	16,299	19,171	122
Greece	23,804	27,125	30,000	35,000	39,500	243
Austria	6760	6850	7150	7400	7530	569
Switzerland	1163	1195	1300	1400	1400	856
Germany	9330	8800	9760	9810	10030	5335
UK	2861	2981	3289	3514	3805	6238
Ireland	167	178	199	205	212	301
Belgium[b]	33,653	35,740	36,400	37,200	38,000	964
Netherlands	1305	1355	1420	1495	1560	736
Denmark	3502	3819	4043	4400	4575	626
Sweden	4771	5145	5700	6020	6300	977
Norway	1982	2294	2769	2950	3242	470
Finland	856	960	1023	1086	1200	280

[a] Billion
[b] Includes Luxembourg
Source: Euromonitor

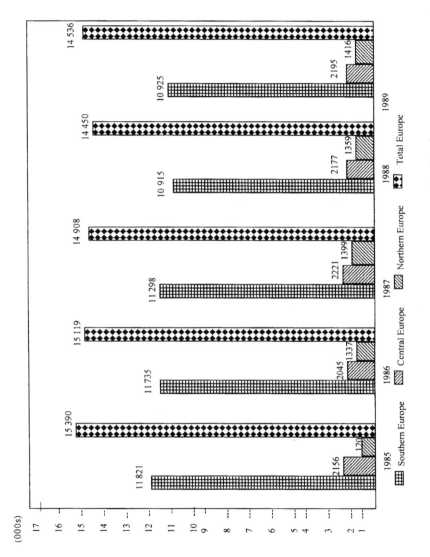

Figure 11.1 Wine consumption in Europe (million litres)

of stabilization. For more than 16 years, the southern wine-producing and traditionally heavy wine-consuming nations had experienced a continuing decline in their home markets. In 1991 the volume consumed in southern Europe was only 72% of the figure for 1973. This region – France, Italy, Spain, Portugal and Greece – accounted for 75% of total consumption. In 1989 the annual average consumption per capita was 74 litres. That was only a tiny amount compared to 1930, when the average Frenchman typically would drink 128 litres a year. For more than 20 years, declining European wine consumption had been balanced by the growth in the northern regions. Traditionally, many consumers in these national markets had had only limited experience but, by 1989, the average per capita consumption in these regions had reached 21 litres per head. For several years, industry experts had been discussing an apparent consumer trend pointing towards a possible European equalization of the per capita consumption level, to converge in the first half of the next century. However, the short-term development indicated a stabilization around the current European consumption rate, primarily determined by France and Italy, which had equally sized markets and together accounted for 57% of total European consumption.

In Eastern Europe, including the former DDR, there was a 4% increase in consumption from 1988 to 1989 – a total of 4.3 billion litres or 30% of that of Western Europe. This growth was solely due to the increased production in the former USSR, which alone consumed 50% of the wine in Eastern Europe. As in Italy and France, consumption in the former USSR had shrunk to 70% of the amount of the mid-1970s. In 1989, the Eastern European average annual consumption was 13 litres per head.

THE INTERNATIONAL WINE TRADE

Beginning in the early 1970s, the imported volume of wine to and among European countries increased steadily at 1–5% per year and in 1989 it accounted for 23% of European consumption (Figure 11.2 and Table 11.3). In 1989, the largest importer was West Germany with 882 million litres; however, the largest volume growth since the 1970s was experienced in the UK, which was the second-largest European importer of wine with 683 million litres. The North

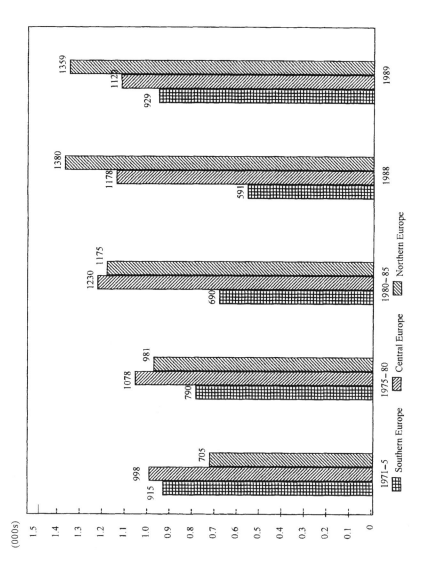

Figure 11.2 European wine imports (million litres)

Table 11.3 European wine imports (million litres)

	1971–5	1976–80	1981–5	1988	1989
France	749	766	650	547	570
Italy	46	22	28	36	66
Spain	20	2	2	7	10
Portugal	0	0	0	0	182
Greece				1	1
Austria	55	29	25	34	25
Switzerland	201	195	218	195	198
Germany	712	840	971	934	882
Luxembourg	18	12	16	15	15
UK	295	362	512	685	683
Ireland	10	10	11	15	15
Belgium	147	188	220	187	185
Netherlands	119	163	207	210	217
Denmark	44	66	93	113	107
Sweden	65	77	89	107	107
Norway	12	13	31	26	26
Finland	13	12	12	17	18
Total	2506	2757	3085	3129	3307

European countries that were not wine producing accounted for 41% of all European wine imports. In the South, France was by far the biggest importer of wine with 570 million litres. Of this amount, 90% was table wine, with most of it being mixed with French table wine which, by legislation, was allowed to contain a maximum of 15% foreign wine. Taking into account that France was the world's biggest market for wine, imported wine accounted for only a small proportion of French consumption. Portugal, on the other hand, had 11 million inhabitants – approximately one fifth of the French population, yet its imports between 1988 and 1989 increased from practically zero to 182 million litres, of which 83% was categorized as quality wine (wine of appellation) according to OIV statistics. Central European countries – although partly wine-producing – were, nevertheless, net importing countries. Traditionally, wine-consuming nations had, since the late 1970s, imported a fairly constant volume of wine; in 1989, the amount was 1120 million litres representing one third of European imports.

In 1989, exports from European countries equalled 3.7 billion litres. From the early 1970s and over the next decade, exports

Table 11.4   European wine exports (million litres)

	1971–5	1976–80	1981–5	1988	1989
France	594	796	1016	1300	1297
Italy	1179	1567	1732	1280	1320
Spain	429	556	590	430	496
Portugal	199	160	140	165	163
Greece	88	100	55	42	138
Austria	19	30	42	4	4
Switzerland	1	1	1	1	1
Germany	64	145	260	279	294
Luxembourg	7	8	8	8	9
Ireland					
Belgium	9	19	23	1	3
Netherlands	12	2	5	4	4
Denmark	3	2	2	4	4
Sweden					
Norway					
Finland					
Total	2604	3386	3874	3518	3733

increased by 50%. Then, through the 1980s, a fairly stable export volume could be observed (Tables 11.3 and 11.4, and Figure 11.3). The largest exporters in Europe were France and Italy, which exported equal volumes of wine. In 1989, Italy experienced a sharp decline in exports – from 1.7 million litres to 1.3 million litres. The decline had several explanations. In 1986, the methanol poisoning of some Italian standard wines had a significant negative effect on domestic consumption; however, after two years exports had increased.

Italy's southern climate made it possible to harvest large quantities of grapes per hectare, which meant that the grapes were most appropriate for production of standard wines. The European market for standard wines had declined seriously in the 1980s, and Italian adaptation towards production of a higher proportion of quality wines had affected the quantity of export. Austria, like Italy, was hit by a serious wine poisoning (diethylene glycol) scandal in 1985 which, for a while, deterred world consumers. This poisoning forced the majority of Austrian producers away from targeting export markets. Exports, only 10% in the beginning of the 1980s, were still quite low in 1989.

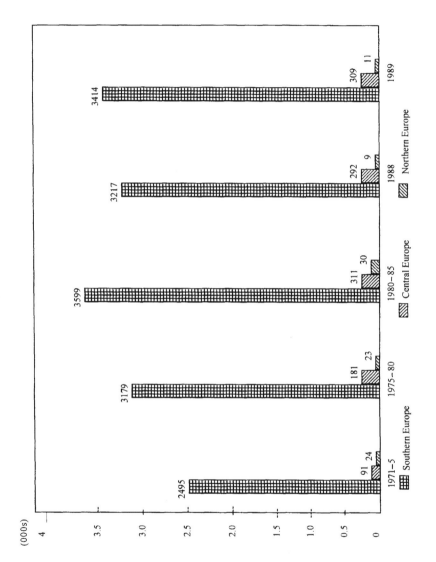

Figure 11.3   European wine exports (million litres)

In general, the three big producers and exporters of wine in Europe (France, Italy and Spain) faced increasing export competition from other wine-producing countries. In Europe, competition came from Portugal and Greece, but a greater threat came from outside the EEC. Despite extra EEC taxation on their wines, younger wine-producing countries like Argentina, Chile, the USA and Australia were able to increase penetration into the European market. In the late 1980s, Eastern European countries – e.g. Bulgaria – dramatically increased wine exports, especially to the UK. With the relaxing of trade restrictions, greater exportation was also expected from South Africa, providing an opportunity for their wines to enter more European markets. The former USSR republics of Georgia and Moldavia were also considering targeting the European market. The EEC could decide to support these young republics by allowing their wines to enter the European market under less competitive conditions.

THE VINEYARDS OF EUROPE

In Europe in the 1850s the amount of land devoted to vineyards (not including Eastern Europe) was very large, covering more than 5 million hectares, while the population was five to seven times smaller than today. However, the vine parasite phylloxera caused a Europe-wide agricultural disaster, which required a complete replanting of all the European vineyards during the last part of the nineteenth century and the beginning of the twentieth. A large part of the destroyed vineyards were never replanted. Between the two world wars, the vineyards in Europe were reduced to approximately 4.5 million hectares. Starting in the 1970s, the EEC subsidized a reduction in the number of vineyards, prohibiting any planting of new vine areas in place of standard vines until 1990. By 1989, the European vineyards had shrunk to an area that was 83% smaller than in the late 1970s (Table 11.5 and Figure 11.4).

EEC regulation encouraged cessation of vine production in low-quality grape regions, while encouraging the planting of better or more suitable vine varieties for wine production in others. In order to discourage overproduction, a certain proportion of the amount exceeding the allocated production quota had to be distilled.

Table 11.5 European vineyards (1000 hectares)

	1971–5	1976–80	1981–5	1988	1989
France	1317	1230	1094	970	948
Italy	1369	1389	1215	1074	1074
Spain	1551	1717	1622	1473	1473
Portugal	354	364	369	385	385
Greece	203	192	192	170	170
Austria	48	54	59	58	58
Switzerland	12	14	14	14	15
Germany	96	101	101	100	102
Luxembourg	1	1	1	1	1
Total	4951	5062	4667	4245	4226

Table 11.6 Average production per hectare (hectolitres per hectare)

	1971–5	1976–80	1981–5	1988	1989
France	52.2	54.7	61.7	59.3	64.2
Italy	50.8	53.7	59.4	56.8	55.7
Spain	20.8	19.7	20.9	15.1	19.7
Portugal	29.2	26.0	24.6	10.0	19.9
Greece	25.7	28.2	26.0	27.8	29.2
Austria	46.7	54.4	48.6	60.3	44.5
Switzerland	79.2	74.3	93.6	79.3	113.3
Germany	84.3	77.5	97.0	93.1	129.7
Luxembourg	150.0	90.0	160.0	140.0	115.0
Ave. (hl/ha)	39.9	40.0	43.2	38.5	42.6

Improvements in cultivation methods increased production and grape quality per hectare. However, according to industry specialists, very large crops per hectare resulted in poorer-quality wines. But, the converse – small harvests – did not automatically produce a higher-quality wine. Improvements that minimized the effects of diseases and parasites in order to produce a sound crop did increase average production per hectare. Normally, there was a trade-off between obtaining a high-quality harvest and a high-quantity harvest. In 1989, the European average production per hectare was 4260 litres of wine. From 1971 to 1985, the average European wine production per hectare increased by 8%. There were wide national differences in the production averages. Spain was the lowest with an average production of around 2000 litres per hectare, nearly one

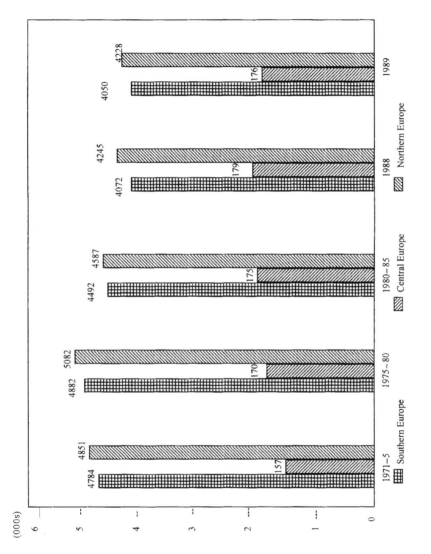

Figure 11.4 European vine areas (million litres)

third that of France and Italy and one sixth that of West Germany. However, one reason for the very low averages in many of the south European countries was poor cultivation. The production range was large. In some south Italian vineyards it was possible to produce more than 400 hectolitres per hectare, whereas the most famous European vineyards – Romanée Contée, Clos de Vougeot, Château Lafite, Cheval Blanc, etc. – rarely produced more than 35 hectolitres per hectare (Table 11.6).

As the production conditions and wine quality varied greatly among and within countries, it was difficult to arrive at cultivation standards per hectare. Despite these differences, the long-term objectives of the EEC were to allocate wine production to the most suitable sites in Europe and to minimize excess production.

ALTERNATIVE USES FOR GRAPES

In 1989, European grape production was 29.9 million tons. But not all grapes were alike. There were three distinct types: wine grapes, table grapes and grapes for raisins.

Wine grapes comprised the majority of all European grapes – 27.4 million tons or 91% of the total (Table 11.7). A small proportion of this segment was used in the production of grape juice. The largest markets for grape juice in Europe were France, West Germany, Italy, Spain, the UK and Switzerland, with a total consumption in 1989 of 194 million litres. Compared to the size of the country, Switzerland was a relatively large market with 13 million litres. The

Table 11.7 Production of grapes in Europe (thousands of tons)

	Table	Wine	Raisins
France	141	7207	
Italy	1403	9977	
Spain	430	4923	3
Portugal	100	1092	
Greece	289	1700	160
Austria		348	
Switzerland	1	225	
Germany		1893	
Luxembourg		29	
Total	2364	27,394	163

European demand for grape juice had been low and stable for four years.

Wine grapes were primarily used for making wine. They could also be used for other bottled alcoholic products (cognac) and for industrial use (such as vinegar, distillation). Of total wine production, approximately 15% was used for the above-mentioned non-wine products.

Table grapes were bigger than wine grapes and not suitable for wine production. European production in 1989 was 2.4 million tons or 7.9% of total grape production. Table grapes were produced in the most southern and sunniest parts of Europe. The largest producer was Italy with 59% of European table grape production, corresponding to 14% of the total national production. The largest relative producer of table grapes was Greece with 17%. Table grapes accounted for approximately 10% of Spanish and Portuguese grape production, while only 2% of the French production was allocated to table grapes.

Grapes for raisins comprised less than 1% of total European grape production. Raisin production required many hours of sun and a dry environment. The largest producer was Greece, with 163,000 tons.

PRODUCTION

World consumption in 1989 was only 85% of the total wine production, corresponding to 29 billion litres. Europe accounted for 18 million litres, of which Italy and France alone accounted for 57%

Table 11.8 European wine production (million litres)

	1971–75	1976–80	1981–85	1988	1989
France	6874	6726	6746	5753	6082
Italy	6956	7462	7215	6101	5980
Spain	3219	3383	3396	2225	2896
Portugal	1033	947	908	384	766
Greece	522	541	500	473	497
Austria	224	294	287	350	258
Switzerland	95	104	131	111	170
Germany	809	783	980	931	1323
Luxembourg	15	9	16	14	23
Total	19,747	20,249	20,179	16,342	17,995

(Table 11.8). Over the last two decades, European wine production had been severely regulated by the EEC in order to control supply and prevent further overproduction. By 1989, European production was down 10% compared to the production level in the early 1980s.

The EEC definition of "wine" stated: "Wine is the product obtained exclusively from the total or partial alcoholic fermentation of fresh grapes, whether or not crushed, or of grape juice." An implication of this definition was that fermented fruit juice – e.g. apple wine – was excluded.

In order to produce excellent wine, high-quality grapes were needed. It was thought that a good winemaker was essential to having a successful outcome. Indeed, an unskilled winemaker could ruin the potential of great fruit but, conversely, a correct winemaking process executed on poor grapes would not automatically result in great wine. The influence of the winemaker's skills on the final product was estimated by experts to be 10–20% of the quality (price).

GRAPE GROWING

The quality of the grapes was, therefore, crucial to the outcome of the final wine. The microclimate and the soil were the given conditions setting the main limitations in the grape growing process. The grower had the choice of grape variety, which could be adapted to the site and, in addition, selected the growth conditions to be used in the vineyard: the number of grapevines per hectare (suitable for mechanization, treatment, harvesting), the number of buds per vine which affected the quantity of the harvest and the concentration of the grape juice, fertilization, treatment of the vines against parasites and diseases, etc. The optimal time for harvesting was related to the maturity of the grapes. Maturity depended on the concentration of sugar, acidity and colour substances, and these factors differed for each type of wine to be produced. It was, furthermore, critical to move the grapes – in an undamaged condition – to the cellar quickly and to begin the vinification process immediately in order to ensure a good quality. Most premium grapes were picked by hand, but mechanical grape-harvesting for standard wine production was becoming common – especially in Germany and France. Mechanical harvesting, although more likely to damage the grapes, was cheaper.

As it was preferable for white wine to have a higher acidity, the green grapes were usually harvested before the blue ones used for red wine.

The Vinification Process

The winemaking process began with the grape harvest, usually in early autumn. The production of white wines often started by mechanically de-stemming the grapes, separating the juice from the skin. The juice was mechanically separated from the remaining solid part of the grapes and treated with enzymes to precipitate proteins or certain polysaccharides. Sulphur dioxide was added to prevent bacterial infection, and the juice was then transferred to stainless steel tanks for the alcoholic yeast fermentation at 12–14 °C. For some premium white wines, the fermentation was executed in oak barrels. The fermentation process lasted 10–15 days, whereafter the wine was treated, filtrated, separated for wine stone crystals and, finally, conditioned and packaged.

For red wine production, the grapes were crushed and sometimes de-stemmed before they were placed in steel tanks for fermentation. The fermentation took 9–20 days and, during this period, the extraction of substances from the grape skin and the stems occurred. The wine was temporarily cleared and then a second (non-alcoholic) fermentation took place to reduce the acidity. This process could take several months, followed by blending, further clearing and filtration. Premium red wines were held in wooden barrels between 3 and 18 months before they were filtrated and bottled, and were often warehoused for further ageing prior to being shipped to the market.

R&D

The wine industry traditionally had little innovation. Evidence of the production of wine went back to the Bronze Age in 3000–1500 BC, to Egypt and to islands in the Aegean – now part of Greece. Wine-related artefacts have been found in the forms of vessels for holding wine (casks, earthenware jars, amphorae, carafes, glasses, cups and goblets), wine presses and cellars. Breakthroughs came in the seventeenth and eighteenth centuries, when the use of glass bottles and cork became common. Sulphur was introduced as a preservative agent in wine and began to be used extensively throughout the industry. This was the reason that some wines, dating to before the French Revolution, were still interesting, very expensive and unique in taste. Pasteur's discoveries in the fields of microbiology and the fermentation process in the latter half of the nineteenth century created additional innovative processes for wine production.

The basic wine production process had not changed for centuries. Even in 1990, the vinification process continued to follow directly after the harvest in autumn, which meant that large parts of the production facilities lay idle most of the year. Furthermore, a large part of vinification had to take place near the vineyards due to legislative constraints. This was a major reason for the scattered production structure consisting of many small producers which existed in the industry. The lack of large-scale production benefits were major reasons that the dairy and beer industries were ahead of the wine industry in process know-how and scientific efforts.

From these industries, innovations such as microbiological process control spread to the wine industry, resulting in new processes which, for example, allowed yeast to be inoculated at the start of the alcoholic fermentation process and lactic acid bacteria cultures to hasten malolactic fermentation. Furthermore, enzymatic treatment of wines started penetrating the industry, leading to the removal or modification of proteins and polysaccharides that were not desirable in wine. These innovations diminished the proportion of "failors" or misfermentations. It helped the winemakers produce a more homogeneous quality of wine.

A new major breakthrough in the vinification process would be to exploit the potential of the complex "hidden pool" of flavour components in wines with a specific enzymatic control. In 1990, several companies and research institutes were involved in research on the flavour chemistry of wines. For example, the French research institute, INRA in Montpellier, was trying to map sources of flavour precursors in wine. Research was also being conducted to improve the grape potential. Research stations like Geisemheim in Germany and ENSAM in Montpellier were attempting to study vine species in order to find new methods that would improve the quality, the harvest and resistance against disease and have more mechanization of production.

PRODUCT CATEGORIES

Within the EEC, several wine quality systems were used. Due to the strongly fragmented wine market, the necessity of providing standards to consumers led to construction of several sub-branding categories. The most famous was the originally French system of citing the "appellation of origin", which to some extent and with some modification, has been adapted in all wine-producing countries.

The most common distinction was between VCC wines (*vin de consommation courante* – wine for current consumption) and wines with an appellation of origin. VCC covered two categories: "*vin de table*" (table wine) and "*vin du pays*" (wine of a region). Wine with an appellation of origin included VDQS "*vin de qualité supérieure*" (wine of superior quality) and AOC "*appellation d'origine contrôlée*" (designated appellation of origin). Within each category, there were more classification systems, especially within the AOC – e.g. the "*Cru*" classification – and the systems differed among national regions. Consumers regarded these systems differently. For example, the French AOC system was considered the most controlled and protected and, among world consumers, the most highly respected. On the other hand, the Italian DOC was less respected by consumers and many Italian producers. It was common that Italian wines of even the highest quality were categorized "*vino de tavolo*" (table wine), which only meant that the producer was not particularly interested in having the DOC (premium) labelling. The "*vino de tavolo*" label was a way to tell consumers that the quality was different from wines that were officially recommended in the specific region. In France, such labelling would be perceived as being of the lowest quality in the market, even though bypassing the AOC system was frequently practised in France as well.

From a business point of view, it was appropriate to divide wine products into the three following categories:

1. Still wines
2. Champagne and sparkling wines
3. Fortified wines (port, sherry, etc.)

Still wine products were divided into three main categories:

1. Standard wines: VDT, VDP

2.   Premium wines: AOC
3.   Super-premium wines (high-priced chateau AOC)

Each of these segments were again divided into red, rosé and white.

Standard Wines

The market for standard wines was the largest market covering more than 50% of European consumption. This market had been the most seriously affected segment in the industry, experiencing constantly declining sales since the 1970s. Increased health consciousness and changing lifestyles in general led many consumers to drink less but better-quality wine. As traditional non-consumers, particularly the northern regions, became more experienced wine consumers, they also became more careful in their choice of wine. This led many consumers from the standard wine segments to the premium segments.

Although, in 1990, the national white wine production was 84% of the total, the proportion was shifting as red wines experienced a growth in consumption. The consumer trend toward red wine was similar in the UK, going from 23% of volume in 1985 to 26% in 1989. Forty-seven per cent of volume consumed was in white wine. The Scandinavian countries consumed more than 60% red wine. French production of standard wines was 54% in 1989, down from 67% in 1985. Consumption of table wine in 1989 was 59% of all wines, down from 67% in 1985. Red wine accounted for the majority of the French production and consumption. In Italy, 40% of wine consumption was white and 81% of wine consumption was table wine.

Premium Wines and Acquisition

It was a common opinion among producers and consumers that premium wine quality was primarily attributed to the site where the grapes were grown. Therefore, acquisitions and mergers rarely led to new names for the domain or the chateau.

It was also commonly believed that it was difficult to expand production without compromising on quality. A company like

Beringer in California (owned by Nestlé and the Labruyère family) kept production facilities separated, benefiting from economies of scale mainly through marketing and distribution. In 1972, Nestlé purchased the crumbling Beringer vineyards for $6 million in conjunction with the Labruyère family. They projected that it would take a decade plus major investments to bring the vineyard to prominence. The facilities were upgraded and more prime vineyards were acquired. Between 1985 and 1987, $21 million were invested to obtain better equipment, greater research capacity and more vineyards. Nestlé's Wine World subsidiary handled six labels. Wine World also ran C & B vintage cellars, which imported a number of European brands. Nestlé's wine companies had sales rapidly approaching $100 million. Nestlé considered Beringer and its other wine properties as strictly American firms. There was no other well-capitalized winery of Beringer's size which generated so little ill will. It was additionally often cited as the best-managed company in the US wine industry.

Acquisitions of prestigious chateaux and real estate in the Bordeaux regions had become very popular over the past 15 years. French banks and insurance companies showed remarkable interest in wine real estate, as did many international buyers like the Japanese, American and British.

Skyrocketing prices in real estate resulted in unrealistic wine prices as costs were passed on to ensure a minimum profitability. Since profit was not obvious, these acquisitions seemed to be connected to the fact that larger organizations outside the wine industry were hoping to enhance their profile by purchasing genuine values like prestigious chateaux and wines. Until 1988, only 10% of the high-quality chateaux changed hands. The rest, about 60 chateaux, were still in family hands, but a newly initiated inheritance tax would force many of these chateaux onto the market over the coming years. The French government considered much of the real estate as patrimony and could, at any time, intervene. When a Japanese company wanted to take over Romanée-Conté – the most famous vineyard in Burgundy – the government prohibited the transaction. When the Danish retailer, Hemming Karberg, integrated backwards by acquiring Chateau Kirwan in St Emilion, the French government resisted the purchase for more than two years. The public resistance against Seagram's purchase of Chateau Latour, categorized as "first growth" (*Premier Cru*) in Bordeaux was but another example of French government/public intervention.

The European Consumer

Fine and standard wines, unlike beer and soft drinks, were seen by the consumer as non-commodity products and therefore commanded higher prices. Among European wine consumers, the overriding criteria in making the purchase decision were seen as:

- Familiarity
- Price
- Reputation
- Value for money
- Curiosity

Personal familiarity remained the most important criterion for purchasing wine, although increasingly curiosity was an important factor among North European consumers. Wine drinking was becoming more of an occasional activity, even in traditional wine-consuming societies. For example, in 1987, only 35% of all adults in France claimed to be regular drinkers versus 46% in 1981.

Furthermore, European consumers were keeping in step with lifestyle changes, such as eating habits, health consciousness, work and leisure, which led to lower alcoholic consumption. This was notable in the UK and Germany and was likely to spread to other European societies over the next decade. In the South, the Italian and Spanish consumer had traditionally consumed wine with their meals. The traditional noonday meal was now changing to lighter fare – such as a sandwich and snack accompanied by a soft drink or a beer. In the evening, the trend was moving towards lighter and earlier dinners. With social occasions becoming less formal, aperitifs were less appropriate. The younger generation of Italians drank less wine and with lower contents of alcohol. In 1991, white wine was still a part of the social drinking scene for younger people. The trend was for consumers to drink less wine but of higher quality, thus favouring the premium wine category. Males were drinking 30% more than women, and the upper class was drinking a little more than the middle and lower classes. Premium wine was primarily related to social events. Surveys showed that consumption in

Northern Europe was more seasonally influenced. In the Netherlands and Germany, sales peaked at the end of the year before the Christmas season. They fell sharply in January and February, rose again in April and May before turning downward in the summer months of June, July and August.

Wine purchasers were, in general, brand conscious due to advertising, and research showed that the primary wine purchasers were women, following a shift towards home consumption of wine and the emerging dominance of multiple retailers. Wine consumers considered themselves to be generally more knowledgeable about wines than they were 5–10 years ago and therefore demanded more of value for money when purchasing wine.

EXTERNAL FORCES

Taxation

As a popular source of tax income, partly fuelled by generally increasing health consciousness, governments imposed restrictive measures on liquor, wine and beer. Alcoholic beverages were differently, but heavily, taxed in Northern European countries – primarily in Scandinavia, England and Ireland. The EEC requested that these countries decrease the tax burden in order to achieve a pan-European balanced level by the mid-1990s. As the European integration process continued, with Austria, Sweden and Finland becoming members of the EEC, a further increase in wine consumption was expected in these regions.

Health Concerns

Due to restrictions on advertising and heavy taxation on alcoholic beverages, wine consumption was seen in most European countries as preferable to drinking stronger alcoholic beverages. Medical studies conducted on deteriorating effects caused by consumption of alcohol were mixed. Exaggerated consumption, of course, could destroy the liver and affect brain cells. But more interesting was the medical debate on moderate use. Some studies indicated that one or two glasses of wine each day contributed to oral and oesophageal

(a)

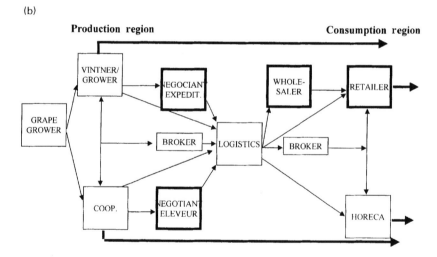

Figure 11.5   (a) Traditionl business flow before 1960. (Business largely operating as separate entities.) (b) 1960–70: wholesalers and supermarkets gain power. (c) 1970–80: supermarkets and hypermarkets integrate backwards. (Wholesalers had to focus on specialty shops and HORECA – hotels, restaurants and caterers.)
(d) 1980–90: increased direct sales to retailers and HORECA. (The power of supermarkets and hypermarkets further eliminates the middleman: high-end vintners and cost-efficient coops enjoy success)

(c)

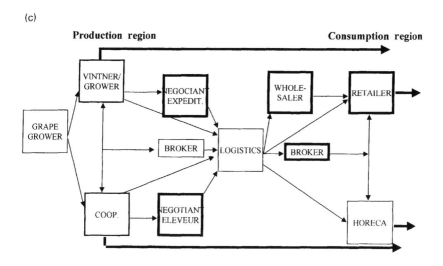

(d)

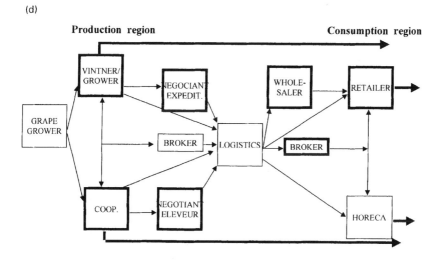

cancer. Others suggested that such quantities aided in lowering hypertension and the risk of a heart attack.

Labelling

Additives like sulphur dioxide had a conserving effect on wines. This substance had been used for more than 200 years and a suitable substitute had not yet been discovered in Europe. The legally determined maximum level of sulphur dioxide in wines had decreased over the last 60 years. Still, the required level for a bacteriostatic effect was so high that one bottle of red wine a day corresponded to the maximum exposure level suggested by the FAQ. By 1993, a label declaring the content of sulphur dioxide was to be required in all EEC countries. Although already required in some European countries, the European wine industry feared that this would have a negative impact on future consumption.

Distribution

The distribution system for fermented grape products was divided into four different chains/circuits:

1. Still wine
2. Sparkling wines (e.g. champagne, cremant)
3. Fortified wines (e.g. Muscat de Frontigan)
4. Ethyl alcohol (distillation of excess production).

This section focuses only on the still and sparkling wines chains. Throughout the last three decades, the evolution in the wine distribution system in Europe had been characterised by a number of breakthroughs in the industry, to some extent broken down by decade (see Figure 11.5).

Until the early 1960s, the traditional business system was strictly separated and specialized. The wine grower produced wine at private facilities or sold the grapes to the local cooperative. The wine was then passed through a local broker to the local wholesaler. The wholesaler normally stabilized the wine, and very often specialized in only standard wines or quality wines. The retailers were mostly specialized stores and groceries. Through the producers to the end user, every part in the value chain was strictly specialized.

PACKAGING AND LOGISTICS

Packaging technology for agronomic products began in the early 1960s, when industrialization and the economies of scale of new packaging and bottling plants became exploitable. This led to a stronger concentration in bottling and distribution (see Figure 11.5(a)) followed by an accelerated introduction of new packaging concepts that affected the wine industry. Packaging and pack design began to play an increasingly important role in the marketing of wine, in terms of both cost reduction and differentiation. This fact lent more power to the wholesaler and the retailer in the consumer regions where the wine was bottled/packaged and distributed.

New, lighter packaging materials than the traditional glass wine bottle decreased the transportation cost of packaged wine. Plastic bottles were lighter, but their use peaked after a short period of time due to the impact on the product's aroma. Plastic bottles were used only for some table wines. Other packaging innovations followed – non-recyclable light glass, then cubitainers or bags inserted into boxes. In 1983, a new packaging technique emerged in the form of aluminium cartons called the "tetrapack" (designed by Tetra Pak). This packaging was suitable for wine marketed in certain new lifestyle segments – fast-food restaurants, leisure beverages, food services, etc.

Contemporary new palleting techniques reduced the cost of transportation and the frequency of waste. This also made it possible to revive the concept of the *"mise en bouteille à la propriété"* (bottled at the site) by doing the bottling at fixed bottling plants, at cooperatives or at larger wineries, and by using transportable bottling plants at smaller domains/chateaux.

CHANGES IN RETAIL DISTRIBUTION

The new techniques and forms of packaging allowed a diversification in the retail distribution of wine. Specialized shops disappeared as commodity wines increased and wine moved into the chains store – "coops", supermarkets and hypermarkets distributing a large range of foodstuffs. Different strategies were applied, but most companies integrated backwards – developing direct purchase within the framework of their purchasing departments. In the early days, the retailers were constrained by the wholesaler. Subsequently, distributors started to dictate and impose restrictions on the wholesalers in terms of packaging, sales price, delivery schedules, type of financing, administration and merchandising (see Figure 11.5(c)).

Until the end of the 1970s, the large retailers and the hypermarkets and supermarkets purchased wine as individual lots. In the late 1980s and early 1990s, these stores had largely evolved to where they were applying sophisticated category management, and were viewing wine as a major store-traffic generator. These department stores began using wine as a major attraction, selling the wine at greatly reduced prices while making a profit on other commodities that the customer bought. These trends contributed to the demise of the speciality shop as the last premium wine bastion. Traditionally, these shops had offered considerably more service in terms of advice, delivery flexibility, aesthetic ambience, etc.

DISTRIBUTION POWER SHIFTING TOWARDS MASS RETAILING

Between 1982 and 1987 there was a significant shift from consumer spending in HORECA (hotels, restaurants, caterers) and small groceries to purchasing wine at hypermarkets/supermarkets, leading to these multiple retailers becoming dominant in European wine distribution. The multiple retailers maintained a low price to ensure increased store traffic, achieving high profitability through greater turnover. The hypermarkets' growing power enabled them to command disproportionately large discounts from producers, allowing the continuation of lower prices. The hypermarkets reinvested their profits in increased efficiency and expansion programmes, which put greater pressure on small and inefficient distributors who became acquisition targets or were under pressure to exit the industry.

- *France*: Approximately 57% of all wines were sold through retail outlets. This proportion was increasing and, as an outlet for quality wines, it was more important than for table wines. Hypermarkets and supermarkets together distributed 71% of retail wine but 80% of the quality wines. Superettes and traditional stores were outlets for VCC wines (*vin de table* and *vin du pays*). The importance of HORECA as outlets was decreasing, and represented 31% of all quality wines and 24% of table wines. Direct sales from vineyards equalled 18.5%, but only 10% of all quality wines were sold through direct sales.

- *Italy*: There were 220,000 licensed premises; 133,000 of them were bars that accounted for 15% of all wines distributed in Italy. Direct sales to consumers represented approximately 31% of all wines sold. 1.25 million vineyards and more than 5000 companies were involved in the wine industry. Independents and multiples were responsible for 27%, and 17% was sold through wholesalers.
- *UK*: Approximately 23% of all wine was distributed through speciality shops. As much as 68% of all wine was distributed through supermarkets. Only 2% was sold through department stores, and only 7% was consumed in pubs and restaurants. Throughout the 1980s, the popularity of wine bars increased in the UK.
- *Germany*: Several sources estimated that German vintners had direct sales of approximately 40%. Retail distribution was also dominant in Germany (44%), followed by discounters like Aldi with 25% and hypermarkets with 15%. Speciality shops accounted for 5% of sales.
- *Scandinavia*: In Sweden and Norway, the state-owned monopolies controlled the importation and distribution of alcoholic beverages through Vin & Sprit AB in Sweden and Vin-monopolet in Norway. This structure led Vin & Sprit AB to be called the most powerful buyer of wine and other alcoholic beverages in the world. With Sweden's entry into the EEC, the government could be forced to abolish this monopoly. Some sources claimed that Vin & Sprit AB had acquired smaller companies in neighbouring Denmark in order to exercise free competition before the market in Sweden was opened for competition. The Danish retail structure was comparable to that of the Dutch or the British structure. The majority of wine was distributed through supermarkets, discounters and speciality stores. About 30% of the wholesale distribution was held by Danisco/De Danske Spritfabrikker, a conglomerate that also covered 70% of the distribution of stronger alcoholic beverages.

THE DEVELOPMENT OF DIRECT SALES BY THE PRODUCERS

The development of direct sales to retailers and end users by the producers had been an important recent development. This was partly due to the new technical development of smaller stainless steel tanks and the application of inert gas, like nitrogen, to cover and protect the wine surface in the storage tank. Nitrogen protected the wine against oxidation and released the producer from having to bottle the wine in a full storage tank at once. Furthermore, the increased demand for authentic wines had been a stimulant. In the 1970s, a large number of cooperatives were created especially for premium wines – like speciality wines and AOC generic wines. These were products where the profitability appeared to be most attractive. The margin per unit was more interesting for table wines, and the turnover of inventory was better than for the "*grands vins*" (fine wines).

A French survey suggested that in 1979 about 25,000 of the 114,000 wine producers in France sold approximately 9% of the production directly (see Figure 11.5(d)). In 1983, this number increased to 10.1%, corresponding to 16% of the AOC (premium wines) and 6.4% of the table wine. This proportion continued to increase throughout the 1980s, while the commercialization of direct sales could be found in more of the larger cooperatives. The degree of differentiation also increased.

DISTRIBUTION IN THE EUROPEAN WINE INDUSTRY

Throughout Europe, the distribution system which carried wine products from vintner to consumer was complex and evolving. Fine wines generally were sold through speciality and traditional wine stores, as well as HORECA, capitalizing on the strong reputation and brand image enjoyed by these products. Standard wines were distributed through "multiple retail stores" such as the hypermarkets (Casino, Carrefour) and chain retail outlets (Marks & Spencer, Harrods, etc.), as well as through low-end discount outlets and speciality stores.

The distribution strategy for common wine was the weakest of the three categories. The common wines were distributed mainly through the multiple retail stores and were promoted through a low-price strategy, leading the distributors to continually seek lower production prices in order to increase their margin and to maintain shelf space for the product.

European Wine Inventory

The European wine inventory at the end of the 1988–9 season (not including Scandinavian countries) was 11,661 billion litres . This corresponded to a European *"réserve"* inventory (to production) of approximately 8 months. The largest reserves were in Central Europe, with Austria at the top holding a 22-month stock. Smallest inventories were in France and Italy, corresponding respectively to 6- and 7-month reserves; of Spanish and French stocks, 50–60% were estimated to be in the wine category appellation of origin.

MARKETING PROMOTION AND ADVERTISING

Promotional activities seemed to be more common in the South European wine-producing countries than in the North. Advertisements for wines and other alcoholic beverages were more restricted in North European countries and in France. Television advertisements were banned in Scandinavia, the Netherlands and France, and were heavily constrained in Germany and the UK. Three product groups were advertised – regional wines, country wines and branded products.

- *UK*: Media expenditures in the UK were £17 million, equal to an average of 0.8% of retail value. This was 12% less than in 1987, when advertising expenditures peaked. The leading brand, Le Piat d'Or, allocated £1.5 million, was equal to 6–7% of retail value for media expenses. The sparkling wine brand, Asti Spumante, spent 5.9% of retail value on media advertising. Other heavily advertised brands included Erben, Eisberg, Mateus Rosé, Veuve de Vernay, as well as fortified wines and vermouth brands. Wines from Bulgaria were supported with a £0.9 million advertising campaign; 52% of all advertising expenditures were spent on table wines.
- *Germany*: Unlike the UK, the German advertising spending on

still wine rose 20% in 1989 compared to 1988 and 1987. The average spending on advertising in 1989 was 1% of retail value. Advertising for sparkling wines increased in recent years and amounted to 6.3% of retail value. Though the volume of sparkling wines only represented 12% of the total volume consumed in 1989, as much as 62% of all wine advertising expenditures was spent in support of sparkling wines. The most important trend in recent years had been the switch to magazine advertising. All other media advertising had declined.

- *Italy*: In Italy, trade-related promotional/in-store activities was common. Brand advertising accounted for the majority of advertising expenditures in Italy in 1989. Headed by the sparkling wine brands, they averaged approximately 15% of retail value on advertising and 75% of advertising funds were allocated to TV advertising, primarily to local TV stations.

- *France*: Advertising of generic wines/regional wines (Vins des Côtes du Rhone, Bergerac, etc.) were far more pervasive and received more governmental subsidies compared to other major wine-producing countries. SOPEXA, the French marketing organ for the agricultural industry, was far more dominant than equivalents in other countries. Furthermore, legislative advertising restrictions were tighter than in other major wine-producing countries. A total ban on advertising for alcoholic beverages had been a heavily discussed topic since the beginning of the 1990s. Promotional activities connected to expositions like Vinexpo, SiteVi, and visits to wine cellars or below-the-line advertising like *prix d'appel* were common.

BRAND BUILDING

The fact that the European consumption of premium wines was growing heavily affected the marketing of standard wines. The strategy of the most dynamic wholesalers – especially in AOC regions – had been to purchase fragmented table wines or *vin du pays* in order to blend a product reminiscent of premium wines (AOC). The products were then marketed using signature conditions (bottled, corked, labelled, packaged and priced in premium style). Some of the wines produced under these conditions were Mouton Cadet, Le Piat d'Or, and Grand Metropolitain. Specialists

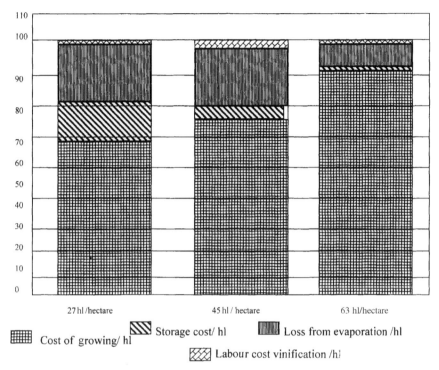

Figure 11.6 Production costs for three qualities of wines

Table 11.9 Production costs of three different qualities of Bordeaux wines

Cost	27 hl/ha	45 hl/ha	63 hl/ha
	Ffr	Ffr	Ffr
Cost of growing/hl	1815	1088	778
Storage cost/hl	266	55	12
Loss from evaporation and treatment/hl	363	218	54
Labour cost vinification/hl	26	26	6
Total cost/hl	2470	1387	850

27 hl/ha represent costs for a super-premium wine, 45 hl/ha a quality (AOC) wine and 63 hl/ha a standard wine, not an inexpensive wine. The numbers are suggested by the famous négociant, Peter Sichel, and date from October 1985. The costs do not include packaging.

within the industry expressed ambiguous opinions about the overall influence of this type of marketing strategy for the global industry. Some industry experts believed that this strategy was confusing the consumer regarding the European quality of *appellation d'origin* (*vin de table, vin du pays*, VDQS and AOC), which also could be influen-

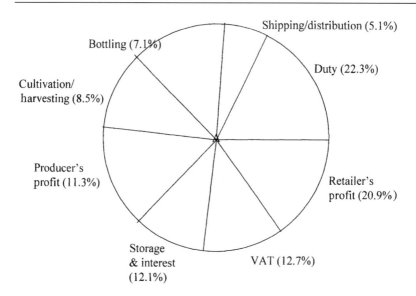

Figure 11.7   Cost allocation for a UK £3.49 wine (75 cl bottle)

tial on the decreasing global consumption of wine (refer to Table 11.1 and Figure 11.1). (For a description of the cost structure for wines, see Figures 11.6 and 11.7 and Table 11.9.)

Different key factors seemed important in the various wine categories. The standard wine business tended to emphasize brand building, often using blended wines in innovative packaging to provide volume products of consistent quality which could be sold through mass-food outlets. Premium wines were sold in upmarket outlets (although volume was still important) with the emphasis on region, village, sort and year branding. The super-premium wines were often used as brand carriers for lesser wines. Quality was of utmost importance. For example, when the management of Chateau Pétrus in Pomerol, Bordeaux, was using helicopters to keep the vineyard and the maturing grapes dry prior to picking, it was to some extent a marketing tool, but certainly also to ensure that the diseases affecting grapes did not spread into the area. In years where the vintage was of lower quality, most of the super-premium chateaux of Bordeaux and Burgundy did not issue wines under the super-premium brand in order to protect the brand image. Moreover, super-premium wine producers were very selective in choosing distribution channels (mostly main outlets or sold directly at the vineyard, often under future contracts). Packaging also used classical labels, bottles, long corks, etc., and prices were set accordingly.

POTENTIAL ENTRANTS

The first companies to diversify into the wine industry were ones already with stronger alcoholic beverages as their core business. This was sometimes due to production synergies, but more often because they could benefit from distribution channels. Until the early 1970s, wines were basically sold through speciality stores, groceries, direct sales and HORECA outlets.

As wine has moved into the supermarkets and hypermarkets, many companies active in the consumer goods business entered the market. The world's largest food company, Nestlé SA – building on product lines in milk products, chocolate, baby foods, coffee and frozen foods – acquired the Beringer vineyard in California in the early 1970s. The French company, BSN – originally in dairy products, beverages, grocery products and biscuits – acquired the champagne house Pommery Greno and Lanson in 1983. Several large retail chains integrated backwards (e.g. Casino in France), and the trend towards direct purchasing from the producer cannibalized the domain of the traditional agent and wholesaler.

The wine penetration into hypermarkets during the 1980s enabled new industries to enter the wine industry. The merging of the strategic approach of the Louis Vuitton Group (luxury leather products and perfumes) and Moët Hennessy took place in 1987, thus creating the world's largest group in prestige products. Its most important advantages were based on having a luxury image rather than on the distribution channels. In stores, leather goods and perfumes were rarely placed beside each other or even on the same floor. Furthermore, less than the majority of products were sold in hypermarkets. This strategy was very successful and would probably be copied by other companies in the future.

As the North European consumer continued to supplement or substitute beer for wine while the South European consumer did the contrary, additional reasons for breweries and soft drinks producers to participate in the wine industry became evident. In the UK, the wine markets were basically led by the three large brewers, Allied-

Lyons, IDV, Bass and Guinness. Carlsberg A/S in Denmark acquired the distributor Vingaarden in the latter part of the 1980s.

SELECTED COMPETITORS

Beaujolais Nouveau: Georges Duboeuf

A wholesaler in Beaujolais was very successful in marketing the wine, Beaujolais Nouveau. This brand of red wine had a special concept, as it was suitable for consumption shortly after being produced. Less than three months after the grape harvest, the wine was ready to be distributed and consumed. To ensure a modicum of quality, the government restricted Beaujolais Nouveau to a release date no earlier than the third Thursday in November.

The wine was fermented under carbon dioxide pressure for a short time. Compared to other traditionally produced red wines, it had lower acidity, lower concentration of the bitter component tannin, less colour and was rich in a few naturally fermented colours (e.g. banana). These features made it possible to consume the wine after a very short time. This type of wine proved to be especially attractive to first-time wine consumers. In countries where there was no wine produced and where wine consumption had low penetration, Beaujolais Nouveau was thought to have prepared the market for other wine segments.

Beaujolais was the first of all vintages to be sold and, although some specialists did not consider Beaujolais Nouveau to be real wine, many considered it to be an indicator of the year's entire red wine vintage of France. Its forecasting role had become a real event. In many countries, the yuppie class waited eagerly for this dramatic moment. Racing-car drivers would bring the wine to where it would be consumed. Competition abounded regarding who could get the wine there most quickly. In Denmark, it was the former world speedway champion who brought the first case of Beaujolais to the country, once even with police escort.

The majority of the production was sold at a relatively high commodity price and consumed over a very short time. This made it possible for Georges Duboeuf and other Beaujolais Nouveau producers to minimize capital cost and the cost of expensive storage, which other producers of expensive wines were not able to do.

Georges Duboeuf was riding on a concept which he invented. The majority of the advertising cost was spent in the weeks before the wine was brought to market and lasted until a few months after the first launch.

In recent years, there had been a trend towards ageing the Beaujolais Nouveau. The popularity of the wine had begun in the early 1970s. In France, sales dropped in 1989 and had also declined in Britain, Germany and parts of Scandinavia. Sales in the USA were forecast to decline 20% in 1990. In 1989, exports accounted for 60% of the total production of 75 million bottles. The only country with a growing demand was Japan, but there too certain problems arose. Airport restrictions related to the coronation of the new emperor caused the volume to decrease by 15%. Nevertheless, Federal Express airfreighted more than 330,000 bottles to Tokyo, while Japan Airlines shipped 900,000.

Although Georges Duboeuf accounted for approximately 10% of the Beaujolais production, the company did have competition from other Beaujolais wine producers. In reality, the Beaujolais Nouveau strategy was to take market share from other wine producers by dominating the market over a short period of the year. This strategy involved having heavy brand support during the brief time when the world's attention was focused on Beaujolais.

Champagne: LVMH Möet Hennessy/Louis Vuitton

The LVMH group was engaged in the production and sale of quality prestige products such as champagne, wines, cognac, spirits, leather goods, accessories, perfumes and beauty products. The holding company contained an array of prestigious champagne and cognac companies as well as perfume brands like Givenchy and Christian Dior.

The major strategic activities occurring in the history of Möet Hennessy reflected, until the merger with Louis Vuitton in 1987, an acquisition policy to gain forward integration of distributors and acquisition of champagne brands such as Veuve Clicquot and Charles de Cazanove. In 1979, they acquired the Dutch distributor Wilmering and Muller and, in 1980, Schieffelin (USA). After the merger between Möet Hennessy and the Louis Vuitton group, distribution agreements between Guinness and LVMH were made

Table 11.10   LVMH Möet Hennessy/Louis Vuitton: (five-year summary)

Year	Sales ($000)	Net inc	EPS ($)
1989	19,635,000	2,932,000	44.69
1988	16,442,000	2,003,000	34.01
1987	13,247,000	1,343,000	23.91
1986	9,797,000	1,101,000	20.86
1985	9,088,000	921,000	18.51
Growth rate	21.2%	33.5%	24.6%

and, in 1988, Guinness and the investor Agache acquired 33% of LVMH. In 1988, Möet & Chandon acquired a 70% stake in a 150-hectare production of quality sparkling wine in Spain – Domaine Chandon.

In 1990, LVMH was one of France's largest companies in market capitalization. It was also one of the fastest-growing larger companies in the world. Some analysts considered LVMH to be a financial miracle (Table 11.10).

With the acquisition of the two champagne houses, Pommery and Lanson, LVMH expanded its market share from 18.4% to 24% of the champagne market. LVMH was the market leader in champagnes, counting an impressive arsenal of premium brands like Dom Perignon, Möet & Chandon, Veuve Clicquot, Mercier, Canard-Duchêne and Henr'iot. LVMH paid a large price for the purchase of the two houses it bought from the French food group, BSN SA. The price was $613.7 million, corresponding to 39 times the company's net income in 1989. But the chairman of LVMH noted that internationally known champagne brands were a limited commodity.

Italian Wines Bolla

Good marketing and advertising played a leading role in the export market of Italy. Taking into account that the industry suffered from a methanol scandal in 1986, Italian wine exports were doing quite well. In the US market, the Italian export volume was number one in 1989 with 10.1 million cases, equal to 42% of imported wine in the USA and representing a $175 million value. Only French wine, at $285 million, exceeded this amount in dollar value. Compared to

Table 11.11 Market shares and sales of leading Italian wine brands 1981–86

| Brand | Worldwide sales (000 cases) | | Sales in Italy 1986 | |
	1981	1986	Cases	Market shares (%)
Zonin	5200	2000	1240	0.24
Folonari	3400	1900	840	0.17
Riunite	10,400	8400	756	0.15
Ruffino	2200	900	530	0.1
Canei	3700	3100	500	0.1
Bolla	1600	1400	168	0.03
Total	26,500	17,700	4034	0.79

Source: Euromonitor/Impact.

1988, volume in 1989 was down by 7%, but Italian wines still retained their market share in imports to the USA (Table 11.11).

The Italian marketing philosophy consisted of bringing out new products, altering old ones, increasing planting and production of such universal favourites as Chardonnay, Cabernet Sauvignon and Merlot. These varieties were strong "sub-brand names" in the USA.

Bolla, which represented a typical Italian wine-exporting establishment, was known for quality, volume of sales and excellent marketing. The company had headquarters in Verona where it had three wineries and 160 employees. Bolla exported 75% of its production to more than 60 countries, and produced 1.7 million cases – up 6% from 1986. Bolla's main market was the USA, followed by Italy second; Canada, the UK and Germany were third, fourth and fifth.

Bolla's brands were Bardolino, Bolla Chardonnay, 100% Chardonnay, Creso and Jago. Traditional brands included Recioto della Valpolicella and Amarone Classico. Other Bolla wines included Pinot Grigio, Valpolicella Classico, Soave Classico Superiore, a "White Merlot" premium blush wine made of 100% Cortese grapes. The current mix of Bolla wines in the USA covered 35% Soave, 15% Valpolicella, 10% Bardolino and 10% Bardolino Classico. Bolla focused on the super-premium segment.

Marketing director for Bolla, Giuseppe Butti, stated that because of its positioning as a premium brand and investments in the USA, Bolla exceeded all other companies in terms of advertising and promotion, at the rate of $3 per case, with $1.5 per case in a market where Gab was second. These marketing resources were targeted primarily towards restaurants.

A Small Vintner, Côtes De Provence: Phillip Croce Spinelli

Chateau Clarettes was a small vineyard (30 hectares) in Les Arcs, Provence, France. Vintner Philip Spinelli produced 1700 hectolitres, equalling FF2.8 million. He was entitled to produce a maximum of 50 hectolitres of wine per hectare within a given range and mix of vine varieties in order to fulfil the requirements to sub-brand his wine "*Appellation Provence controllée*". There was a restriction on new planting in the region, and the only way to expand was to obtain the right from someone else.

In order to differentiate his vineyard from other small vintners in an appellation area producing more wine than the whole Bordeaux region (55 million cases), Spinelli chose to produce a wine based on 100% pure Mourvedre. He said that he was probably the only one in the region making a pure Mourvedre. Normally, it was mixed with other varieties because, as a marketing tool, it was more important than the quality of the product. Provence was not the most prestigious region for wine in France. Until recently, it had largely been associated with wines bought in petrol stations.

Spinelli's vineyard and type of competition was similar to that of most vintners. He tried to differentiate by using his right to claim that his product had a taste which appealed in ways not found in the wines made by neighbouring vintners. However, when it came down to the bottom line, all the vintners in the region were competing in the same limited market.

The most effective strategy for Spinelli was to focus on a few well-selected distributors who would take good care of his brand. Good relationships with distributors, keeping high prices and then selling directly where his margins were considerably better than on sales to retailers were the major elements of his strategy.

Allied Lyons plc

The British Allied Lyons plc was a large conglomerate with three divisions. The food division, J. Lyons & Co. Ltd, had main products

Table 11.12 Allied Lyons results 1984–90 (£million)

Year	Turnover wines & spirits	Turnover beer	Turnover foods	Consolidated turnover	Consolidated profits pre-tax
1984				2850	195
1985				3175	219
1986	1124	1058	1205	3302	269
1987				3615	341
1988	1484	1585	1233	4236	436
1989	1531	1671	1345	4504	502
1990	1670	1700	1080	4700	565
Average Annual Growth	10.5%	15.1%	− 2.5%	10.8%	31.6%

in tea, coffee, bakery products and other foodstuffs. The Allied Brewery division included several breweries, an important range of beer brands and the second largest brewery pub chain in the UK. The Allied Vintners Ltd division's main products were wines and spirits. Main product groups were British wines, perry, whisky, rum and other spirits, port and other wines. Allied focused on new product development, particularly in the light and low-strength drink sectors. A serious attempt was made to build up its internationally branded light wine business. This attempt was reflected in the company's purchase of Hermann Kendermann in Germany with its Black Tower brand. In 1990 for a reported transaction of £545 million, Allied purchased Whitbread's 50% shares in European Cellars (Holdings) which included European Cellars, Handling Stowell's Wine boxes, Black Tower and Piemontello, and Jr Philips, Handling Harverys and Lanson (Table 11.12).

Seagram Company Ltd

Seagram, based in Montreal, Canada, was controlled by Canada's Bronfman family. It was one of the world's largest wine and spirits businesses, with a corporate turnover around C$5.6 billion in the year 1990. The company was one of the most aggressive global players in the alcoholic beverages industry.

With the acquisitions of Martell and Tropicana, and the joint ventures with Suntory of Japan in the Far East and Allied Lyons in

Europe, Seagram led the assault on global brands and global distribution channels. Seagram was aiming to be the worldwide leader in every sector in the alcoholic beverages industry. The name of the game was premium brands, market leadership and strong distribution channels. Seagram also owned the French champagne producer, GH Mumm et Cie, and other brands including Sterling Wines, B & G, Perrier-Jouet Champagne and Sandermann products. In the USA, Seagram was, together with Gallo, one of the leaders in the wine-cooler market.

Seagram appeared to be streamlining its ownership of distribution channels. The money invested in brands and the development of licensing agreements worldwide paid off handsomely for the company. This meant that Seagram could be interested in disposing of its direct ownership of distribution outlets such as Oddbins, a major off-licence chain, with principal outlets across the UK.

12
The World Flavour Industry

The term "flavours" is applied to any of a number of chemical products added to processed foods or beverages to impart taste and aroma. Flavours were usually classified as either natural, nature identical, or artificial depending on the production method used. A flavour was classified as natural if it was extracted from animal or vegetable products using physical means including standard kitchen activities like cooking, heating, boiling, etc. Flavours produced through fermentation were generally considered natural. Nature-identical flavours or enzymology consisted of synthesized substances but which occurred naturally in food. Artificial flavours were substances derived from any source which did not occur naturally in food.

Traditionally, the manufacturers of flavours, known as flavour houses, had also supplied fragrances (for perfumes, personal hygiene products, soaps, detergents, etc.) because both flavours and fragrances were extracted from raw materials using the same fractionation and distillation processes. However, the changing market and technology was eroding many of the synergies between the two segments. Not only was demand for flavours increasing as the food-processing industry became more competitive, but the food industry also demanded more sophisticated flavours, able to withstand the

This case study was prepared by Research Associate David Hover, under the supervision of Professor Per V. Jenster, as a basis for class discussion rather than to illustrate either effective or ineffective handling of a business situation. Copyright © 1991 IMD. International Institute for Management Development, Lausanne, Switzerland. IMD retains all rights. Not to be used or reproduced without written permission directly from IMD, Lausanne, Switzerland.

rigorous food-processing procedures and meet government and consumer standards. The market conditions made creating suitable flavours much more difficult and technologically demanding than creating fragrances. As one executive noted:

> Everyone knows what green peas taste like – coming up with the exact same flavour is challenging. However, with fragrances you can be more creative.

At the same time the market for fragrances was static and in the case of designer perfumes actually declining.

The impact of the market changes was felt in the performance figures of the industry. Until the late 1970s, the world flavours and fragrances (F & F) industry had shown consistently strong results. Industry profitability approximated 15% of sales in the mid- to late 1960s and 10% in the 1970s. In the 1980s, however, slower growth and increased competitive pressures had reduced profitability to about 6–7% industry-wide and real sales growth averaged 5–6% per year, reaching an estimated $6.7 billion in 1990. Projections into the 1990s estimated growth rates to remain in the 5% range. Flavours comprised nearly 45% of the total F & F market and were valued at approximately $3.1 billion in 1990. Western Europe and the USA were the largest regional markets, together accounting for 63% of the world flavour sales. Japan was the third major market. Consumption in the rest of the world was significantly lower. However, Eastern Europe and the Far East were identified as having significant growth potential.

In the flavour segment of the market, the growth of processed foods as a percentage of total food consumption was expected to drive up demand through the 1990s. An increase in sales of savoury flavours (25% of the total flavours market) was anticipated as well. Because of the high cost of research and development, the food-processing companies were increasingly contracting out product development to flavour houses, seasoning houses, and ingredient suppliers, further strengthening demand. The considerable increase in demand for convenience foods was also likely to continue to grow throughout the 1990s, creating new opportunities to expand the market.

Other developments had also influenced the industry in the late 1980s, including changing customer profiles, evolving competitive environment, and more sophisticated end-consumers. Together, these factors acting on the industry were forcing flavour houses to re-evaluate the way they did business.

IMPORTANCE OF FLAVOURS

Although the flavour component usually represented only a small fraction of the total cost of a food product, its benefit to the final product was very large. Price, image, nutrition, convenience, and texture were also important, but taste acceptance by the consumer was essential to the creation of brand loyalty. Food processors placed considerable pressure on flavour houses to deliver consistent, high-quality flavours at low costs.

Major research was also conducted to develop more efficient delivery systems. The natural and nature-identical flavours favoured by the producers were difficult to protect from degradation in processing, packaging, and reactions with other ingredients. High-temperature short-time (HTST) food processing, restoring and microwave cooking, in particular, were harsh environments for the delicate flavours. The price premiums paid for the natural products also increased demands for efficient delivery systems. New techniques to enhance stability and shelf life were also important. The leading-edge technologies such as micro-encapsulation were expensive to develop and tailor to different types of applications. The high capital costs associated with many of these technologies necessitated large end-user markets frequently only possible through a global presence and product consumers were also changing their demands. Natural healthy foods, low cholesterol, low fat, low sodium, high fibre, and low sugar were increasingly in demand and able to command a price premium. As the population in most of the developed world aged, tastes became more sophisticated. Rising interest in tea-flavoured drinks was one of the manifestations of this development.

Convenience (largely related to the microwave) was also a major interest of consumers, despite their otherwise increasing demand for natural ingredients. Furthermore, the flavour houses had to work with the packaging companies so that the combination of ingredients, flavours, and packages would have the flavour, texture, browning ability (appearance), and shelf life demanded by the consumer. For the flavour houses each of these trends placed demands on the R&D activities of the flavour houses.

LABELLING AND REGULATION

The distinctions between natural, nature-identical and artificial flavours were frequently subtle and no firm international standards existed. For example, flavours which were non-declarable (nothing had to be mentioned on the label) in some countries might have to be labelled or were even prohibited in others. Few international standards existed on acceptable ingredients. Until recently, German brewers, for example, were unable to use any additives in beer. Other countries were much less restrictive in potential ingredients. Individual product requirements forced flavour houses to reconfigure their product lines for some countries. With the exception of some EC regulations coinciding with the realization of the European Common Market in 1992, industry experts did not anticipate comprehensive coordination of national food regulations.

Emphasis on natural products by end-consumers was having its own impact on product rationalization. In response to the changing market and regulatory trends, most major flavour houses had re-oriented their development programmes to focus on natural flavours. Natural flavours, however, were more technologically demanding. Artificial and nature-identical flavours generally cost less to manufacture and were more able to withstand the modern food-processing techniques such as ultra-high-temperature (UHT) and industrial-scale microwaving which degraded many natural flavours. Despite the advantages of artificial flavours, they were increasingly shunned by the market and the market share of artificial flavours had fallen from 75% in the 1960s to 25% by the late 1980s.

COMPETITORS

In 1990, International Flavours and Fragrances (IFF) was the largest flavour house with 12% of the worldwide market. Quest was a close second with 11% market share. (see Figure 12.1). The market share of the two companies, however, differed from market to market. Quest was market leader in a number of smaller European countries while IFF's market leadership was primarily a result of its dominant position in the USA. In other countries, notably Japan and Germany, neither IFF nor Quest had significant market shares.

In the F & F industry overall, 14 companies had sales of $100

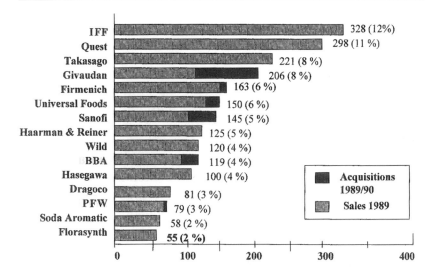

Figure 12.1   The top fifteen flavour houses by sales (market share in parentheses). (Source: Quest International)

million or more. The remaining sales were dispersed among some 100 other major producers and nearly 1000 smaller companies around the world. Most of the smaller companies were very specialized and closely held. New entrants were constant. It was relatively easy for companies to enter the market (especially in fragrances) as niche players in specialized products or for individual producers. As new product development became more costly and complex, strategic acquisitions had become an important means of company growth in the flavour industry. Acquisitions were also made for other reasons: accessing a base in a particular regional market, acquiring a market niche, expanding R&D in a particular field, or retaining a talented flavourist or a key food account.

Despite the high level of merger and acquisition activity, the world flavour industry (and the F & F industry in general) remained highly fragmented in the early 1990s. This was not expected to change. Arthur D. Little, a management consulting firm, even predicted a slowdown in the rate of acquisitions in the first part of the decade. Continued success in the industry required as enhanced working relationship with customers and mergers and acquisitions were one way for flavour houses to obtain the necessary range of products and knowledge to meet customer demands.

CUSTOMERS

Competitive strategies and changes in the flavour industry were
partly in response to the fast pace of change in the food-processing
industry, the primary flavour market. Concentration and globalization, frequently through mergers and acquisitions, were the dominating trends as the food processors tried to enhance their competitive position. The search for global products and associated
economies of scale was motivated by such factors as the emergence
of free trade areas like the European Community and the
US–Canadian Free Trade Association, and increased interest in
ethnic foods. In Europe, the industry was responding more slowly to
the market trends than in Japan or the USA, but already the
aggressive European producers had begun to establish a Europe-
wide (and occasionally global) base of operations.

One result of the new industrial order was an increased level of
competition. In the past, regional political and physical boundaries
had sheltered many companies from outside competition. The gradual erosion of many of these barriers had allowed companies to
expand into new markets more efficiently. As in the flavour industry,
meeting the new competitive challenge frequently meant acquisitions either for additional market share, national presence, or product range extension. With many of the acquisitions, however, also
came increased debt loads which put pressure on the companies to
allocate funds away from such "investment" areas as R&D. Because
of the cutbacks in R&D spending at many of the food processors
and greater cost efficiency, the flavour houses came to spend significantly more on R&D than their customers. R&D spending varied
by company size: the large flavour houses spent 7–12% of sales on
R&D, while the smaller companies spent 2–5%.

Global branding had an impact on the food-processing industry.
Food products companies, interested in reducing costs, continuously searched for product concepts that could be applied transcul-
turally. Although David Stout, the head of Unilever's economics
department, claimed, "There is no such thing as an edible Walk-
man," some products were more suitable to global branding and
marketing than others. Many beverages, snacks, fast food and some
dairy products were relatively easy to sell across national borders.
Despite sharing the same product concept, the product inside the
can or package was frequently modified (sometimes substantially)

from country to country to satisfy local tastes, cooking habits, and/or cultural norms.

The structural changes in the food industry had led to increasing polarization between the very large multi-product companies (Kraft, itself a division of Philip Morris, CPC International, Nestlé BSN) and the small, highly specialized niche players. The large multinationals strove to enlarge their market shares while the remaining niche players specialized further. Medium-sized companies. if they were to survive, found themselves forced either to expand or specialize. As the food-processing companies went international they wanted their flavour suppliers to be there with them.

Providing international service to their customers was not easy for the flavour houses. Because of the extensive resources needed, it was important to identify which customers were going to be successful in the 1990s and the decades beyond. Limited resources did not allow all options with each customer to be pursued. Working hard and expending limited resources to maintain extensive relations with a customer unable to compete in the long term was potentially disastrous for a flavour house. Consolidation in the food-processing industry also reduced the number of potential alternative customers, further increasing the risk associated with a failing customer.

Declining numbers of customers, besides increasing the proportion of business associated with one customer, changed the nature of the sales relationship. Fewer sales people were needed but the necessary level of expertise and interaction increased. Sales personnel had to interact with managers and technicians at many levels and functional areas including R&D, production, operations, purchasing offices and marketing. These interactions had to be managed carefully: each area had different interests, needs and concerns which had to be addressed if the relationship was to work effectively. Effectiveness was also dependent on a complete understanding of the customer's business needs. It was no longer sufficient to just sell a product; the supplier also had to know how it integrated with the rest of the customer's operation.

FLAVOUR INDUSTRY DEVELOPMENTS

In the latter part of the 1980s a number of notable trends were becoming apparent in the flavours industry which had long-term implications for industry players. The trends included more emphasis on flavour systems, high rates of new product introduction and the breakdown of traditional distinctions between competitors in different segments.

Total Food Systems

As they concentrated internal activities on marketing, food-processing companies were increasingly interested in flavour houses which were able to offer solutions to particular problems rather than just individual flavours. The development of low-fat, low-calorie ice cream was a typical example of the services food processors wanted from their suppliers. Removing fat from ice cream was technically not difficult. However, the fat was the basis for both the taste and mouth feel of the product. Creating the same sensation the customer experienced when eating ice cream but without the fat required developing a complete system composed of flavours, food ingredients and additives. Companies that had previously operated only as suppliers of specific products like emulsifiers, colours, or preservatives began to find that their customers, lacking the ability to develop flavours systems on their own, wanted more than just the basic product.

A total food system combined various products (flavours, food ingredients, and additives) to create an end product with certain desired flavour, texture, and appearance qualities. Food ingredients, to replace bulk or assist in product enhancement, were a fundamental part of many systems although the actual costs of the flavour or ingredients frequently only constitute 5% of the final and consumer product price. Few flavour houses had the necessary expertise and production facilities in ingredients yet they had to begin adding food ingredients and additives (such as fats, fat substitutes, emulsifiers, preservatives, etc.) to their product range.

In 1990, however, only six flavour houses were serious players in food ingredients and together held only 34% of the market. Their share, worth $1.029 billion, was, however, growing quickly (it had increased 42% from 1989) primarily through acquisitions (see Table 12.1). Many in the industry believed the best way to get the necessary expertise in ingredients was through acquisitions. Quest and others in the industry believed the ability to offer complete systems

Table 12.1   Food ingredient sales of flavour houses: sales and market shares

Food ingredient sales (US$ million)		Including 1989/1990		
	1989	% share	Acquisitions	% share
Sanofi	412	14	414	14
Haarman & Reimer	–	0	231	8
Quest	98	3	158	5
Universal Foods	67	2	83	3
PFW	75	3	75	3
Takasago	68	2	68	2
Subtotal	720	24	1029	34[a]
Others	2280	76	1971	66
Total	3000	100	3000	100

[a]Acquisition effect: 43
Source: Quest International

was increasingly a prerequisite to remaining a worldwide competitor in the industry.

Previously, food ingredients had been produced by speciality chemical companies. Just as flavour houses began investing in food ingredients, food ingredient manufacturers began investing in flavours. Many chemical companies had found food ingredients a natural outgrowth of their speciality chemicals operations. Grindsted and Gist Brocades had made investments with varying levels of success in the area of flavours.* It was becoming apparent that the successful flavour houses and food ingredient companies would be those that could provide global one-stop services or particular niche products.

Product Innovation

Redoubled efforts to reach new consumers had caused a significant jump in the number of new food product introductions. According to Productscan/Marketing Intelligence Service, more than 8000 new

---

*Biotechnology was another industry which was encroaching on the flavour houses. While flavour houses had spent considerable sums in developing the technology themselves, companies with a biotechnology background were still at an advantage in applying the technology to the production of natural flavours. (Most regulations treated flavours made through enzymology or fermentation as natural as long as the flavour met the other requirements.)

food products were introduced in European markets in 1987. The trend towards expanding product offerings was expected to continue, and in turn, increase the demand for new flavours and flavour systems. Many flavour houses predicted that the 1990s would bring a continuation of the flavouring fads of the 1980s – exotic flavourings, natural flavourings and easy-to-prepare foods. However, the area receiving the greatest interest was in natural flavourings and "healthy" foods. Product obsolescence, due to changes in consumer preferences, habits, and lifestyles, was also occurring faster than before. Together, combined with the competitive pressures stemming from the food industry, these factors were forcing flavour suppliers to improve their customer service in product application, research and development, technical assistance, and marketing.

EXTENDED PRODUCT LINES

Blurring of the distinctions between different fields in the industry was also having a major impact on the competitive structure of the food industry and created an excellent opportunity for flavour houses. Companies were expanding existing product lines utilizing either existing technological expertise in a particular area (such as chocolate or tea) or a successful brand image (such as Mars bars or Lipton). The occurrence of blurring industry definitions was especially marked in the area of soft drinks. Companies from many previously unrelated fields were becoming interested in obtaining a piece of the market. For example, the "healthy-athletic" trend in parts of North America, Japan, and northern Europe had prompted pharmaceutical companies to develop nutritional and "sports" drinks as alternatives to traditional soft drinks. Also, as soft drinks like Coca-Cola were increasingly marketed as alternative morning beverages to coffee, coffee producers tried to develop iced coffee as an alternative to soft drinks for consumption throughout the day (see Figure 12.2).

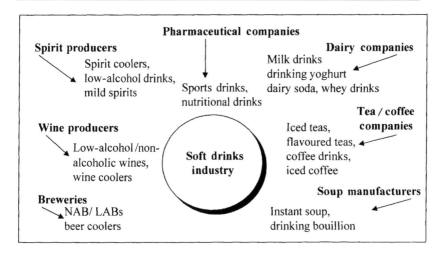

Figure 12.2 Examples of sources of new entries from other industries

13

The West European Car Rental Industry

By 1990 the revenue of the West European car rental industry was expected to reach £3.1 billion ($5 billion), 12% more than the previous year (short-term rental in Europe, excluding Warsaw Pact countries and commercial vehicles) (Figure 13.1). The year 1989 had been an exciting one for the major players in the business. Hertz, the largest worldwide car rental company, had dramatically ensured its presence in the UK by reaching exclusivity agreements with British Rail (representation at 2500 stations) and with British Airways through their BABS reservation system. Avis, the second largest worldwide operator, showed a 31% increase in pre-tax profits for its European car rental network. Budget, the third worldwide operator, had increased its European fleet by 33% over a 12-month period. Europcar, by merging with Interrent in January 1989, had become the largest European operator with an overall 13% market share.

MARKET SEGMENTS

There were two dimensions of customer usage patterns which industry executives viewed as important market segments: usage scope and usage purpose.

This case study was prepared by Manuel F. Colcombet, IMD MBA research assistant, and Professor Per V. Jenster as a basis for class discussion rather than to illustrate either effective or ineffective handling of a business situation. It is based on industry sources and the work of Laurent Bachmann, Regina Erz, Gustavo Fernandez Bonfante, Barbara Lauer and Manuel Ordas Fernandez.

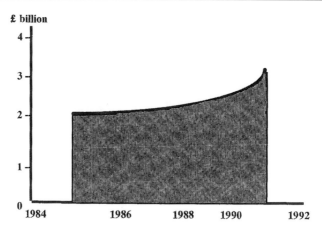

Figure 13.1 Market size

Usage Scope

The first dimension referred to the location where the car was booked and where it would be used. "Local usage" was when the car was booked and used in the same city; "incoming" rental was when the booking was made in a different city. Industry operators realized that serving incoming customers required a different infrastructure and commercial approach from what was needed to serve local customers. One manager explained:

> For the "incoming" customers, the most important sites of car rental outlets were airports, where more than 30% of European car hires were generated. Travellers also required outlets at major railway stations and hotels. Stations were expected to increase in importance with the expansion of high speed rail lines and the completion of the Channel Tunnel projected for 1993. The supra-local customers were eager to be able to book the car in their home country and even pay for the service with their own currency. These customers were keen to avoid anything going wrong in a city that they might not know well; therefore, they would choose the operator that instilled the most confidence from among the ones they managed to contact.

Local renters looked for convenience and price. These customers knew the place, managed the environment, and were aware of the other means of transportation that could substitute for car rental such as taxis and public transportation. Finding a telephone hook was nearly all they needed to price shop, check proximity and the opening time of outlets.

Usage Purpose

The second dimension was divided into the following categories: business, car replacement and repair, and tourism. The relevance of each segment varied among countries and seasons, but the business segment was the most important with 50% of the overall market value, 30% for replacement and local traffic, and tourism 20%.

The demand for rental cars for business purposes was higher on workdays, especially Mondays to Thursdays and throughout the year from September to June. The industry viewed business people as emphasizing the following factors: reliability, convenience, image and status. They expected to have no hassles, speedy delivery, easy check-ins and rapid check-outs. To attract this segment, car operators constantly made efforts to improve their service standards. As part of this programme, they issued personal cards such as Budget's "Rapid Action" and Hertz's "Number One Card" (7 million in circulation). Avis had established a self-imposed standard maximum check-in-to-rent time of 5 minutes. At certain airport locations like London's Heathrow where customers had to go elsewhere to collect their vehicles, this was obviously not always possible. In an effort to increase convenience, Hertz had experimented with "Travel-pilot", an in-car electronic vehicle navigation system.

Industry sources stated that, in selecting a car rental company, half of the business people were restricted to using the operator that had a corporate account relationship with the employer. Additionally, these sources mentioned that secretaries would make all the travel arrangements in one out of five occasions.

Tourism and leisure was a particularly active segment in summer. Tourists welcomed reliability and convenience; however, if the consumer were young, price mattered more. In the UK, 60% of those under 34 years of age shopped around for a "better deal", but only 40% of those over 45 years old bothered to do so. In choosing a car rental company, customers preferred those which offered all-inclusive rates, eliminating surprises on tax and mileage expenses.

The car replacement segment was particularly active at the beginning of every week, as Monday was the day people most often took their car in for repair. In some countries, like Germany, this segment was important because insurance companies were compelled to offer a replacement for cars damaged in an accident. In recent years, this segment was declining because there were fewer car accidents, and car insurance companies were attempting to reduce costs by compensating people who did not rent a replacement. In the early 1970s, consumers who were replacing cars that were out of order or hiring an extra car for short-term usage represented 60% of the German car rental business; in the late 1980s this figure was approximately 40%.

In selecting a car rental company, the garage owner exerted some influence, particularly if his garage offered a replacement service. This service tended to be "free" or included in the repair bill.

MAIN GEOGRAPHICAL MARKETS

More than 70% of the West European car rental revenue was generated in six countries, the biggest market being West Germany, followed by the UK, France, Italy, Sweden and the Netherlands. (Figure 13.2). Prices tended to vary across borders, according to the following index (UK = 100):

Netherlands	135
Sweden	131
Italy	123
France	110
UK	100
Germany	97

Usage also varied. In Britain, customers typically rented a car for four days (versus an average of three days on the Continent), predominantly for private use. In northern France and in Germany, business and replacement were the main segments with one-way rentals constituting 30% and 23%, respectively, of all rentals; these were the highest in Europe. In the Mediterranean area, foreign visitors (both tourists and business people) were the main client groups, representing over 40% of the market; the average driven rental distances covered were the largest in Europe.

Industry operators also studied differences in consumer attitudes across countries. For example, for Germans the car's characteristics such as model, luxury, maintenance, and cleanliness were important in addition to the speed of service. British customers were viewed as price shoppers; their interests also focused on convenient locations (pick-up points) and all-inclusive rates. The French generally viewed

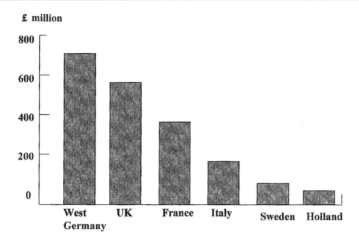

Figure 13.2   1989 revenue by country

the industry with scepticism and, therefore, preferred all-inclusive rates (as opposed to base rates plus additional charges for distance, insurance, tax, etc.). Payment mode, one-way rentals and having a selection of models to select from were also considered relevant in the French market.

There were also notable differences according to gender. In Europe, France had the highest rate of cars being rented by women, with 24% of the market. In the UK, even though women represented only 6% of the rental market, they were believed to play an important role in the purchasing decision; for example, it was found that women made half the inquiries about car rental in the leisure market.

MARKET OUTLOOK

Industry observers expected the market to continue growing by 10–13% over the next three to five years, up from a 7% growth rate in previous years, due to the following factors:

- General growth of the overall economy (based on a moderately strong increase of 4% for GNP). Improved business conditions would generate more business travel; increased income would expand the leisure industry and growing car ownership would also increase replacement rentals because of more trips and breakdowns.

- The "1992" phenomenon was also seen as a factor which would stimulate rental, because cross-border trade would be easier in a single market.
- Car rental executives also saw business opportunities coming from industry consolidations. A range of factors was contributing to more growth such as better reservation systems, better services, different pricing, new products such as cabriolet cars. Industry members resisted disclosing the financial results due to the new products. But one Central European operator increased business by 10% just from luxury cars and evening hire. Another area where operators were seeking new opportunities was in car ownership replacement.

One Budget executive reached the following conclusions after an extensive analysis of the UK market:

> For town or country dwellers, car rental is also an efficient alternative to owning a second car which might be idle most of the time but still incurring tax, insurance and maintenance costs. With many car rental companies able to deliver a car to the doorstep, the rental alternative offers good value and convenience. An Escort, for instance, could be rented for 134 days a year, including delivery and collection, within a 15-mile radius of an office at the same cost as owning it. If the second car is actually used less than 134 days a year, renting as needed offers significant savings

Several industry experts based their outlook on comparisons with the US market. They expected that the single market would result in a narrowing of differences between Europe and North America. Cross-border differences in car taxation and car rental taxation were expected to disappear. One-way cross-border rentals would not be restricted. Air transportation was going to be deregulated, thus providing additional opportunities for car rental firms.

Alan Cathcart, chairman and chief executive of Avis Europe, clearly expected greater prosperity from a unified Europe:

> The USA is an excellent precursor of what 1992 could lead to in Europe. Consider the following statistics: less than 5% of the European drivers has ever rented a car, compared to 10–20% of US adults. Further, there are only 1.5 rental vehicles per 1000 Europeans, compared to 5.5 for every 1000 Americans.

Others felt, however, that the US market would not necessarily be replicated in Europe. The differences in distances, lifestyle and the

Table 13.1 Country indicators: population, number of cars and rental cars

Country	Population (millions)	Cars (millions)	Rental cars (thousands)
Belgium	9.9	3.6	7
Denmark	5.1	1.6	5
France	55.9	22.5	90
Germany (West)	61.5	29.2	80
Greece	10.0	1.4	12
Ireland	3.5	0.8	10
Italy	57.5	23.5	45
Luxembourg	0.4	0.2	2
Netherlands	14.8	5.3	17
Portugal	10.3	1.4	23
United Kingdom	57.2	21.3	140
Spain	38.9	10.5	30
Total EC	325.0	121.2	461
Austria	7.6	2.8	3
Sweden	8.5	3.5	23
Switzerland	6.5	2.7	9
USA	247.0	140.0	1380

Sources: Eurostat, ECATRA, industry estimates

European transportation system were sufficient reasons to explain this point of view (i.e. in Europe only 30% of the car rental business was generated at airports, compared to 70% in North America). (See Tables 13.1 and 13.2 for key country indicators and sizes of the private and rental car fleets.)

INDUSTRY STRUCTURE

Even though global competitors dominated the market, there was no clear market leader. Large local markets with regional differences in preferences, rental patterns, taxation, historic development and low barriers to entry were seen as key reasons for significant market fragmentation. Traditionally, firms had entered the car rental business as a sideline to auto retail or petrol station operations, where the overhead costs could be kept to a minimum through operational synergies. Garages handling car repairs were an excellent example of the local company that competed within the replacement segment. The garage owner could keep a few cars on

Table 13.2   Per capita country indicators: income, number of cars and rental cars

Country	GDP per capita[a]	Cars per 100 persons	Rental cars per 1000 persons
Belgium	16	36	0.7
Denmark	17	31	1.0
France	17	40	1.6
Germany (West)	18	47	1.3
Greece	9	14	1.2
Ireland	10	21	2.9
Italy	16	41	0.8
Luxembourg	19	40	5.0
Netherlands	16	36	1.1
Portugal	9	14	2.2
United Kingdom	17	37	2.4
Spain	12	27	0.8
Total EC	16	37	1.4
Austria	16	37	0.4
Sweden	19	41	2.7
Switzerland	21	42	1.4
USA	25	57	5.6

[a] Gross domestic product per capita at current prices and purchasing power parities.
Sources: Eurostat, ECATRA, industry estimates

hand which he then rented out to a customer having repairs made.

Another reason for fragmentation was that national borders prevented the global competitors from fully exploiting their relative size. Economies of scale through volume discounts on car purchases and insurance were not always possible because of frontiers. In addition, country regulations significantly increased the cost of cross-border rentals because the car had to be returned to the country of origin at the company's or the consumer's expense.

Some local operators (licensees) had franchise agreements whereby they could use the brand name of global players. This arrangement benefited both parties. The licensees enjoyed the benefit of using a recognized name, won access to computer reservation systems and to international clients. As the licensees supplied themselves with outlets and vehicles, these agreements enabled the licensor to extend its presence with little capital expenditure and to benefit immediately from a 3–4% fee on gross licensee sales. Additionally, the licensor enjoyed the strategic advantage of penetrating an area that might not have been accessible to him. Another way of extending coverage without too much increase in fixed costs was by establishing agencies; that is, independently owned firms that operated the outlets, received a commission, but did not own the hired cars.

The existing market structure was far from static. A growing number of mergers as well as many new entrants indicated that this industry was undergoing significant changes. The previously mentioned Europcar–Interrent merger was only one example of the industry's restructuring. Increased concentration was also occurring as local firms joined global companies or departed from the industry. In 1989 alone, almost 1000 companies (12%) left the industry (i.e. discontinued the business or were absorbed). The primary reason appeared to be the fight for market share by the international companies. In an effort to increase their business base, these firms tried hard to enter new regions and to approach new customer sub-segments. Using the USA as a comparable single market, major companies clearly expected gains from 1992. The top four companies in the USA had an 80% market share versus only 43% in Europe. With this comparison in mind, an industry marketing director asserted that the "big four" would command 70–75% of the European market by the year 2000. Yet Europe still faced new entrants coming from the USA: Eurodollar, Alamo, and Thrifty were looking for a stake in the market before the consolidation process ended. All three companies had entered the market through partnerships or franchising, and had competed in the USA on a price platform. Some operators feared that Japanese car rental companies, backed by the powerful vehicle manufacturers of that country, would also try to enter the market.

SALES AND MARKETING

The industry used a wide range of channels to maximize the speed and availability with which customers could book their services, including travel agents, corporate accounts arrangements and dedicated sales people. Travel agents accounted for 20% of the bookings. In return for their selling services, travel agents and tour operators received a commission, ranging from 5% to 25%. The highest fee corresponded to the sale of a full-rate car rental package.

CRS Systems

Travel agents would either call the car rental company or use their computer reservation system (CRS). When receiving a telephone reservation, the larger car rental companies immediately booked the reservation on their in-house CRS. These CRS systems were continuously developed and improved. Avis asserted that its Worldwide Wizard system enabled the company to offer improved service, because customers could "check out" (rent a car) in just two minutes, and "check in" (return it) in only one minute.

When a travel agent reserved directly on a CRS, it was generally through an "outside" system, to which the car rental firms did not have direct access. However, changes were taking place for some industry participants. Budget was proud to claim that it was the first international car rental company to sign up with both the Amadeus and Galileo airline reservation systems. These two systems, Amadeus and Galileo, founded by the major airlines, were backed by groups of European carriers. Commenting on the effects of CRS systems, Robin Gauldie, editor of *Travel Trade Gazette*, stated:

> There is no doubt that these systems will become vital to the survival of the travel agent in the complex environment of post-1992 Europe. They will give agents an enhanced sales tool, will speed up their reaction time to fare changes and, importantly, in view of the threat of increased paperwork, provide them with a vastly more powerful back office facility, as well as faster and more comprehensive reservation facilities. Agents who adopt the new technology are likely to become increasingly hostile to principals who are not themselves accessible through CRS, a move which will have profound implications for tour operators, hoteliers and other travel service providers.

Robin Gauldie's forecast implied that small car rental operators would encounter an increasingly tough environment, as these systems would not be able to carry more than 20 car rental companies. The range of alliances was extending beyond the airlines and travel intermediaries. Railways were willing to provide selling services to the car rental industry and, on some occasions, signed agreements providing exclusivity. Examples included a contract between the SNCF in France and Avis, and between British Rail and Hertz. In another type of arrangement, the car and hotel CRS CONFIRM had a development agreement with Budget as an equity partner along with Hilton, Marriott and AMR.

Corporate Accounts

Industry sources estimated that corporate accounts represented nearly one fifth of the car rental industry. In some countries, such as France, Germany and Italy, this segment represented nearly 30% of all car rentals. To obtain these agreements, car rental companies offered discounts between 10% and 40%. In France, where a price war was raging for corporate accounts, these discounts reached 30% in 1990. In return, the car rental companies received first choice on all rentals and thus were ensured a non-seasonal captive market. These corporate accounts, in addition to favouring the market share of a particular operator, could increase the size of the rental market by providing a corporate fleet.

Gentlemen's Agreements

Industry operators often maintained informal agreements with car mechanics and hotel receptionists, who served as sales intermediaries by referring clients. These intermediaries could receive a commission of 10%, or even 20%, for a full-rate sale. Regarding this type of sale, global companies did not show any sizeable advantage over local companies.

"Walk-in" and Telephone Sales

Direct contact between the car rental company and the consumer, where telephone reservations were made by the customer directly, accounted for more than half of total sales. To attract the customer's attention, firms relied on good advertisements in telephone books and on billboard postings in multiple urban locations.

In this area, local operators had the same advantages as global players, especially when there were synergies with existing businesses, such as when garages rented replacement cars to customers having repairs done. The major companies were slowly gaining market share by offering affiliated garages repair and maintenance work on the operator's fleet, as well as a commission of 10% for referring clients.

Table 13.3   Price list for international customers: *Budget Rent A Car,* 1990

	Unlimited mileage tariff, per day			Unlimited mileage tariff
	1–3 days	4–6 days	7 days +	Friday 12:00 to
	Special offer – not discountable			Monday 9:00
Opel Corsa	142	108	96	182
VW Golf				
Opel Kadett	195	152	136	213
Opel Kadett Stationwagon	196	157	137	215
Opel Kadett, Automatic	210	161	147	223
Opel Vectra				
Toyota Corolla wagon 4 × 4	227	182	167	247
Opel Vectra Automatic	205	205	180	285
Opel Omega	268	207	181	310
Opel Omega Stationwagon	323	250	225	385
VW Microbus				
Isuzu Bus	375	315	275	400
BMW 316i				
Opel Vectra 4 × 4	379	316	285	430
Mercedes 190 E Automatic				
BMW 525i Automatic (sunroof)	281	230	199	550
Mercedes 230 E Automatic A/C	512	440	385	590
Mercedes 300 SE Automatic A/C	583	496	436	670

Source: Company price list 1990

Pricing

Car rental rates varied by country, city, season, day of the week, rental length and mileage requirement. Prices were also affected by the booking mechanism and the pre-delivery booking period, creating complex pricing schedules which even employees found difficult to manage and apply. The extra cost options and insurance charges made pricing even more complicated. (See Tables 13.3 and 13.4 for a typical tariff structure for one company in one country.) Pricing had little relation to operating costs, in part because the cost related to a particular hire was difficult to allocate, and because pricing was a tool used to attract different segments and increase the utilization of the rental fleet.

The pricing policies of the various competitors in the industry were also designed to charge, when possible, as much as the "market will bear." As in other service industries, one way to support this marketing policy was by rewarding the employees when clients chose higher margin products from the firm's portfolio, i.e. upgrad-

Table 13.4 Price list for international customers: *Budget Rent A Car*, local tariff 1990

	Unlimited mileage tariff, per day			Week-end tariff	
	1–3 days	4–6 days	7 days and more		
		Special tariff		2 days	3 days
Opel Corsa	71	54	47	119	156
VW Golf					
Opel Kadett	91	73	63	146	188
Opel Kadett Stationwagon	94	74	65	147	190
Opel Kadett, Automatic	96	76	66	157	203
Opel Vectra					
Toyota Corolla wagon 4 × 4	115	89	81	175	224
Opel Vectra Automatic	124	97	87	188	244
Opel Omega	136	112	97	207	270
Opel Omega Stationwagon	182	147	133	259	339
VW Microbus					
Isuzu Bus	195	159	142	302	392
BMW 316i					
Opel Vectra 4 × 4	184	146	132	278	359
Mercedes 190 E Automatic					
BMW 525i Automatic (sunroof)	233	188	170	336	435
Mercedes 230 E Automatic A/C	290	236	214	419	541
Mercedes 300 SE Automatic A/C	361	293	267	499	651

Source: Company price list 1990

ing, ordering additional options, or selecting a more luxurious car. For example, customers perceived that rental rates corresponded to the prices for different new car models, even though the operator's costs did not correlate proportionally. A customer might also walk into an outlet in a hurry and with no advance booking, and be willing to take a more expensive model, even if initially attracted to that contract claiming a special offer. The following simplified pricing example provides an illustration:

	Regular	Contract[a]	Weekday	Weekend
Business	100	80	100	80
Tourist	100	70	100	70

[a] Corporate account contracts were arranged through the head office. Reservations were booked in advance.

Table 13.5   USA–Europe rate comparison

Region	Sub-compact	Compact
Germany	440	580
UK	430	575
Spain	335	415
New York	290	315
Florida	160	180

Note: Prices in US dollars including taxes, unlimited mileage and insurance.
Source: Avis Supervalue weekly rates at April 1990 exchange rates

Prices also varied significantly among the European countries, although they were always much higher than those in the USA (Table 13.5). Tax differences explained only a small part of the difference (Table 13.6).

Other Marketing Tools

Creating brand awareness through advertising was considered important to attract the cross-border traveller. It was estimated that global companies spent around 2% of sales on advertising. Achieving the right spending balance posed continued problems, as advertising was not uniformly recognized as an order winner. One industry observer commented that Budget Switzerland had difficulties in 1987 and was subsequently sold, largely because of its belief that it could win increased sales only through heavy advertising and promotion.

In addition to pricing discounts, most large companies were willing to spend more than 5% of sales on various promotional activities. The main objectives were to:

- Maintain an information flow about the company's products to the market, that is, point of sales offerings, brochures, maps, etc.
- Meet clients' expectations and attract the repeat client segment by offering free gadgets, better service, etc. Some operators also launched so-called "internal promotions", such as training programmes for personnel.

Table 13.6   Value Added Tax by country

Country	On short-term car rental (%)	On car purchase (%)	On car insurance (%)
Belgium	25	25–33	a
Denmark	22	22	–
France	25–28	25	–
Germany	14	14	7
Greece	16	6	a
Ireland	10	25	Nil
Italy	19–38	19–38	12.5
Luxembourg	12	12	12
Netherlands	20	18.5	a
Portugal	17	17	–
UK	15	15–25	Nil
Spain	12	33	Nil
Austria	20	32	10
Sweden	23.5	–	–
Switzerland	Nil	6.2	–
USA	6–12	6–12	–

Note: This list does not include import duties and other special taxes on vehicles.
[a] The Value Added Tax is replaced by a specific tax.
Sources: Hertz, ECATRA

OUTLET MANAGEMENT

Outlet management involved the on-going management of the rental outlets, including activities such as "checking out", "checking in", invoicing, car cleaning, and staffing. Selection of the site and the people were considered the key factors because of their promotional impact. The main outlet costs (totalling 35% of revenues) were maintaining properties (offices and garages) in key locations, and supporting a trained staff with long working hours (e.g. the Avis location in Amsterdam Airport employed over 120 people).

Airport administrations, aware of their control at key locations and having only limited space, charged car rental firms a premium of 10% of their sales for an outlet on the premises. Some companies, in an attempt to avoid this charge, established outlets just outside the airports and relied on a shuttle service to transport their customers (e.g. Heathrow) with resulting delays.

Major companies carried an extensive network of outlets in order to meet the needs of the supra-local traveller and to fully capitalize on their established brand names (e.g. Hertz had more than 150 locations in Germany). In addition, these companies regarded increased distribution as a way to gain market share. To help reduce investments and swap fixed costs for variable costs, they relied on sub-contracting in less critical locations. In contrast, local firms minimized outlet costs through synergies with other lines of business such as car sales or repairs.

CAR CONTROL

Ensuring that a given car was in the right place at the right time was considered critical for the large firms in order to obtain high utilization rates. This was not easy, considering the amount of one-way travelling, the need to wash and service the cars, and the industry's practice of not penalizing clients who did not respect their reservations.

All international companies made extensive use of information technology to optimize car utilization. By considering booked reservations and historical sales figures, they determined the mix and number of cars at any given outlet. When adding the expenses of redistribution of vehicles and staff needed, 10% of revenues were typically spent performing this operation. In smaller firms, this activity was either limited or unnecessary.

FLEET MANAGEMENT

Fleet management represented up to 30% of revenues. It involved the purchase of the vehicles, maintenance and repair of the fleet, as well as insurance and, eventually, resale. The large rental companies were important customers for the vehicle manufacturers. An estimated 4–7% of all new cars were purchased by the car rental industry. In addition, car rental represented an important test opportunity for potential new car buyers. The large volume of cars purchased resulted in significantly reduced prices for the car rental companies. The importance of these firms as customers had led to acquisitions by the car companies. For example, Avis was partially owned by General Motors, Europcar by VW, Hertz by Ford and Volvo.

New cars were purchased and resold every 6 to 12 months by the large companies. Market conditions within the new car and resale market tended to move together. Thus, if the resale market were soft, the new car market would also be soft, offsetting any arbitrage risk for the rental companies. Repair and maintenance costs tended to be minimal for the larger companies, because their cars were generally sold within the normal warranty period. In addition, the companies tended to contract insurance only for damages to third parties, thereby self-insuring their own fleet. Local rental companies tended to keep their car fleet longer, thus reducing their acquisition costs, but increasing maintenance and resale expenses.

MAIN COMPETITORS

The industry could be divided into three groups of competitors: the "big four", the other international firms, and the local operators.

The "Big Four"

This group consisted of Avis, Hertz, Budget and Europcar. The first three had started operating in the USA and now enjoyed market leadership positions in that country; Europcar was, as its name suggests, European and owned by major European car manufacturers. The "Big Four" could be called pan-European in the sense that they were present in all West European countries. Their market share, size and structure differed somewhat (as indicated in Table 13.7). In some countries (West Germany, France, the Netherlands, Spain, and the UK), their presence was diluted by the existence of hundreds of competitors. In other countries like Sweden and Italy

Table 13.7 Profile of major competitors in Western Europe

	Avis	Budget	Europcar	Hertz
Market share (%)	12	7	13	11
Fleet (000 cars)	80	35	75	70
Outlets	1700	1200	1850	1600[a]
Airport market share (%)	25	10	20	25

[a] Plus 3300 railway representations

Sources: Company brochures, company directories, press releases, industry literature and estimates

where competition was concentrated, the "Big Four" managed to control well over half the market (see Tables 13.8(a) and 13.8(b)).

In the most rewarding segment, "the walk-in customer", the major companies enjoyed large shares (approximately 80%), but the percentage was even higher in the commercial traveller segment. Such high shares were the result of efforts made by this group of competitors to cater to these customers at every airport and to capitalize on the selling power of their international network. Industry observers named Hertz as the most successful in following this strategy, with nearly two-thirds of their turnover generated at airports. Hertz was supposed to be closely followed by Avis, then Europcar and, finally, Budget where less than one-third of the turnover was generated at airports (see Table 13.8(b)).

For all these companies, the segments reached and the strategies being used varied from country to country. As a result, price positioning also varied. Observers perceived that Avis was situated at

Table 13.8(a) Market share and number of competitors by country

	Big Four (%)	Others (%)	Number of competitors
Germany	46	54	***
UK	39	61	***
France	46	54	***
Italy	67	33	*
Sweden	60	40	*
Netherlands	34	66	**

Notes on number of competitors (orders of magnitude):
* *Italy, Sweden*: 100:** *Netherlands*: around 300: ****Germany*: 1000:
the UK and France: *more than* 1000

Table 13.8(b) Market Share by major competitors by country

	Avis (%)	Budget (%)	Europcar (%)	Hertz (%)
Germany	10	9	19	8
UK	9	8	12	10
France	14	4	15	13
Italy	27	5	15	20
Sweden	10	13	19	18
Netherlands	10	9	6	9
West Europe	12	7	13	11

Sources: Budget, ECATRA, industry estimates

Table 13.9 Examples of car rental prices in £ (all prices valid on 31 March 1988 (VAT included); one day's rental of a category A car, 200 km and CDW)

	Avis	Budget	Europcar[a]	Interrent[a]	Hertz	Local[b]	Local[c]	Local[d]
B	98.41	86.93	98.41	91.53	99.56	75.76		
DK	106.74		83.77	82.26	108.74	73.74		
D	89.55	67.33	83.61	83.55	89.09	72.78		
GR	54.03	49.77	49.77	50.98	69.50	44.71		
E	63.57	60.56	64.98	61.13	63.77			
F	111.19	106.06	111.71	105.64	111.15	87.74	99.61	84.17[d]
IRL	96.93		85.55		101.06[c]	38.76	34.23	
I	134.72		147.41	135.08	137.14	134.06	100.38	130.37
L	87.68		86.62	56.81	105.86			
NL	96.63		94.11	85.21	98.17			
P	43.13	41.83	42.45	51.18	43.00	33.92	37.71	41.08
GB	92.57		84.82					
A	113.63	93.10	100.87	101.09	83.75	91.92	79.86	
CH	114.57	105.04	111.39	95.56	112.57			
YU	50.34		43.11	52.01	59.80			

[a] Europcar and Interrent have merged
[b] Locally owned firms
[c] Becomes 115.26 when driver is under 23 years of age (CDW more than doubles)
[d] PAI included as well
Source: BEUC, car rental price survey, 1989

premium price points followed by Hertz and Europcar, with Budget having the lowest prices among this group (see Table 13.9).

Avis Europe

In 1988 this company became public and independent of its parent, Avis US. By the end of 1989, however, it returned under parent control of Avis Inc, Lease International SA, and General Motors. Throughout the period of independence, Avis Europe had continued to use Avis's reservations and marketing network.

Avis Europe's 1989 annual report revealed that its short-term rental operations had increased profits by 31% despite an 8% price drop and only 19% increase in revenue. Employee morale was high (70% owned company shares). The company was known for its slogan "We try harder" and enjoyed an "international", "upmarket" and "good service" reputation.

Though already enjoying a dense location network with more

than 1700 outlets, industry observers were expecting Avis to "buy more market share". The goal was "to grow ahead of hungry opposition" and at the same time meet its objectives of being present in all communities of over 50,000 inhabitants. It was felt that one of the key issues for Avis was to rethink its international pricing policies.

Hertz Europe

Hertz was the largest worldwide car rental company, with about half of its fleet in the USA. Represented in 120 countries, Hertz had a network of around 400,000 vehicles in 4700 locations. Its major strength was the control of the airport market and the consequent share of visitors to Europe, particularly those coming from North America.

The ownership of Hertz had continued to change. In 1987 the Ford Motor Company took control of Hertz. By 1989, Ford had sold 26% of its stake to Volvo North American Corporation and 5% to Commerzbank. The Hertz management team owned 20%, with Ford's remaining share amounting to 29%.

In the industry, it was believed that Hertz was performing well and was consolidating its presence in the European market. Hertz's West European network consisted of around 1600 locations of which 350 were served on a contract basis or operated on a reduced schedule (i.e. seasonal outlets open for holiday periods, reduced-hour outlets for low traffic airports). Hertz had also made an effort to be present at railway stations, in addition to its traditional airport locations. Hertz obtained 3300 representations resulting from its agreements with British Rail and the Swiss rail system. Hertz was permanently installed at 140 airports, but was also present at another 210 airports, some of which largely served private aviation.

With Hertz's caption, "Number one", it held a market perception of being "big", "American", and "upmarket". One industry observer commented that Hertz's management was faced with an organization which risked becoming bureaucratic because of its size. On the other hand, it was credited with excellent media advertisement and positioning.

Europcar/Interrent

On 1 January 1989, Europcar, a French operator with an international network, and Interrent, also international but mostly German, merged to create the largest European network. By the end of 1989, the combined organization had more than 1800 locations in Western Europe. The merged company was then controlled by Wagons-Lits and by Volkswagen, a German car manufacturer. The intent of the merger was to build strength through:

- An extensive coverage and a clear leadership position in the major European markets: Germany, the UK and France
- The alliances built by Europcar with "National Car Rental" in the Americas and the Pacific, "Tilden Rent a Car" in Canada, "Nippon Rent a Car" in Japan and the Pacific
- Their established name and reputation
- Synergies from operations.

An industry observer noted that the integration of the two operations was slow to come, because of cultural differences, differing goals of the shareholders, and different management and operating systems. Another asserted that the companies would have been stronger if they had remained separate:

> Merged operations will mean reduced desk occupancy at the airports, and half the offerings on the CRS screens of travel agents and airline personnel. Also, there is the risk of redundant personnel and that subcontractors will migrate to the competition. Remember what happened to Hertz when it restructured its German operations in the mid-'70s; Interrent and Europcar profited from that opportunity.

Because much work still had to be done to complete the merger, Europcar's results were quoted as being poor, and the fruits of the merger were yet to be seen.

Budget

Budget was the most recently founded company of the big four (Los Angeles, 1958). In October 1988 the Ford Motor Company financed a management buyout of the company. By 1989, its worldwide operations served 3400 locations with 200,000 cars. The European network consisted of 1200 locations, with a majority held by licensees and their agents. Budget made extensive use of franchising. The result was that the company was less homogeneous than its major competitors in most areas – from marketing practices to operating performance. One example of this heterogeneous approach was the situation at Madrid Airport. In contrast to all the other major European airports, Barajas Budget only offered a "pick-up" service from the airport. Budget's franchising policy, however, provided a network of highly motivated entrepreneurial companies, such as Sixt/Budget in Germany. This strategy had resulted in a growth of 38% over recent years.

Every country had to adhere to the overall strategy of providing "Good value for the money". Hence, Budget was well regarded, especially in the leisure segment of the market. Some felt, however, that it relied too much on this particular segment. Yet Budget claimed that it was getting the highest operating performances in the industry with utilization rates above 70%, in contrast to the industry average of 60%. In general, Budget used less media advertisement than its competitors, but this savings was compensated by more discounts and promotion (internal and external).

Other International *Firms*

A series of other companies were trying to establish themselves as pan-European, or even international. In pursuing that objective, they joined forces with other European or North American players.

Thrifty, regarded as number five in the USA and clearly competing on price, had moved into the UK, France, Greece, Belgium, Spain, Portugal, Italy, Ireland and Scandinavia. In Germany, it had reached an agreement with *PROcar*. But, industry observers considered that, after achieving this network, Thrifty had become somewhat "stretched" and "coverage was very thin". *Dollar*, another US operator, had been able to merge with Swan (UK) and also signed convenient licensing and franchising agreements on the Continent. The resulting network operated 11,000 cars in the UK and 4000 on the Continent. Another kind of alliance was "reciprocal marketing and representation agreements" which, for example, had been achieved between *General* (Florida) and *Kenning* (UK). Industry observers pointed to *Ansa International* as the most successful medium-sized company operating in more than 50 countries worldwide. Its shareholders were 40% American, 40% EC, 10% Swiss, and 10% Pacific based.

Local Companies

The overwhelming majority of these companies were small independent concerns operating at a regional or purely local level. For these firms, renting cars was generally an ancillary activity to vehicle repair and sales. Not generally "geared up" for the business executive, these local operators received most of their turnover from accident replacement rentals and had suffered from the contraction of this market. Their relative inflexibility, the debilitating effects of insurance companies' cost-cutting on the industry and increasing competition from the multinational rental leaders also contributed to the continuous rationalization process which had occurred. Nevertheless, some of them benefited from the major players' appetites and sold their telephone numbers and client accounts for healthy amounts. Thus, the local company's clients would be referred to the major one. Still others continued the operation as a strong contributor to the profitability of their main business.

Index